To,
My big sister
Happy birthday
1999
Lots of love
Jenny.
x.

THE COMPLETE

STEP-BY-STEP

CRAFT
BOOK

THE COMPLETE
STEP-BY-STEP
CRAFT
BOOK

MORE THAN 450 CREATIVE IDEAS FOR GIFTS AND FOR THE HOME

PUBLISHED BY
SALAMANDER BOOKS LIMITED
LONDON

—— A SALAMANDER BOOK ——

Published by Salamander Books Limited
8 Blenheim Court
Brewery Road
London N7 9NT
United Kingdom

1 3 5 7 9 8 6 4 2

ISBN 1 84065 065 6

All correspondence concerning the content of this volume should be addressed to Salamander Books Ltd.

CREDITS
Project managed by: Charlotte Davies
Designer: John Heritage
Introduction by: Amanda O' Neill
Typeset by: SX Composing DTP
Printed in Spain

CONTENTS

In recent years, the growing interest in crafts has seen more and more people trying their hands at new craft-based hobbies. In response to the increased demand for craft materials that this has created, manufacturers have developed an increasingly wide range of products and materials. As a result, decorative crafts like fabric painting or stencilling, which used to require a high degree of technical skill and a great deal of expensive equipment, are now much more accessible and attractive to the general public, thanks to the vast new range of colourful, easy-to-use products.

One of the great delights of craft work is that it enables you to create your own unique style in the home rather than having to conform to a prevalent trend, as you do when buying manufactured designs. You can introduce your personal touch everywhere. Inventive painting techniques such as ragging, sponging or stencilling transform plain walls, while fabric paints can convert soft furnishings, from curtains to cushions,

Below: *A sumptuous design such as this does not have to be expensive; it owes more to a can of gold spray paint and a little ingenuity than to large amounts of money.*

into artistic creations. With a paintbrush and a little imagination, you can have new lamps for old - in fact, you can give a new lease of life to old pieces of furniture and uninspired household objects of every kind.

Craft work also comes into its own in the festive season. A handmade gift will always have a more personal touch than a bought one - and you can take matters a stage further by creating your own unique giftwrap and greeting cards. Party time takes on a special air when guests find not just a delightful meal on the table but an individual look created by a decorative centrepiece, personalized placemats, lovingly folded napkins or a little gift by each plate. You can produce stunning effects at a low cost, and in the colours and styles to suit your décor.

Let's start by looking at the materials and equipment you will need. Some items you will have in stock already. Old newspapers, empty cartons and cereal packets, boring old plates or an unloved and uninspiring kitchen chair are all materials for exciting craftwork. Most households will also contain some form of drawing kit, scissors, brushes and so forth, although you may need to extend your collection. For certain

projects, such as fabric painting, you will need to go out and buy the specialist kit required: everything in this book is readily available from art and craft shops.

Choosing Paints

One of the joys of modern craftwork is the vast range of paints now readily available from craft shops and good department stores. Although, on the whole, the various products are intended for use on specific surfaces, you will find that some paints work well on more than one surface: for example, ceramic paints are suitable for use on glass, metal and wood, as well as china.

Glass paints are solvent-based paints which give a stained glass effect on glass, or a translucent finish on china and pottery. They are thick and sticky, so they require some practice to apply correctly, and they should always be used and left to dry (for at least 24 hours) in a relatively dust-free environment. The item to be decorated must be totally free from grease or dust before you begin. If necessary, wash the surface with warm, soapy water, rinse and dry it, then wipe it with a cloth soaked in petroleum essence or methylated spirits. Apply the paint with

a good quality, soft, clean sable brush, well loaded with paint. A second coat may be necessary once the first has dried, to achieve a strong enough colour. These paints are best reserved for purely decorative items, as they are not intended to stand up to heavy wear and tear.

Ceramic paints are solvent-based paints designed for use on clay and pottery, though they are also suitable for glass, metal and wood. They need at least 24 hours to dry, and give a glossy, opaque finish. A final coat of ceramic varnish will protect the design to some extent, but these paints will not stand up to much wear and are best reserved for decorative items. Avoid using cutlery on painted plates as this will scratch the surface, and never put decorated objects in a dishwasher, but wash them by hand in warm soapy water.

Acrylic paints are ideal for painting small wooden objects. They are easier to use than the oil-based gloss paints usually used for larger wooden objects such as doors and skirting boards, they

Below: *Choose from the wide range of craft paints now available. You will also require artist's brushes, a craft knife, masking tape, acetate, masking peel, a sponge and varnish.*

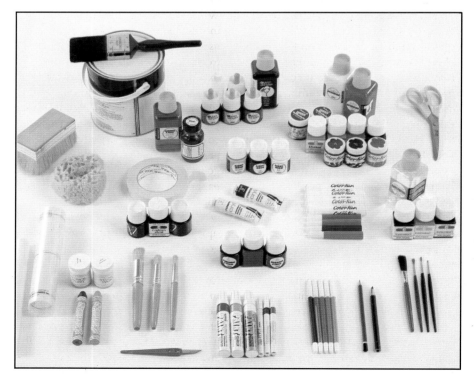

come in a wide range of bright colours, and dry very fast to give a rich glossy finish. Unlike gloss paints, they do not require the surface to be prepared with primer and undercoat beforehand: they can be painted straight on to bare wood. They are fully waterproof and are suitable for use both indoors and outdoors. They can also be used for painting designs on walls. One word of warning, though: be sure to clean your brush in water immediately after use, otherwise the paint will soon dry hard and ruin the brush.

Fabric paints come in various kinds. Most need to be used on unbleached white or naturally coloured fabrics for the colours to remain true, but there are also paints available which are suitable for use on dark fabrics - these 'opaque' paints sit on top of the fabric as opposed to being absorbed into it. Fabric felt tip pens are very easy to use, but always remember to tape the fabric down before you begin, to prevent it moving around. Transfer paints are for use on synthetic fabrics, though natural fabrics can be used if they are specially treated first. Silk paints can be used on wool as well as silk. Start by stretching the fabric across a silk or batik frame, available from craft shops. Use special silk pins to attach it. Then you can draw your design on the silk in gutta, a gum-like substance which comes in a special applicator bottle. You have a choice between clear gutta, which is removed when the design is complete, or coloured gutta, which outlines each colour in the design in the same way that lead outlines stained glass. Be sure to make the lines continuous - any gaps will allow the colour to seep through. Leave the gutta to dry for one hour before painting.

Once a design has been completed, fabric paints must be 'fixed' so that the colours do not run when the fabric is washed. Manufacturers will recommend the method best suited for fixing their products, which may include heat or chemical treatments.

For stencil work, manufacturers produce quick-drying water-based stencil paints and oil-based wax stencil crayons in a wide range of colours. The paints are very economical, and you can use them sparingly to create a subtle cloudy effect or to build up layers, making it possible to stencil a pale colour over a dark background. They are also intermixable, so you can make virtually any colour you need. The crayons are ideal for a beginner to use, as there is no danger of runny paint leaking under a stencil. The colours blend beautifully and can be quite subtle or bold.

Many paints not made specifically for stencilling can also be used in this way, including fabric and ceramic paints. Ordinary household emulsion paints are ideal for large, simple designs and can be applied with a sponge. Artists' acrylic paints are good for stencilling flexible surfaces such as roller blinds and shower curtains. Cellulose car spray paints can be used on a wide range of surfaces including walls, floors, plastics and fabrics. They are very durable and you can blend the colours as you are stencilling, but you must mask around the stencil carefully to avoid overspray. Household spray paints are similar and offer further options of pastel shades such as pink and peach.

For papier mâché shapes, emulsion (generally white) is the best choice to prime the surface before decoration. Without this, the colours tend to sink into the paper. Alternatively you can use ready-prepared gesso, obtainable from artists' suppliers. This is more expensive, but it provides a thicker layer and has an attractive, soft appearance. Once the surface is primed, you can use a wide range of paints and colours. Many of the papier mâché projects in this book are finished with gouache colours, while others are painted with household paints - gloss or emulsion. You can also use artist's watercolours, children's chalks, felt tipped pens, acrylics and artists' inks to good effect.

Other colouring products suitable for decorative painting techniques include multi-purpose felt tip paint pens, designed for a range of surfaces - china, glass, wood, leather, plastic, etc. The pens are easy to use, fast drying and available in a wide range of colours. They are solvent-based and their strong smell can prove slightly overpowering, so you are advised to use them in a well-ventilated room.

Finally, to finish off your decorative paintwork, you may require a coat of varnish to protect the surface. Polyurethane varnish is ideal for wood and comes in a matt or gloss finish. Ceramic varnish is specially designed for use on china and pottery. Patina varnish is used to build up a high gloss, lacquer-effect finish on wood. Crackle varnish is applied over patina varnish that is not quite dry, so that the difference in drying rates between the two varnishes causes the crackle varnish to craze, giving an 'antique' effect. For papier mâché, acrylic varnish is ideal since it is very clear, but it makes gouache colours run, so it is best to use polyurethane, matt or gloss, over these. If the slightly yellowing effect of polyurethane varnish would spoil the look of the piece you can obtain clear varnish, designed for use with watercolours and gouache paints, from artists' suppliers.

Creating Stencils

You can buy ready-made stencils, or make your own. Virtually anything which masks out an area of background will serve as a stencil - a pattern of masking tape, lace, paper doilies or even something with an interesting outline such as a leaf. But the usual stencil is cut out from cardboard or plastic film.

Stencil card is a brown, flexible oiled cardboard which is very easy to cut, but opaque. This means you have to transfer the design directly on to it and that you cannot see through it to match up the patterns when stencilling. It is inexpensive, but becoming increasingly hard to find as it has been superseded by modern plastic materials. It does not last very long when used with water-based paints but is excellent for sprayed designs.

Plastic film is usually referred to as acetate but its correct name is Mylar ®. You can buy it in sheets ready printed with guidelines, especially for stencilling. If you are going to do a lot of stencil cutting, it is more economical to buy large sheets or rolls of special film sold for use in drawing offices. All these plastic films are transparent, which means you can lay the film over a drawn design and cut straight

Below: *To change the colour scheme of an existing stencil, don't bother making a new one. Mask off the unwanted areas of the old stencil to convert bluebirds into robins!*

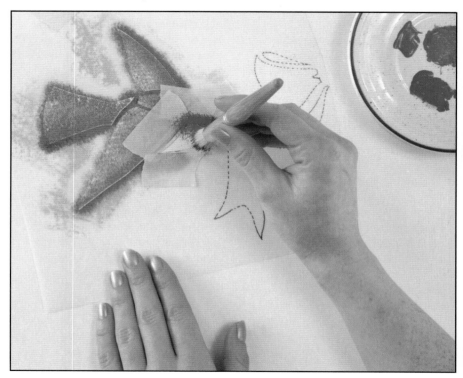

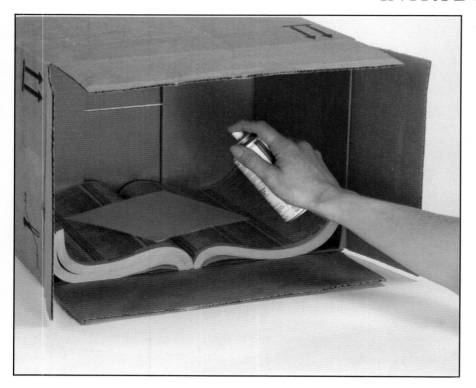

Above: *Always use a 'spray booth' when spraying glue or paint. It is easy to set up by placing a cardboard box on its side. Choose 'ozone-friendly' spray glue or paints.*

through. You can also see through when stencilling, which is a great help when lining up a set of stencil patterns.

Adhesives and Tapes
It is important to use the right glue for the job. Read the manufacturer's instructions carefully and test glues on scraps of paper first. When sticking thin papers together, make sure the glue does not seep through the paper. Also take care with printed papers as some glues will smudge the pattern. Use a plastic spreader or strip of cardboard to apply glue evenly over a flat surface.

For a professional finish use spray adhesive. Either put your work on newspaper spread over the work surface or place it inside a box to protect the surrounding area from spray. Spray an even film over the surface and then stick in place. The sprayed paper can be repositioned which is very useful, and any tacky areas can be cleaned up with lighter fuel. Always use an ozone-friendly spray adhesive and work in a well ventilated room.

PVA (polyvinyl acetate) medium, also known as white glue, has many purposes. It is a non-toxic, white solution that does not stain, and is quite suitable for children to use. It can be used as a glue and to make papier mâché. As it dries to a clear, glossy finish, it is also useful as a protective varnish.

For papier mâché, wallpaper paste is used to paste the layers of paper pieces. Most brands contain fungicide, and are therefore unsuitable for use by smaller children. Non-toxic paste powder can be obtained from craft shops and educational suppliers. To strengthen the mixture, you can add a little white glue.

Double-sided tape is sticky on both sides and provides a neater, cleaner alternative to glue. Clear sticky tape is very functional but remember that it does yellow and become brittle with age. An alternative is an opaque tape sometimes called magic or invisible tape, which is longer-lasting but does not adhere so well.

Masking tape is a low-tack tape which is handy for holding paper and cardboard in place while you are working, and it does not leave a mark. It is ideal for stencil work, to attach

your stencils to the wall without damaging the surface, to mask areas of the stencil quickly and easily - and to repair any stencils which are torn or cut. It is also useful in papier mâché work, to hold pieces together while glue dries, although where tape is intended to form part of the finished construction - attaching pieces of cardboard, or neatening edges - brown paper tape is recommended.

Paper and Card
Many of the projects in this book require paper or cardboard. If you look around your home you may be surprised to find how many suitable materials you already have from which to make your designs - from left-over wrapping paper and wallpaper to cardboard packets and boxes which can be cut up and re-used. Even old newspapers can be pressed to use for papier mâché objects. You will find that different papers give varying degrees of success, but in general broadsheet papers are of better quality than tabloids.

Art and craft shops stock an inspiring range of special papers. Apart from plain coloured papers, there is a wide variety of handmade papers and exotic

Above: *In addition to the range of papers available in craft shops, consider too using wrapping paper or wallpaper for your designs. Ribbons add a finishing touch.*

gift wraps which will add a touch of sophistication to any design. Textured and flock papers are also available to add a third dimension to collages. Crepe paper is very adaptable because of its stretchy quality, and comes in a wide range of colours. When cut against the grain, the cut edge can be gently stretched to give an attractive fluted edge. Tissue paper and iridescent film, although delicate, can be used to stunning effect on mobiles or as a lining for handmade boxes and bowls. Paper doilies and pictures cut out from greeting cards or magazines are perfect for making gift tags and greeting cards or for decorating boxes.

Brightly coloured gummed paper squares are easy to apply - you simply moisten the back and stick them in position. This type of paper is particularly convenient when working on an intricate design.

Generally, where cardboard is required for a project, you should use thin, lightweight cardboard, roughly the same thickness as that used for cereal packets. Where thick cardboard has been suggested, it should be sturdy enough to crease when bent. Some cardboards have a thin coating on one side which has an attractive shiny, metallic or textured finish. These are particularly good for making party hats and masks. Mounting board can be used for items that will be handled a lot. It is composed of layers of cardboard and comes in a selection of thicknesses.

Brushes and Tools
For decorative painting, use good quality paintbrushes, and always clean them immediately after use. Brushes used with solvent-based paints should be cleaned in white spirit or turpentine substitute; those used with water-based paints should be washed in water.

Specially made stencil brushes are available in different sizes, and can be supplemented with real sea sponges for creating a sponged texture on walls before stencilling. Small pieces of the same can be used to create a mottled texture on larger stencils.

A sharp, pointed pair of scissors is essential for working with paper. A small pair is more useful and easier to handle than a large pair. For cutting thick cardboard, and for cutting stencils, you will need a sharp craft knife with replaceable blades, or a scalpel available from art shops. Always cut on a cutting mat. A purpose-made rubberized, self-healing cutting mat is the perfect base to draw on. It has a printed grid which is very helpful for drawing accurate guidelines and register marks, and has a non-slip surface. Cutting mats are, however, rather expensive, and a sheet of thick cardboard makes a good substitute. When cutting through thick card, do not try to cut right through in one go but make several cuts, going deeper

each time, for a clean line. Cut straight lines against a steel rule, preferably a safety one to protect your fingers. When cardboard just needs to be folded, first score the surface lightly with a craft knife, making sure not to cut too deep.

A hole punch is useful for making decorative holes, punching out circles from coloured paper to be glued on to a card or for making holes in gift tags, through which ribbon can be threaded and attached to parcels. A pair of dividers or a stout needle is useful to make holes in card to sew on buttons, etc. Tweezers are highly recommended for keeping hold of small items when applying glue.

When selecting pencils and drawing aids, you will find an HB pencil the most versatile, but a softer lead such as 2B is better for sketching. Always keep pencils sharpened to a fine point so that your drawing is accurate. Be sure to use

a ruler for drawing straight lines, and a set square for drawing squares and rectangles so that the angles are correct. Draw circles with a compass or, for tiny circles, use a plastic stencil. A fine, waterproof felt-tipped pen is ideal for drawing thin, accurate guidelines.

Modelling Material
For a few projects, modelling clay is used to mould small forms. Fimo modelling clay can be moulded and cut into the desired shape, then baked in an oven for a few minutes to harden, following the manufacturer's instructions. A small rolling pin and board are useful for rolling out the clay, and a palette knife can be used for lifting flat shapes from the board.

Below: *Look out for unusual materials. Toy shops, haberdashery departments or charity shops may be a source of decorative trimmings to brighten your designs.*

Left: *Old china plates, ceramic tiles, books, magazines, postcards, fabrics and attractive packaging can all prove a source of inspiration for designs.*

Trimmings and Ribbons

It is often the finishing touches that make a handmade item so special, and you will find craft shops are a treasure trove of suitable decorative objects – many of them very reasonably priced. Cotton pulp or polystyrene shapes are lightweight and suitable for decorating in many ways. Similarly, coloured pipecleaners, tiny pom-poms, stick-on eyes, beads, sequins and jewellery components all add interest to a design.

Doll's house specialists are invaluable for finding tiny accessories, and stationers can supply an exciting range of attractive stickers and transfers.

Nowadays, there is an exciting range of Victorian scraps that are ideal for paper crafts, plus a wide variety of decorative sticky tapes that help give a professional finish to a project.

Ribbons have many uses, and come in a great many widths and colours, including floral, tartan and printed themes. Ribbon can be curled over scissors, woven, plaited and glued. Giftwrapping ribbons can also be used to great effect. The wide ones can be moistened so that they will stick to themselves, and the narrow ribbons will coil attractively when pulled smoothly over the blade of a pair of scissors. Braid is another very useful and more unusual material and again is available in a variety of forms and colours.

Flowers are ever-popular motifs, and you can achieve quite different effects by using different sorts - dried, fabric, ribbon, etc. Paper doilies come in a whole range of sizes and patterns and can also be used to striking effect.

Sources of Inspiration

To begin with, you will probably want to follow the designs featured in this book. But as you become more confident and adventurous, you will find inspiration from a wide range of sources. Old china plates, ceramic tiles, books, magazines, postcards, fabrics and attractive packaging can all spark off ideas for creating designs of your own.

Visits to museums, craft shops, haberdashery departments can all provide themes, motifs and jumping-off points or new ideas. Special occasions such as weddings, christenings or birthday parties all provide their own inspirations.

What to decorate? The possibilities are endless. Junk-shops and charity shops are an inexpensive source of plain plates, boxes, lampshades and shabby old furniture which cry out to be metamorphosed with an imaginative new paint finish. Specialist craft suppliers stock plain wooden items specially designed for decorating. Or you can always start right from scratch and create your own unique objects in papier mâché.

How to Make Cards and Stencils

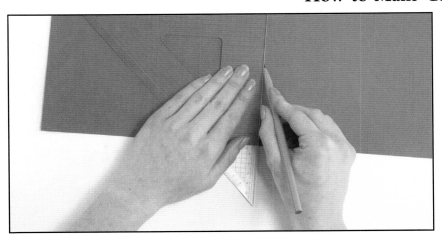

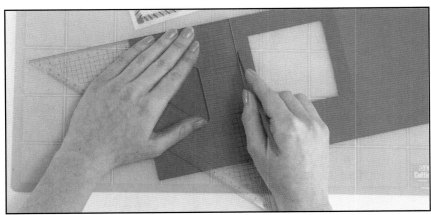

Above: *Decide on the size of the card and multiply the width measurement by three. Draw out on a piece of chosen card. Mark the fold lines. Measure the piece of work for mounting and cut a window to fit. Score the two fold marks on the right side of the card. Cut off a 1mm (¹/₈in) strip from the left side.*

Above: *Choose a design from a piece of fabric, wallpaper, giftwrap, a book or magazine, then use a pencil to carefully trace the shape on to tracing paper. Now convert the motif into a stencil by redrawing it with 'bridges', so that whole areas of the design are enclosed within a continuous line.*

Choose two or three warm colours and subtle textures to create a rich, elegant mood in a small room. Decorate with simple stencils to prevent the designs becoming too distracting. Accentuate pictures with a two-colour rope border to make an attractive "frame". Simple accessories can complement the whole theme with touches of the rope border in the same shades or with gold and copper lustre to add sparkle. Select stencils from the Template Section (page 243) to transform any room in your home.

Experiment with stencil designs in a range of colours and situations to change the mood and style of any room. In this study the stencilled wall decorations and soft furnishing accessories bring an air of simple elegance to the once-plain surroundings.

If the present you have bought is an awkward shape, don't waste time trying to wrap it neatly. Instead, make a box or a bag and put the present inside. With the minimum of fuss and effort you can create an attractively presented gift and the person who receives your present enjoys the added bonus of being able to use the box or bag again afterwards.

In the Gift Wrapping chapter you will find instructions for making an assortment of cardboard boxes. The templates for these boxes can be found on pages 252-253 and by scaling them up or down you can make a box in any size you like.

Why not try your hand at making an original container from this varied selection of gift boxes and bags. They are completely professional in finish, yet remarkably straightforward to make and will suit presents of any size or shape.

Usually it is easy to guess the contents of a gift if the gift is a recognisable shape – but not if you disguise it. Throughout this book you will find ideas and inspiration for turning a bottle into a pencil for example, a record into a cushion, a cube into a dice or even a circular gift into a hat.

Many of the present wrapping ideas in this book can be used at any time but there are also a number of projects especially devised for celebrating special occasions. Wrapping gifts for Christmas, Easter, weddings, christenings or Valentine's Day usually requires extra inspiration. There are plenty of exciting designs to choose from to bring a touch of originality.

Whether your present is for Christmas, Valentine's Day or a christening, you can have great fun wrapping it to match the occasion. You can even disguise it as a birthday cake or a domino. No-one will ever guess what is inside.

The huge selection of gift wraps now available from a range of outlets should give you plenty of scope for covering your presents. You don't have to use ready-made gift wrap however – for a more stylish, individual touch you can easily make your own. There are plenty of ideas to choose from in the pages that follow. For example, what about stencilling your own design, creating a collage, or printing a pattern with a humble potato?

And once you have your wrapping paper, there are plenty of useful tips on how to use it most effectively, such as wrapping a cylindrical gift neatly, or what to do with a spherical shape.

There's no excuse for an unimaginatively wrapped present with such a spectacular range of gift wrap available. Choose from plain, matt, shiny, pastel or bold colours, glossy or glittery designs, to make the most of your gift.

15

INTRODUCTION

To ensure that your greeting cards have a professional finish, you must select the correct weight of card - not too thin so that it curls or fall over, or too thick. To make a neat fold in card, score on the right side with a light cut using a sharp craft knife and a steel ruler, just piercing the top layer of card. The card will then fold in a straight line. Unless otherwise stated, all the cards in the chapter on Greeting Cards are folded vertically. Always measure carefully and mark with a sharp pencil to create a fine line. Should your finished card be crooked, trim a new straight edge using a set square and with the card folded so that you can cut through back and front thicknesses at once. Draw the blade twice along the cutting edge.

Card comes in a variety of finishes, cloud effect, metallic, parchment style, textured, glossy and matt. Tissue, brown paper, origami, marbled, wall and wrapping paper, foil and plastic bags can all be used to create different effects.

INTRODUCTION

The decorative details on a gift can make all the difference to the finished article. The wrapping paper might be bright and attractive, but if the present is lacking decoration it can still look dull. Even a pretty bow can provide the finishing touch you need to turn a plain parcel into a chic gift.

Buying manufactured ribbon pom-poms to match your paper can make gift wrapping highly expensive. In the chapter on Gift Wrapping you will find instructions on how to make all sorts of ribbon decorations for yourself that look just as good as the shop-bought kinds. You can also create your own tassels, foil stars, paper ruffles, and flowers of all kinds.

Reels of gift ribbon can be turned into an array of different decorations, from stunning rosettes to individual and original pom-poms. Braid, cord, tissues and even sweets can be used to decorate your gifts and make parcels look extra-special.

This is something we probably all learned at school but many of us have long forgotten! First you need to choose a bowl or some other receptacle that is roughly the shape you wish to achieve. Tear up lots of newspaper into narrow strips, and then make up a flour and water paste, not too stiff, not too runny. You will soon discover the correct consistency when you get started.

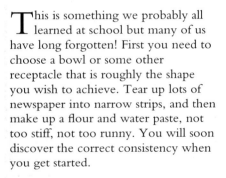

These little carnation-shaped flowers are useful for adorning all sorts of decorations, or can be used by themselves to make a lovely floral centrepiece. Take an ordinary paper tissue and cut it in half lengthwise. Concertina-fold it down its length, as shown, then tie it in the middle with a piece of wire or twine.

Dip the newspaper into the paste and start placing it on the bowl, working your way around it until the whole surface is covered. Keep working over it, in all directions, until you have built up at least six layers. This will give you a firm mould. Make sure to keep it smooth as you go along.

Fold the tissue in half, and wrap one end of the wire firmly around the base to hold the shape in position. (The other end serves as the stem.)

When you have finished, leave the papier-mâché to dry in a warm dry place. It will take about 24 hours to dry completely – more if it is particularly thick. When it is ready, ease it off the bowl. You may have to sand down the rough edges, but this is best done after the first coat of paint, as this will show up any lumps and bumps.

Now simply fluff out the paper, teasing it with your fingers until it resembles a carnation.

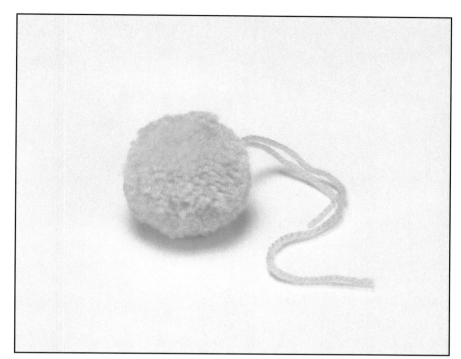

Tassels are useful for trimming hats or the edges of hanging decorations, and they are very easy to make. Cut several strands of yarn or cord; the more you cut, the fuller the tassel will be. The strands should be twice the finished length of the tassel. Tie them firmly in the centre. Leave the tying strands uncut, and fold the tassel strands in half.

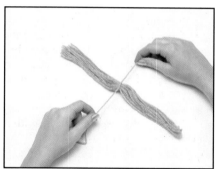

These jolly trimmings, ideal for party hats, can be made of wool left over from knitting projects. First cut two circles of cardboard with a diameter the size you wish the finished pom-pom to be. Cut a fairly large hole in the centre. Now wind wool (doubled, to speed up the work) over the cardboard rings until you can barely push the wool through any more.

Now wind a cord several times around all the strands, about 2.5cm (1in) from the top (or less, for a small tassel). Tie it firmly and cut off the ends.

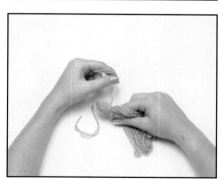

The more wool you use, the bushier the pom-pom to be. Cut a fairly large hole in the centre. Now wind wool (doubled, to speed up the work) over the cardboard rings until you can barely push the yarn through any more.

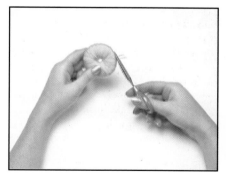

Trim the ends off the tassel so that they are all the same length. Use the top cord to attach it to whatever you are trimming.

Wind a piece of wool between the cardboard rings around all the strands. Pull firmly and make a strong knot, leaving long ends. Now take out the rings. Finish by trimming off any straggling ends of wool.

FOR THE HOME

SPONGING

Sponging is one of the easiest paint finishes to achieve. You can use one, two or more colours. When choosing colours, go for a light, mid and darker shade of the same colour. Here, rose white has been used as a base for soft peach and dusky apricot. It is a good idea to buy some small samples of emulsion paint to practise with before you start. First, apply the base cost with a brush or roller.

When your base colour is dry, take a natural sponge and dampen it. Now dip the sponge into the second colour, being careful not to overload it with paint. Remove any excess paint by dabbing the sponge on to waste paper, then apply paint to the walls with a light dabbing motion. Don't press hard or the paint will smudge. Continue in a random pattern, re-applying paint to the sponge as necessary.

Wash out your sponge and apply the third colour, overlapping the second colour. When you have finished you should have an even blending of the three colours. If the last colour is too dominant you can soften it by sponging over with some of the base colour.

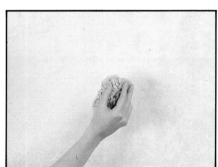

RAGGING

There are two main methods of ragging: 'ragging off', in which you apply rags to a wet wall of paint, so removing the colour and leaving a pattern; or 'ragging on' as shown here. In the latter, the colour is applied with bunched-up rags, in a similar way to sponging. First apply a base coat of emulsion paint with a roller or a brush.

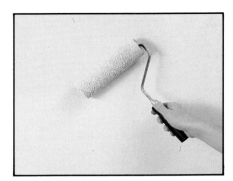

Use dry rags for this technique – it is the crisp folds in the fabric that form the pattern. Make sure you cut up lots of rags before you start and have plenty of waste paper around. Clasp a rag in your hand and dip it lightly into the paint. Dab off the top layer of paint on to some waste paper, then apply the cloth to the wall with a dabbing motion.

Continue to apply paint in a random pattern, replacing the rag with a fresh one as soon as it becomes too damp. When the first colour has dried, apply a second colour as before: a contrasting colour can look particularly effective.

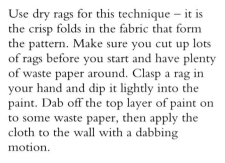

FREE-HAND FLORAL TILES

A very easy way of painting tiles is to use multi-purpose felt tip paint pens. Assuming each square represents one tile, square up your design and transfer it on to the tiles using a chinagraph pencil. Draw over this line with a fine line felt tip paint pen. Try to keep the paint flowing once you have put the pen on to the tile so that the line is continuous.

Colour in your design using both thick and fine line pens. Be as outrageous as you like with your use of colours, placing reds, oranges, and pinks together, and adding a sparkle with gold and silver.

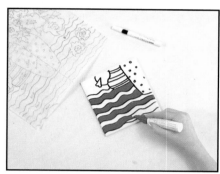

Add to the range of tones and colours with plenty of dots and lines in contrasting colours. To finish, protect your design with a coat of ceramic varnish once the paints are dry.

MARVELLOUS MARBLING

This must be the easiest way of achieving a stylish effect. All you need are some plain white tiles, ceramic or glass paints, white spirit, a large bowl full of water, a small mixing bowl or saucer and a paint brush. You may also wish to wear rubber gloves to protect your hands. Thin some paint with white spirit and begin to drop it on to the surface of the water with a paint brush.

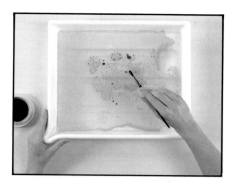

Using the handle of the paint brush or an old stick, mix the colour round so that it creates a swirling pattern. If you wish, you can dilute a second colour in the same way and add this to the first.

Carefully hold the glazed side of the tile against the surface of the water and then quickly lift it away. The tile will pick up the swirls of paint to give a marbled effect. Leave the tile to dry then give it a coat or ceramic varnish to protect the finish. You may find it necessary to practise this technique for a while before you perfect it.

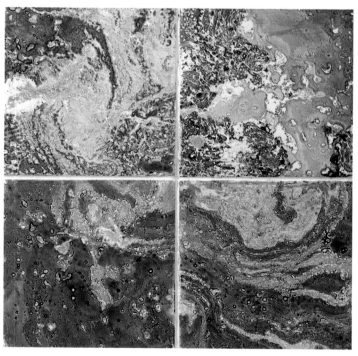

These attractive full-length curtains will add style to any modern living room and can be painted in any colour to match the decor. You will need lots of space when painting the fabric so cover your floor with plenty of newspaper before you begin. Now rip sheets and sheets of newspaper into long strips. It is best to use broadsheet newspapers as they are wider and have more pages.

Sew together enough fabric to make a curtain and lay it out on the floor. Tape several strips of newspaper together so that they fit across the width of your fabric. Now, using loops of masking tape on the underside of the paper, stick the strips to the cloth, leaving gaps between the rows. As you work your way towards the top of the cloth, break up the rows with small 'islands' of paper.

Pour some opaque black fabric paint on to a saucer or plate and, starting at the bottom of the cloth, sponge the paint between the rows of newspaper.

With each new row, mix a little white opaque fabric paint into the black before you dip the sponge in. Keep adding white with each successive row so that the colour gradually changes from black to grey as you print up the cloth. By the time you get to the top where you have the islands of paper the colour should be light grey.

Leave the fabric paint to dry before removing the paper. Repeat the whole procedure with the second curtain. Iron on the back of each piece of fabric to fix the colour and then make them up into curtains.

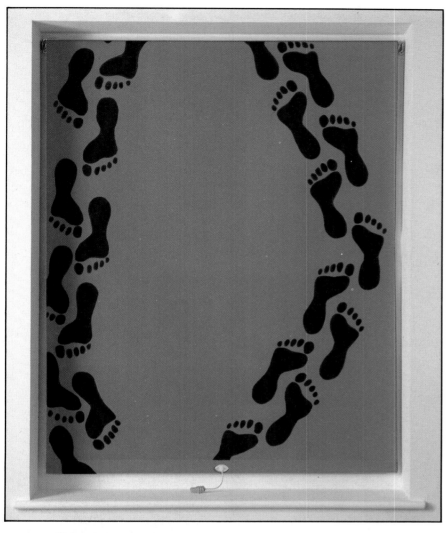

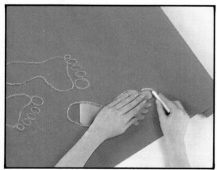

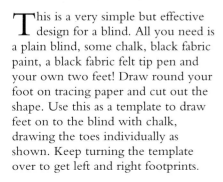

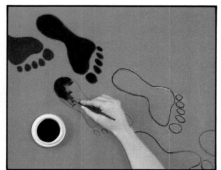

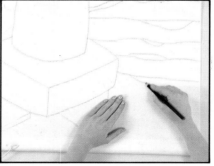

This is a very simple but effective design for a blind. All you need is a plain blind, some chalk, black fabric paint, a black fabric felt tip pen and your own two feet! Draw round your foot on tracing paper and cut out the shape. Use this as a template to draw feet on to the blind with chalk, drawing the toes individually as shown. Keep turning the template over to get left and right footprints.

When you have chalked your design going up and down the blind, draw over the chalk with a black fabric pen. Fill in the centre of each foot with black fabric paint then iron on the reverse side of the fabric to fix the colour.

Forget city life and make-believe you live in a cottage by the sea with this colourful blind. A photograph of a sea gull is a useful reference when drawing the bird. Create your design at a reasonable size first then square it up to full size (see Introducton) so that it fits on the blind. Draw the design on to a plain white blind in pencil.

When painting such a complex picture, it is a good idea to paint the background first, so start with the sky. This is a mixture of white and blue fabric paint, sponged on quite densely. The clouds are sponged on more lightly. Once the background is painted, start painting in the details. When you've finished, iron the back of the fabric to fix the paints.

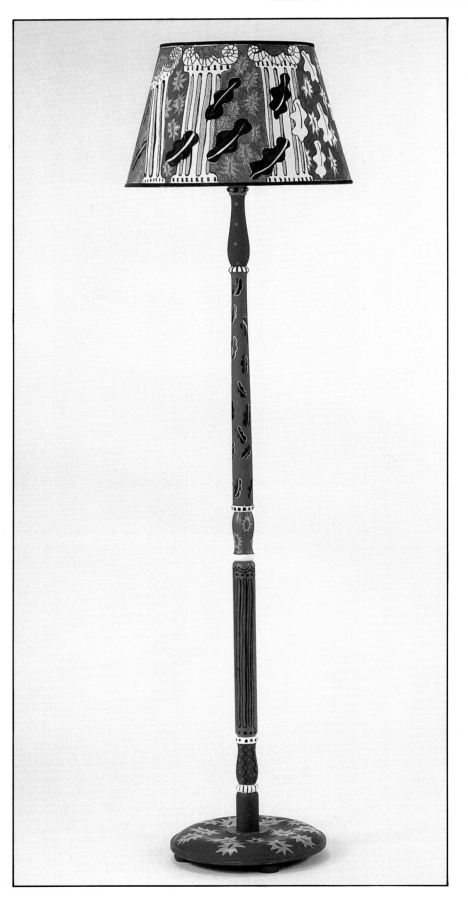

Here's something for those who enjoy the outrageous and the avant garde – an old standard lamp eye-catchingly decorated with Doric columns and oak leaves. Following the maker's instructions, strip the original finish off the lamp-stand with varnish remover. Use an old toothbrush to get into difficult corners. Rub down the surface with wire wool then sand it to give a smooth finish.

Paint the stand with primer and, when this is dry, apply some undercoat. Alternatively, you could use two coats of combined primer/undercoat. Leave the stand to dry before you begin to apply the colour.

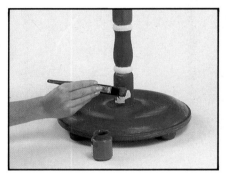

Decorate the standard lamp with acrylic paints, using bold, primary colours. Paint different parts of the lamp different colours, and break the colours up with rings of white, using the carved features as guidelines.

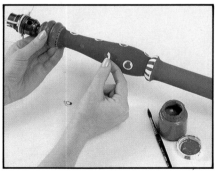

Now decorate the base colours with dots, dashes, spots, leaves and columns, using both acrylic paints and multi-purpose felt tip paint pens. Paint the spots by sticking ring reinforcements on to one section of the stand and filling in the holes with a brightly contrasting colour. Paint black oak leaves on another section and outline them in bright yellow using the felt tip pens.

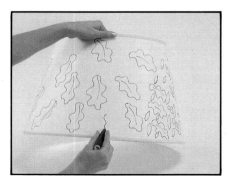

When the stand is dry, apply a coat of protective varnish. Outline your design on the shade with a fine line fabric felt tip pen, repeating the patterns used on the stand. Now fill in the design with thick fabric pens, continuing to use brightly contrasting colours.

Cover the base with black tissue paper, torn into squares of approximately 10cm (4in). Paint one side of the paper and apply this side to the lamp, overlapping pieces slightly. Give the feet three coats of poster paint, and then paint the entire base with matt polyurethane varnish. Finish with fire retardent, available from threatrical suppliers.

Using a craft knife, make two more holes in the base – one at the top for the light fitting, and one about 2.5cm (1in) away from the hole at the bottom, to carry the flex. When you wire the lamp, fit a cord grip inside the lamp to secure the flex.

For the shade, it is simplest to use an existing shade to make the pattern. Mark the outline on thin paper, such as newspaper. Cut this out and place over the existing shade to check for fit. When you are satisfied, mark the outlines on thin cardboard or thick cartridge paper, making sure that there is a sufficient crossover.

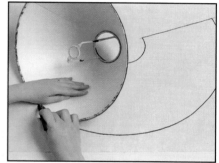

A cheap plastic beach ball, approximately 35cm (14in) in diameter, is used for the base. Coat it with petroleum jelly and then apply six layers of papier mâché all over, using pieces about 7.5cm (3in) square. When the last layer has dried, mark a line around the shape and carefully cut with a craft knife, then remove the papier mâché.

Tear tissue paper into 10cm (4in) squares and apply it to the cardboard – the pencil outlines will still be visible through the paper. Pink tissue paper was used first, and these were overlaid with strips of blue and yellow, to create purple and orange tones. Cut out the shade and hold it over a lighted lamp – add more pieces if needed (we added some black).

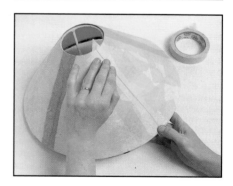

Glue the edges and hold them with masking tape until set, then remove tape and cover the join with two layers of papier mâché. Using a small bowl, mark a circle, large enough for your hand to fit through, on the ball shape and cut it out. Make three large balls (see page 78). When dry, slice a small section from each, so that they can lie flat. Attach the feet around the hole with epoxy glue.

Paint the overlapping edges with white glue; hold with masking tape until dry. Using new supports or those from the old shade, attach them with white glue, having first given them a coat of white emulsion. Treat the finished shade with fire retardent, available from theatrical suppliers.

IVY LEAGUE

A plain lampshade is decorated with a simple ivy motif, coloured in with pearlized fabric paints. First, draw the design on to tracing paper, then pencil over the shapes on the reverse side. Tape the trace in position over the shade and transfer the design by following the outline once more.

Go over the motif in pencil to make the images stronger. When this is done you can colour in the design. If you cannot buy pearlized fabric paint, use opaque fabric paint on dark background colours, or ordinary fabric paints on light backgrounds. When the design is complete, fix the colour by holding the shade under a hot hair dryer for a few minutes.

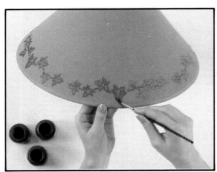

DRAGONFLY LAMP

The inspiration for this lamp came from a small evening bag. Either copy the design used here or find an alternative source of inspiration, such as a piece of fabric, a greeting card or a porcelain plate. Then experiment with the colours you are going to use, colouring in the design with felt tip pens.

Trace your design on to the shade and colour it in using brightly coloured fabric felt tip pens. Edge the motifs in stronger colour. Now paint the design on to the lamp base using ceramic paints. If you do not feel confident about painting the shapes straight on to the surface, draw them on first with a chinagraph pencil

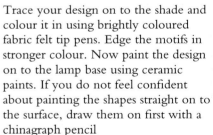

Leave the first colour to dry before edging the design in a lighter shade. You will need to fix the paint on the lampshade by heating it with a hair dryer for a few minutes.

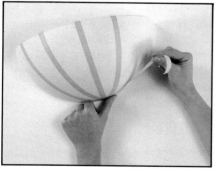

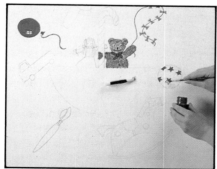

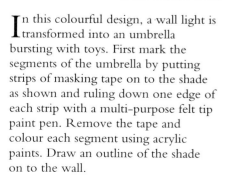

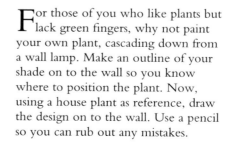

In this colourful design, a wall light is transformed into an umbrella bursting with toys. First mark the segments of the umbrella by putting strips of masking tape on to the shade as shown and ruling down one edge of each strip with a multi-purpose felt tip paint pen. Remove the tape and colour each segment using acrylic paints. Draw an outline of the shade on to the wall.

Draw the various elements of the design in pencil on to tracing paper – restrict your shapes to balloons, balls and kites if you are not too confident about more complex shapes. Pencil over the reverse of each trace and transfer the images on to the wall. As before, use acrylic paints to colour in the toys. Complete the picture by fixing the shade in position.

For those of you who like plants but lack green fingers, why not paint your own plant, cascading down from a wall lamp. Make an outline of your shade on to the wall so you know where to position the plant. Now, using a house plant as reference, draw the design on to the wall. Use a pencil so you can rub out any mistakes.

If you are using a translucent lightshade like this one, you can draw some of the leaves within the outline so that they show through the shade. Paint the leaves using acrylic paints or even artist's oils, though the latter will take a little longer to dry. Use dark colours to create shadow and depth, and light colours to add highlights. Finally, fix your shade in place. As you can see, the effect is stunning.

KITCHEN LAMPSHADE

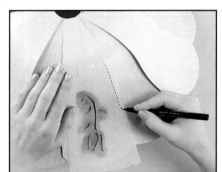

Stencil a pretty pine lampshade to hang over the corner table and complete the setting. Sand the wood smooth and paint with two or three coats of pale blue satin varnish. Use a single flower motif and trim the acetate to fit one section. Place the stencil centrally and draw in the outline of the section to align the stencil accurately each time.

Tape the stencil on one section and stencil all over with quick-drying stencil paint in pale blue. Use a clean brush and lightly shade the base of the flower and leaves with a darker blue–grey paint. Leave to dry and give the whole shade a coat of clear matt varnish to complete it.

Size as required: suggest one square represents 2cm (¾in)

An old piece of utility furniture, long past its prime, is transformed with a beautiful paint finish and some new china handles. Choose a light coloured emulsion paint for the base colour, plus a medium and a dark shade for the sponging on. Before you can start to redecorate, you will need to remove the old finish.

Place the piece of furniture in a well ventilated room, standing it on plenty of newspaper to protect the surrounding floor. Apply paint stripper according to the manufacturer's instructions; leave for the required length of time and then scrape off the old paint. Wash down the surface with liquid detergent and water and, when dry, sand it until the wood is smooth.

Next, apply a primer, an undercoat and then an emulsion base colour, leaving the cupboard to dry between coats. Take a natural sponge, wet it and squeeze it so it is just damp. Dip it into your second colour and dab any excess paint on to waste paper before applying paint to the cupboard. Use a light dabbing motion so that you do not smudge the paint, and leave lots of gaps for the next colour.

Apply the third and darkest colour with a clean sponge, filling in any gaps and overlapping other sponged areas.

Finally, using ceramic paint, decorate some plain white china handles with a pretty leaf or floral pattern. If you need inspiration for your design, try looking at an old china cup or plate.

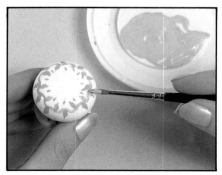

Using red, green and blue acrylic paint and a fine paint brush, paint the cross pieces, the central dowels and the ends of the legs and arms in alternating bright colours. Acrylic paints dry very quickly so clean your brush instantly between each colour.

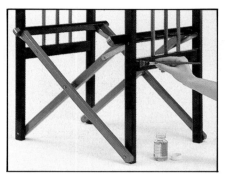

When the paint is completely dry, give the frame a couple of coats of varnish to protect it. Leave the first coat to dry before applying the second one.

Using either the original covers or some new fabric cut to size, put strips of masking tape across the canvas, masking off a series of rectangles both large and small. Rub the tape down with the back of a spoon to give it extra adhesion.

A striking 'Mondrian' inspired design in bold colours gives a new lease of life to a battered old director's chair. Even if you don't have an old chair to do up it's still worth buying a new one to customize. As well as paint brushes, masking tape and a sponge, you will also require varnish, acrylic paints, opaque fabric paints and a black fabric paint pen.

Pour some opaque fabric paint into a saucer and dip a sponge into the colour. Dab the paint on to a masked area of the canvas being sure not to get any paint on the adjacent squares. Use a sponge rather than a paint brush to avoid brush strokes. When you have finished applying one colour, take a clean sponge and apply the next. Continue like this until all the rectangles are filled in.

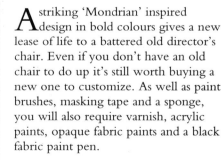

Remove the canvas from your chair; if it is old, you can replace it later with new deck chair canvas. Sand down the chair frame until the wood is smooth and fill any cracks with wood filler. Now paint the outline of the frame with black acrylic paint, applying a second coat if necessary.

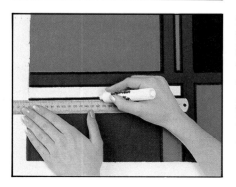

You may find you have to use more than one coat of paint if you are working on a very dark background. When the paint is completely dry, tear off all the masking tape. Finish by drawing a black rule round each of the rectangles, using a fabric paint pen. You can now put the canvas back on the chair.

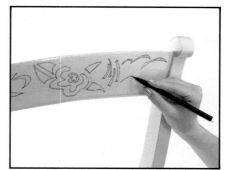

This chair was inspired by designs of the 'Bloomsbury Group' (a London-based group of artists and writers). First, give a plain wooden chair a fresh coat of gloss paint. Then referring to the pattern in the main photograph, draw the design on to the surface using a fine black felt tip pen.

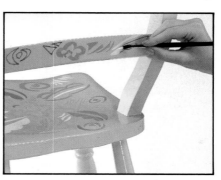

Using gloss paints, colour in the design with a fine brush, making sure you just cover the black outlines so that the design remains soft, rather than hard-edged.

Here's a cheerful way to decorate some inexpensive plastic chairs for a party or kid's playroom. All you need are some fine multi-purpose felt tip pens and a chinagraph pencil. Using the chinagraph pencil, draw your design on to the seat and the back of the chair, creating bold shapes and patterns. Rub out any mistakes with a soft cloth soaked in lighter fuel.

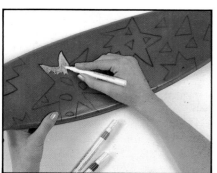

Colour in your outlines with the multi-purpose pens, using brightly contrasting and even clashing colours. Decorate the stars with dots, spots, dashes and triangles of black.

Outline the edges of the shapes in black to make the images sharper. Finally, link up the various elements of your design with colourful streamers and more dots and dashes.

Bambooing is a simple but effective paint technique which can add interest to a plain piece of cane furniture. Before you start to paint, remove any varnish from your furniture with varnish remover. Dilute some brown acrylic paint with water to make a wash, then, using a 20mm (¾in) brush, paint bands of colour at intervals along the cane.

Next, using the same colour undiluted and a fine brush, paint on the markings. First, paint lines of colour in the centre of the band of wash. Next paint elongated 'V' shapes in pairs at right angles to the lines, finishing off with tiny dots by the sides of the Vs. When the bambooing is complete, apply a coat of varnish to protect the paintwork.

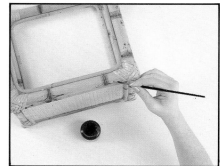

In recent years, Lloyd loom chairs such as this have become collectors' items. But because so many of them are now in poor condition, they are often renovated and painted with an attractive motif. The flamboyance of this design is intended to reflect the warm sunny conservatory for which such chairs were originally intended.

You can either paint the chair using aerosol spray paint or apply paint in the traditional manner with a paint brush. Draw your rose design on to the chair, using a soft pencil and keeping the flowers big and bold. Colour in the design with acrylic paints, mixing the colours to get a wide range of shades. Use dark shades to add shadow and depth, and lighter shades for the highlights.

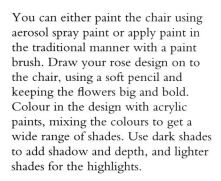

Trace off the Florentine motif from page 247. Draw out the pattern carefully, spacing the motifs evenly about 9cm (3½in) apart vertically and 7.5cm (3in) apart horizontally. You will need two motifs minimum for small areas but you will greatly speed up the stencilling if you cut a sheet with six or eight motifs. Also draw on vertical guidelines and dotted motif outlines.

Find the centre of the wall and use a plumb-line to mark a vertical pencil line down to the dado rail. Join up the pencil marks with a long ruler and use this line to begin stencilling.

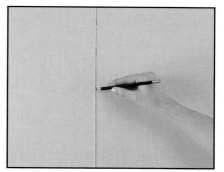

Start near the top of the wall and work one row of motifs vertically down the plumb-line. Make pencil marks first so that the design starts about 5cm (2in) from the ceiling and leaves a 11.5cm (4½in) space above the dado rail for the border. Mix up some grey quick-drying stencil paint and brush stencil lightly to give a soft, grainy texture.

When using a small, two-motif stencil, overlap the lower motif you have stencilled with the top one on the acetate sheet to space the first row accurately. The small stencil is useful in tight corners and close to door frames to prevent bending the acetate too much.

Work the next vertical row of motifs matching up the dotted areas with the first row of stencilling. Continue all over the wall. Adjust the space between rows very slightly to accommodate awkward corners. Stencil within 13cm (5in) of the mirror edge. If there are large gaps near the curved area, leave them and add another motif later when the border is complete.

You will need to adapt the original bluebird pattern for this prettily decorated chest of drawers. Trace off the central bow from page 247 and turn the design slightly so that the ribbon tails hang vertically. To balance the bow, sketch in another loop of ribbon on the left. Also use the bow design on page 38.

Trace off the new bow design on to a small piece of acetate using a fine waterproof felt-tipped pen. Mark the position of the bird stencils on either side to align the design when stencilling. Cut out the shapes carefully using a sharp craft knife and a cutting mat. Also make a bird stencil. Alternatively, use part of the complete stencil if you have one already made.

If you are only using part of a complete design, mask off the areas of stencil you do not want with paper and masking tape. Mark the centre of the drawer with a pencil line and stencil either side, reversing the stencil as needed. Use quick-drying stencil paint over a base coat of emulsion and, once dry, finish off with a coat of clear varnish.

A painted Lloyd Loom chair is an ideal accessory for this child's bedroom. As the wall stencil is too detailed for the texture of the chair, a bolder version of the design has been chosen. Use the pattern on page 247 to cut three stencils from acetate. Tape the bow stencil centrally on the chair back and mask all around. Spray with household spray paint in soft peach.

Position a bird stencil on the left of the chair beside the bow. Tape in place and mask as before. Spray the bird in white. Spray several thin coats from about 30cm (12in) away, until the weave of the chair is well covered but not clogged. Leave to dry, then carefully remove the stencil and mask. Repeat with the other bird stencil to complete the design.

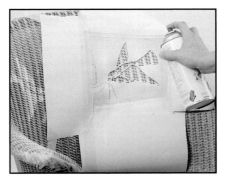

BLUEBIRD BORDER

Follow the pattern opposite to make your full-size stencil. Trace off the bluebirds on to a sheet of clear acetate using a fine waterproof felt-tipped pen. Also trace off some parts of the peach bows, using a dotted line, to help position the stencil. Mark the top and side lines as register marks, then cut out the bird shapes using a craft knife.

Make another stencil for the bows. Mark a faint horizontal pencil line along the wall to line up with top register mark on stencil. Tape the stencil in position and, using soft peach quick-drying stencil paint, stencil the bow design. Keep the paint fairly thin and leave to dry. With a clean brush and terracotta paint, dab the areas where the ribbon twists to give a 3-D effect.

Using the bluebird stencil, tape the acetate in position, lining up your register marks and matching the dotted lines with the stencilled bows. Carefully dab slate blue stencil paint over the birds. Make sure the whole design is covered but keep the brush fairly dry to avoid paint seeping underneath. Wipe the surface often to prevent small holes in the stencil becoming clogged.

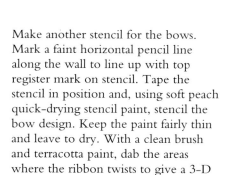

One square represents 2cm (¾in)

RIBBON BOWS

Use this delicate bow to 'hang' small pictures in your bluebird bedroom. The ribbons at the side interlock so you can also use it as a pretty border pattern. Trace off and cut out the design opposite on acetate. Tape the stencil just above the picture so that the ends of the ribbons will disappear behind the frame. Stencil with quick-drying stencil paint in soft peach.

When the paint has dried slightly, use a clean brush to lightly dab on some terracotta colour stencil paint. Do this where the ribbons twist and overlap to give a 3-D effect and make the ribbon look almost shiny. Blend the terracotta paint into the soft peach to avoid a sudden colour change.

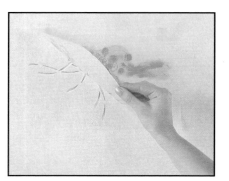

The plain flush doors in this modern hall looked very boring, so to add a little character they have been stencilled with four grey borders to give a panelled look. Start by marking out the panels with pencil lines, using a long ruler and set-square for accuracy. The borders should be about 1.5cm (⅝in) wide, with the space at the bottom of the door greater than the top and sides.

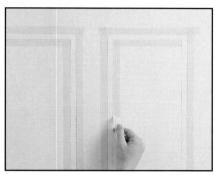

Use long strips of masking tape to mask off around the border, on both sides. Press down the tape with your fingertip to prevent paint from seeping underneath and cut the corners neatly with a sharp craft knife. On an old plate, mix up some white, grey and black quick-drying stencil paints. If the door paint is very shiny, lightly sand the border area first to key the stencilling.

If your light source is on the right, start by stencilling the left hand side of each panel in a medium grey, dabbing the paint on thinly and evenly. Mask the top and bottom corners of this line with tape to form a 45° angle (like the mitred corner of a frame). (If the light comes from the left hand side, start stencilling on the right hand side of each panel.)

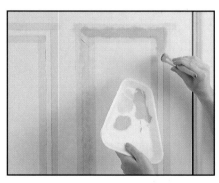

Leave to dry for a few minutes and remove the angled corner tapes. Then stencil the top and right hand border in dark grey. (Top and left hand border, if light comes from the left.) Mask the corners at an angle, as before. Stencil a thin, even coating of colour, getting slightly paler towards the bottom of the panel.

Lastly, stencil the lower border in pale grey as it will theoretically get the most amount of light. Leave to dry and very carefully pull off the masking tape. For economy, these tapes can be used several times. Stencil all the other panels on the door and then clean off the pencil marks with a damp cloth when the paint has dried.

To create this beautiful effect, first paint your walls in white silk vinyl and then sponge pale, sunny yellow emulsion paint over the top to make a warm, cloudy effect. Dip a large, damp natural sponge into a saucer of paint, taking care not to overload the sponge. Dab off the excess on to a spare piece of cardboard, then dab on to the wall in an even pattern.

Enlarge and cut two stencil sheets from the design on page 41. Lightly mark the desired level on the wall and tape the flower stencil in place. Use a small piece of natural sponge and dip it into a saucer containing pale peach or yellow stencil paint or emulsion paint. Tester pots are ideal for this purpose. Dab on to the stencil around the edge of each circle of flowers.

Mix up a subtle pinky-orange and sponge-stencil this on to the centre of each group of flowers. Gradually blend the pink with the yellow to make a soft orange. Stencil all the flowers around the wall like this, linking the design with the dotted lines on the stencil.

Tape on the leaf stencil and mix a few shades of green from lime to emerald on an old plate. Use another piece of sponge to stencil the leaves and stems. Try to vary the shades of green over the design, to give added interest. Dab lightly for a mottled texture that blends with the wall sponging.

BATHED IN FLOWERS

Enlarge and cut out two stencils from the honeysuckle design opposite. Clean the outside of the bath thoroughly – you can spray paint this first if necessary. Spray glue over the back of the first stencil and tape in place. Mask all around with plenty of waste paper to protect from overspray. Using household spray paint, held about 30cm (12in) away, spray the flowers lightly in yellow.

Leave to dry for a few moments. Meanwhile, shake a can of pink spray paint to mix it thoroughly. When the first colour is touch-dry, spray the centre of each circle of flowers with a burst of pink to subtly shade it.

Tape the leaf stencil in place, lining up the flowers with the dotted lines on the acetate. Tape waste paper all around as before and lightly spray the leaves in green. Add a little extra green in a few places to liven it up. Stencil all around the bath, then leave the paint to dry thoroughly before use.

Draw a door plate shape on cardboard (you might draw around an existing plate). Draw a simple squiggle down the middle, as shown. Cut the shape out.

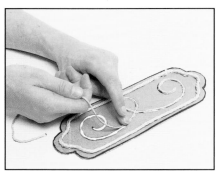

Using sizal, for thickness, glue string around the shape, just inside the edge. Glue thinner parcel string along the squiggle shape.

Using small pieces to maintain as much definition as possible, papier mâché over the string and on the front and back of the plate. Apply up to four layers.

Give the door plate two coats of emulsion and then a coat of light green gloss.

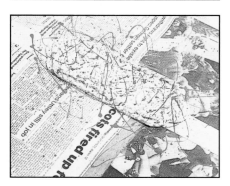

When this has dried, sponge on darker green paint. When dry, lay the door plate on a sheet of newspaper and splash red gloss paint over it, creating a 'Jackson Pollock' effect. Make a hole at the top and bottom, so that it can be attached to the door.

This decorative column is based on one seen in Savannah, Georgia. Start by drawing the shape, which measures approximately 25 by 52.5cm (10 by 21in) on a drawing board. Roll out a clay sausage about 2.5cm (1in) thick, and press it along the line, flattening the base to make the roll D-shaped. Coat the shape and 5cm (2in) of board on either side with petroleum jelly.

All at one go, apply four layers of 10cm (4in) square papier mâché (you may require smaller pieces on inner curves). The vertical lines are made from lengths of semicircular wooden dowel, sanded into rounds at each end. These are simply given two coats of white emulsion. When dry, cut the papier mâché from the board and remove the clay. Clean the flat edges with white spirit.

Sand and seal the surface, and apply two coats of emulsion. Draw a line 6mm (¼in) out from the raised surface and trim away the excess. Position the pieces on the wall with masking tape and draw around them. Take them down and apply impact adhesive to the column pieces and the wall, then fix them in place, filling any gaps with ready-mix plaster.

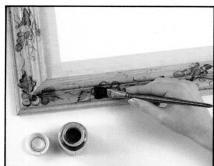

A brightly decorated clock makes a novel gift for a child. Self-assembly clocks like this one are available from some craft suppliers (particularly by mail order) so check in craft magazines for stockists. First, sand down the clock so that it is perfectly smooth, then draw your design in pencil. Use bright acrylic paints to colour the design.

When the painting is complete, assemble the clock according to the manufacturer's instructions. Apply a coat of polyurethane varnish for a glossy finish.

A vine leaf design is used to enhance a plain mirror frame. The design can be painted with acrylic or a combination of ceramic and glass paints, using different shades of green, plus brown, white, yellow and black. Protect the glass before you start painting with a layer of paper stuck down around the edges with masking tape.

To age the frame, stain it with brown and green glass paint diluted with turpentine. When the stain is dry, finish with a coat of varnish. Another way of ageing the frame is to use the 'crackle' varnish method.

Firmly tape all the pieces together around the outer edge. Give the resulting frame four layers of papier mâché and leave it to dry.

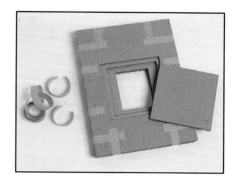

Using a quarter of a broadsheet each time, crumple nine pieces of paper and leave them in paste overnight. Squeeze out the excess paste and form them into sausages, pointed at each end. When dry, after several days, cut each in half with a breadknife, making 18 points of slightly varied sizes.

Using epoxy glue, fix the points around the frame, spacing them evenly. Work on one edge at a time, supporting the frame so that the edge on which you are working is horizontal. When you have finished, leave the glue to harden before decorating the frame.

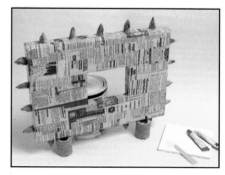

Paint the frame with five layers of ready-prepared gesso. Draw the surface lines with a pencil, and then paint lines on the front and the edges with three coats of gold poster paint. When this has dried, apply a coat of matt polyurethane varnish, giving the white a slightly aged quality.

M ade with an ordinary mirror tile, this would be ideal for a hallway. Instead of emulsion, the white ground of the frame has been painted with gesso to add textural interest. Cut eight pieces of cardboard, each measuring 30 by 40cm (12 by 16in). Cut windows from each, as shown in the diagram, discarding all the centres except for the largest.

When the varnish has dried, place a 15cm (6in) mirror tile in the back of the frame. You may need to back it with a piece of cardboard the same size. Finally, fix the spare cardboard window over the tile, using epoxy glue to hold it in place. Brass eye screws can be used for hanging the frame.

Cut two more circles, this time with a diameter of 18.5cm (7½in), and glue them to one end of the cylinder. Make a base from two 22.5cm (9in) squares of cardboard, with side pieces 5cm (2in) high.

For the top, cut a 27.5cm (11in) square of cardboard. Using compasses and leaving 4cm (1½in) at the middle of each side, mark and cut curves from the corners. Bend a length of cardboard along one of the curves. Mark the length of the side, then complete the shape, finishing in a 7.5cm (3in) circle at each end, as shown. Cut four, and assemble as shown.

To fill the gaps at the rounded ends, cut strips of cardboard 4cm (1½in) wide and tape them in position. To finish the top, glue two more 17.5cm (7in) squares to the top of the column. Cut two 27.5cm (11in) squares of cardboard and join them with sides 6cm (2½in) high. Add this to the base of the column.

Cover the column with six layers of papier mâché, not forgetting the bottom, and then apply two coats of emulsion.

This attractive plant display column could be brought outside on a fine day, but is really intended for indoor use. First, make a cylinder, 30cm (12in) high and with a diameter of 15cm (6in), using two circles and a rectangle of cardboard. Use white glue and tape to assemble the cylinder.

Paint to suit your decor. This particular column was painted with pink wood primer, which gave it an attractive matt finish. It was then stippled with a piece of screwed-up rag soaked in dark grey wood primer.

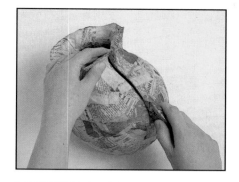

When dry, use a pencil to draw a line dividing the shape into two equal halves. You can erase any unsatisfactory attempts. When you are satisfied, cut along the pencil line with a sharp knife.

Lay each half on cardboard and mark around it, then cut out a back.

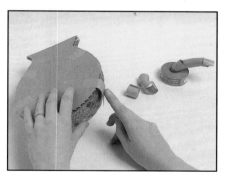

Paint the matching edges with white glue, then hold them together with brown tape. Papier mâché the back and edges of each vase, applying three layers over the back and as far inside as you can reach, all at one go. Allow them to dry, preferably on a cake rack in the airing cupboard.

With this technique, you can make two attractive wall vases at the same time. First cover a balloon with five layers of papier mâché. When this has dried, pierce the string end of the balloon and remove.

Cut a small hole at the back of each vase, about 2.5cm (1in) down from the top. Sand and seal the vases and give them two coats of emulsion. The vases can then be decorated, either with black and white emulsion, finished with three coats of acrylic varnish; or with gouache, finished with polyurethane.

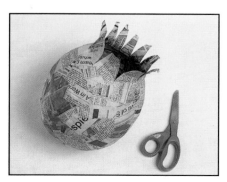

Cut into that end, as shown, gently bending out the resulting teeth. Cover this toothed edge with two layers of 7.5cm (3in) square papier mâché. Allow this to dry overnight, then add a further two layers.

Once the parts are roughly taped together, go over them again with brown tape, covering all the joints and edges. This gives a better finish.

Measure the length of a shelf front and the top. Make paper templates for a shelf frill and scroll top. Using a craft knife, cut three shelf frills (these are used singly) and three scrolls (joined together, like the shelves).

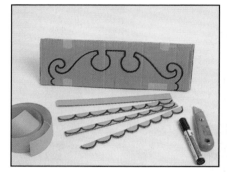

Again with brown tape, add the break-top scroll and shelf frills to the unit.

Laying the unit on cardboard, mark and cut out a back piece. Attach this with white glue and brown tape. For greater stability, add a base, again using three thicknesses of cardboard. Cut the base pieces 1cm (⅜in) wider and 2cm (¾in) longer than the existing base. Also, for fun, glue three table tennis balls to the top. Apply six layers of papier mâché.

This antique-style shelving unit makes a charming showcase for small ornaments. The main frame of the shelves is made from cardboard. Cut twelve pieces measuring 35 by 7cm (14 by 2¾in) and six pieces 40 by 7cm (16 by 2¾in). The shelves and sides are all made from three layers each, fitted together as shown and held with brown tape.

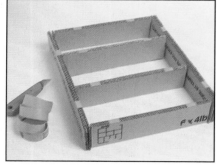

When dry, give the unit two coats of emulsion and leave it to dry. Paint with yellow ochre gouache and then add the lines in alizarin crimson. To complete the unit, give it two coats of mahogany-stained varnish. Further coats will give a progressively darker effect, if desired.

To make this clock, you will require a clock movement with a screw fitting behind the hands, available from craft shops. The top and base are octagons, made by trimming the corners from 20cm (8in) squares of cardboard; the side pieces are all 25cm (10in) high, cut to the width of the octagon sides. Cut crenellations into the top edge of the side pieces. Cut a circle from the base.

Tape the pieces together as shown, taping the circle that was cut from the base to the front, to become the clock face.

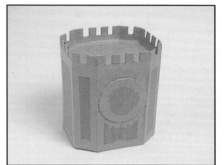

To make the spire, cut four isosceles triangles, with a base of 9cm (3¾in) and a height of 20cm (8in).

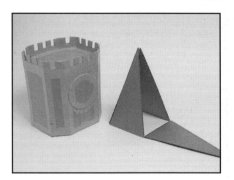

Tape the pieces together and tape the spire to the tower.

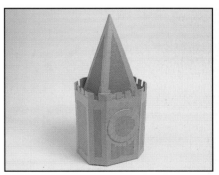

Apply six layers of papier mâché. When dry, give the tower two coats of emulsion and then a coat of sand-coloured gloss paint. Dry-brush a dark brown gloss over the sand to create the stony look. Make a hole in the front and fit the clock movement, adding the hands once this is secure. Paint the numerals, winding the hands round to see where they should go.

POTATO PRINT CUSHIONS

You probably think of potato printing as something you used to do in primary school – well think again! It can be used to great effect when decorating soft furnishings for the home. Cut a potato in half and draw the design on to one half with a felt tip pen. Now cut around the motif so that the design stands proud of the background.

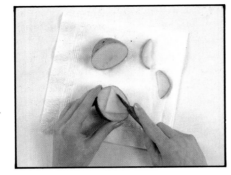

Paint some fabric paint on to the potato motif with a brush. Stamp off any excess paint on to some waste paper then print the motif on to your chosen fabric, leaving plenty of space for a second and even a third motif.

Cut another simple motif from the other half of the potato. Apply the colour as before and print on to the fabric. When the fabric has dried, iron on the back to fix the paints. Your fabric is now ready to be made up into cushions.

'QUILT' CUSHIONS

These cushions are based on designs taken from American patchwork quilts. With a soft pencil, copy the design on to tracing paper then position the trace, pencil marks down, over your chosen fabric. Transfer the image on to the fabric by tracing over the back of the design.

When the design is on the material, go over it with a pencil if the image is not strong enough. Apply the first colour using a fabric felt tip pen.

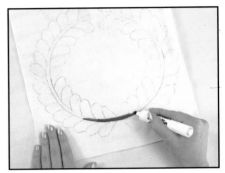

Fill in the other colours. If you are using alternate colours, as on these leaves, it is a good idea to mark each leaf with the correct colour so you don't make a mistake half way through. Iron on the back to fix the design and make the fabric up into cushions.

The inspiration for this vase comes from a beautiful piece of Victorian embroidery. The designs are similar except the white and black have been reversed so, instead of white stalks on a black background, there are black stalks on a white background. You can either copy this design, or find a similar piece of embroidery to copy.

As it is always difficult to paint directly on to a curved surface, first draw the design on to the vase using a chinagraph pencil.

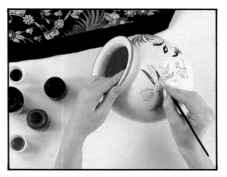

Colour in the design with ceramic paints, mixing the various colours together to get the right shades. Use very fine paint brushes for the stalks and slightly thicker ones for the leaves and flowers. Clean the brushes carefully between each colour.

Decorate a plain ceramic planter with bamboo stems and leaves, painted in a Chinese style. You will need green and yellow ceramic paint and green and black glass paint. Paint wide vertical lines of green around your pot, using a 20mm (¾in) decorator's brush and both the glass and the ceramic paints to give different depths of colour. Make the lines uneven and slightly crooked.

Add yellow highlights to some of the green stripes. Mix some green and a little black paint and, with a fine pointed brush, paint slightly curved horizontal lines at intervals across the vertical lines. Finally, using a soft pointed Chinese art brush and the green/black mix, paint groups of leaves radiating out from the stems.

An elegant but inexpensive vase is transformed with the simple use of a sponge and some ceramic paints. Take a small piece of natural sponge and dip it into some white spirit. Squeeze the sponge out and lightly dip it into a saucer of ceramic paint. Dab excess paint on to a piece of waste paper, then apply the colour to the vase with a light dabbing motion.

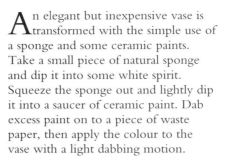

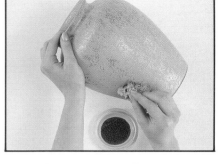

Sponge the whole of the vase, leaving space for a second colour, and reapplying paint to the sponge as necessary. Use a second sponge to apply the next colour, making sure to overlap the colours for an even finish. As an alternative to ceramic paints, you could use high gloss gold lacquer and ordinary emulsion paint.

With a combination of ragging and flicking you can transform a plain china vase or jug into a work of art. You will need a piece of cloth for the ragging, a couple of fine artists' brushes and some ceramic paints. Dip the rag into one of the paints and then blot it onto some waste paper to remove any excess paint. Now begin to dab paint on to the vase.

Leave gaps between the dabs of paint to allow the background colour to show through. When you have evenly covered the surface, leave it to dry. Now spatter the vase with white ceramic paint, flicking the paint on with a fine brush. Once again, leave to dry.

Finally, apply some gold ceramic paint with a fine paint brush, forming clusters of little gold dots across the surface of the vase. Be sure to clean your brush thoroughly in turpentine when you have finished.

Using a pencil or a medium-sized knitting needle, lightly score across each side piece, from one inner angle to the other. Paint first one side and then the other of all five pieces with white glue. This will seal the card and help to prevent warping.

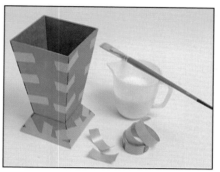

When the pieces are dry, paint all the sides and base edges with white glue. Fit the pieces together as shown, using strips of brown tape to hold them in place. Leave the vase to dry overnight.

Layering the pieces alternately vertically and horizontally, cover the vase, inside and out, with three layers of papier mâché, each piece approximately 2.5 by 7.5cm (1 by 3in). When dry, sand and then seal with thinned white glue.

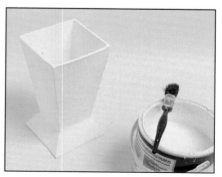

Paint the vase all over with white emulsion. The first layer may crack, but when this has dried, apply a second layer, which should be flat and white.

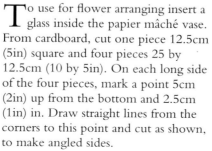

To use for flower arranging insert a glass inside the papier mâché vase. From cardboard, cut one piece 12.5cm (5in) square and four pieces 25 by 12.5cm (10 by 5in). On each long side of the four pieces, mark a point 5cm (2in) up from the bottom and 2.5cm (1in) in. Draw straight lines from the corners to this point and cut as shown, to make angled sides.

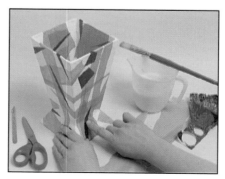

Use the thinned glue to apply pieces of torn coloured tissue paper, inside and out, and then pieces of cut foil sweet wrappers. When dry, apply three layers of acrylic varnish, putting your hand inside the vase for the outer layers, and standing it on its base for the inside. Finish by varnishing the bottom.

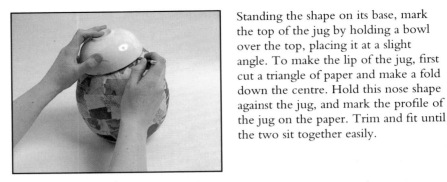

Standing the shape on its base, mark the top of the jug by holding a bowl over the top, placing it at a slight angle. To make the lip of the jug, first cut a triangle of paper and make a fold down the centre. Hold this nose shape against the jug, and mark the profile of the jug on the paper. Trim and fit until the two sit together easily.

Use the template to cut a card lip, adding tags as shown, and cut a corresponding notch from the jug. Sketch a handle for the jug. Cut one from cardboard, making adjustments for a good fit as necessary, then cut three more identical handles from cardboard. From thin card, cut two more handles, with tabs at either end.

Glue and tape the handle together, hold it to the jug; mark the top and bottom, then cut slits and push the tabs through, gluing them to the inside with epoxy glue (use a pallete knife for the lower tags). Also attach the lip. Hold with masking tape until the glue has dried.

This elegant decorative jug is painted with a 1950s-style design. To make it, papier mâché a balloon, mark the bottom (a reel of brown tape was used here), and cut out the section to create a flat base.

When the glue is dry, remove the tape and apply three layers of papier mâché, all at one go, to the handle and the lip, covering all tags. Sand and seal the jug, then apply two coats of white emulsion.

Supporting the balloon shape in a bowl and using strips approximately 5 by 15cm (2 by 6in), cover the hole with four layers of papier mâché, applied at one go. Leave the shape to dry overnight.

Draw the pattern in pencil and then paint with gouache, starting with the palest shade and ending with black. Finish with a coat of matt polyurethane varnish.

These two candlesticks are shaped like pyramids and marbled. From cardboard, cut eight rectangles measuring 17.5 by 10cm (7 by 4in). One one short side of each, measure in 2.5cm (1in) from each corner and mark a line down to the lower corner. Cut as shown, angling all eight rectangles. Also cut four 5cm (2in) squares. Glue and tape the eight pieces into two pyramids.

For each, mark the shape of the bottom on cardboard and cut out. Take a 4cm (1½in) length of cardboard tube, such as the inner tube from a roll of freezer bags. Using scissors, cut 6mm (¼in) nicks at 3mm (⅛in) intervals around one end. Also cut a circle the diameter of the tube from one small square of card, then glue it to a complete square.

Using white glue and brown tape, fix the bases to the pyramids, then the candle holder tubes into the recessed top pieces. Finally, fix the tops in position. When both candlesticks have been assembled, paint all over with a coat of thinned white glue, to prevent warping.

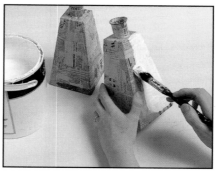

Cover with three layers of papier mâché, applied all at one go. When dry, sand and seal again with thinned white glue. Apply two coats of white emulsion, then paint with thinned black gouache, adding touches of blue and green while the black is still wet. This overall wash forms the base for the marbling.

Next, apply stronger black lines of gouache, flattening the loaded brush on the edge of the paint pot to shape the end into a chisel. Add more lines with a gold felt-tip pen. Give the candle holder three layers of gold poster paint. Finish with matt polyurethane varnish, brushing along the gold pen lines with light strokes. Give the finished candlesticks a coat of fire retardant.

Glue and tape together the matching squares. Centre the smaller square on the flat side of the larger, and glue and tape it to make the lid. Coat a rubber ball with petroleum jelly and apply four layers of papier mâché, using fairly small pieces. To check for gaps, allow the paper to dry between layers.

Apply three layers of papier mâché to the box at one time, using pieces measuring about 2.5 by 7.5cm (1 by 3in). When the ball is dry, mark the circumference and cut around it.

Remove the papier mâché and immediately glue the two halves together, holding them with masking tape. When dry, cover the join with two more layers of small pieces.

Glue the dry ball to the lid recess with epoxy glue. Sand and seal the box and lid, then apply two coats of white emulsion.

This marbled box has a golden handle on the lid. From cardboard, cut four (side) pieces 15 by 10cm (6 by 4in), two (lids) 13.8cm (5½in) square and two (inside lids) 9cm (3½in) square. Join the sides with white glue and tape, and then mark and cut out a base. Join this to the sides. At the centre of one of the large squares, mark and cut a hole 2.5cm (1in) in diameter.

Paint the inside of the box and lid with gouache. Decorate the outside with brown and orange chalk, then brush all over with clear water. Repeat two or three times for depth of colour. Give the ball three coats of gold poster paint. Finish with a coat of matt polyurethane varnish.

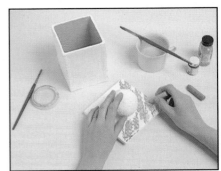

This would make an excellent holder for pencils or brushes. Cover your chosen shape – perhaps a plastic cream or yoghurt container – with petroleum jelly. Apply five layers of papier mâché to the outside at one time, using strips measuring about 4 by 15cm (1½ by 6in), setting each new layer at right angles to the last.

When the papier mâché has dried, mark down the centre line on each side. Cut with a sharp knife down the sides but not across the bottom, slightly sliding the blade under the paper to help to release the paper shape.

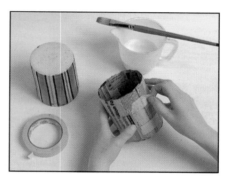

Remove any traces of petroleum jelly with cotton wool and white spirit. Immediately paint the cut edges with white glue. Hold them together with masking tape until the glue has dried. Remove the tape and apply another couple of layers of papier mâché, inside and out.

You could simply bind the edge, but this rolled edge is created with paste-soaked pieces of paper measuring about 7.5cm (3in) square. Work around the edge, holding two of these rolls against the outside edge of the beaker and binding them in place with 2.5 by 10cm (1 by 4in) strips.

When the edge has dried, sand and seal the beaker, and then apply two coats of white emulsion. First draw the pattern on the surface with a pencil, then paint with gouache colours. Paint the black lines of gouache last. Finish with a coat of matt polyurethane varnish.

GOLDEN HONEY POT

Transform a rather plain ceramic honey pot into something striking. Using a fine paint brush and black ceramic paint, paint some bees on to the lid of the pot. If you are worried about painting free-hand, first draw the bees on with a chinagraph pencil. And if you are not even sure how to draw a bee, copy one from a picture.

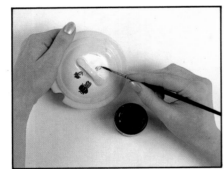

Now paint the stripes with black ceramic paint. If, like this one, your pot is ridged, use the raised surface as a guide for your lines of paint. Otherwise you can use strips of masking tape to mask off those areas which are to be yellow. In order not to smudge the work, you may find it easier to paint the lower half first and then leave it to dry before painting the top half.

When all the black has dried, apply the yellow ceramic paint, carefully filling in the bee's striped body with a fine brush. Fill the pot with honey and have a nice breakfast!

TORN TAPE PLATE

Create a stunning design by using a very simple but effective design technique, known as masking. Cut a strip of masking tape the width of your plate and very carefully rip it in half lengthways, creating an uneven edge. Place the two torn pieces back to back across the centre of the plate. Then add further double strips of tape either side, leaving gaps in between each set.

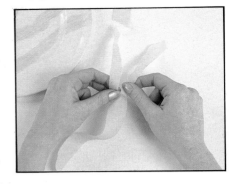

When you have covered the plate in torn tape lines, make sure that all the edges are stuck down properly. Apply ceramic paint to the exposed areas, using a dabbing motion so that the paint does not seep under the tape.

Leave the plate to dry for at least 24 hours before carefully removing the tape. Clean up any smudged edges using a rag dipped in white spirit, then apply a coat of ceramic varnish. The black lines on a white background gives a striking 'zebra stripe' effect, but other colour combinations look equally attractive so try experimenting a little.

Who's been eating my porridge . . . and left footprints all over my plate? You can have great fun decorating china like this, using bird prints, paw prints, wellington boots or even human footprints. To make the paw print plate, first draw a spiral on to the plate as shown with a chinagraph pencil.

Using the spiral as a guide, paint the outline of the prints in black ceramic paint: you will need a very fine paint brush for this. Once the paint has dried, rub off all trace of the chinagraph line.

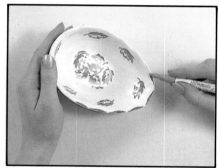

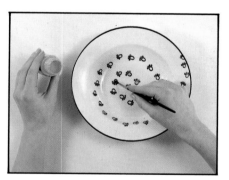

Colour the centre of the paws with a brightly coloured ceramic paint. When the plate is completely dry, finish off with a protective coat of ceramic varnish.

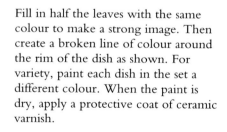

Brighten up some plain avocado dishes with an attractive leaf design. Such dishes are ideal for decorating as, although functional, then tend not to be used daily. Also, because you eat from the skin of the avocado, you are unlikely to scratch the design with your cutlery. Decorate the dishes with multi-purpose felt tip paint pens. First, draw the outline of the leaves in the bottom of the dish and around the sides.

Fill in half the leaves with the same colour to make a strong image. Then create a broken line of colour around the rim of the dish as shown. For variety, paint each dish in the set a different colour. When the paint is dry, apply a protective coat of ceramic varnish.

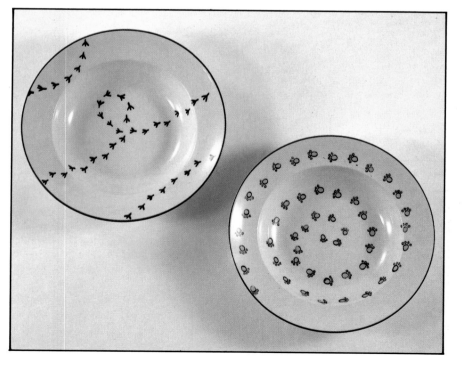

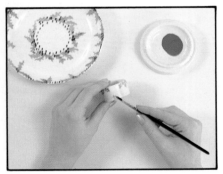

Choose a simple motif, such as holly, mistletoe, or bells, and create your own unique festive tea service. For this attractive holly design, you will need plain white china, red and green ceramic paint and a fine paint brush. Paint the outlines of the holly leaves with green paint, grouping the leaves together in threes, Now fill in the leaf outlines with more green paint.

Join up the leaves with garlands of red berries made by applying dots of red ceramic paint with a very fine brush. Also add clusters of berries at the base of the leaves. When the paint is completely dry, finish off with a coat of ceramic varnish. To complete the picture, you can even paint the motif on to the corner of your paper napkins.

These candlesticks are designed for those in a party mood; they are bright and fun, and especially suitable for a teenage party. You will need some self-adhesive ring reinforcements, candlesticks, and multi-purpose felt tip paint pens in a range of bright colours. Stick the ring reinforcements all over the candlestick as shown.

Paint the centres of the circles in various colours. Once the paint is dry, pull off the reinforcements to reveal a series of coloured dots. Complete the design by painting a border line round the base of the stem in one of the bright colours you have been using. Finally, apply a coat of ceramic varnish.

ZIG-ZAG TUMBLERS

These octagonal glasses look very stylish with a band of colour rotating around the glass. You will need either ceramic or glass paint. Cut four or five strips of masking tape long enough to wind from the top of the glass down to the bottom. Stick the first strip down then add successive strips, leaving a gap between each one.

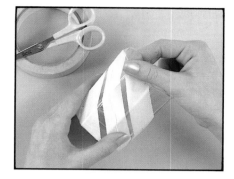

Apply the paint to the exposed areas, holding on to the masking tape while you rotate the glass. Now leave the glass to dry.

Remove the masking tape. If some of the paint has seeped under the tape, clean it off with a cloth dipped in turpentine.

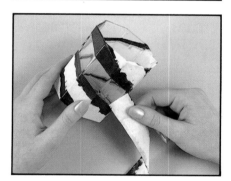

ART NOUVEAU GLASSES

Paris goblets are the cheapest wine glasses you can buy, yet you can transform them into these stylish drinking vessels with no more than a little ingenuity and some glass paints. Working from either the top or the bottom of the glass, paint on a winding plant stem using a fine brush. You may have to leave the glass to dry between painting the bulb and the base so you do not smudge the paint.

Once the stem has dried you can then decorate it with intricate leaves and curling tendrils. Use a very fine brush to achieve a delicate finish.

HERB STORAGE JARS

HARVEST STORAGE JARS

Bring the countryside into your kitchen with these charming storage jars. Cut out a piece of paper to fit round the side of the jar and then, using the template on page 251, draw your design on to the paper. To work out your colour scheme, colour the design using felt tip pens. Trace off the design on to the jar and outline the pencil with a fine black felt tip pen.

Colour the corn with the coloured felt tip pens, leaving the middle of some of the husks the natural wood colour so that the corn looks more rounded and realistic. Paint the centre of some of the other husks yellow to add more interest. Do not press the pens too hard as the colour will bleed.

Colour in the animals and butterflies and decorate around the top edge of the jar with green, as shown in the main picture, to suggest hills. Paint the lid with swallows soaring in the sunshine and, when the inks are dry, finish with a coat of polyurethane varnish to protect the colour.

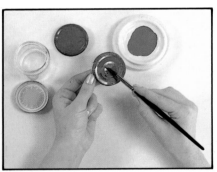

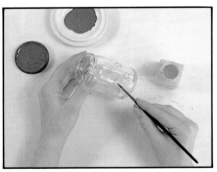

When you buy herbs in jars you are paying more for the packaging than the contents, so why not make your own storage jars and save money? Collect some old glass jars with lids and wash them in hot soapy water, removing any tough labels with a scourer. Dry the jars thoroughly, then use a medium-sized artist's brush to paint the lids with ceramic paint.

Using either ceramic or glass paints and a much finer brush, paint a series of tiny yellow dashes in clusters of five to form petals. Leave these to dry.

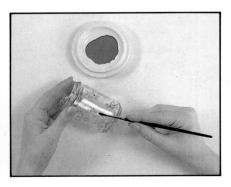

Now dot the flower centres with the same colour of paint you used for the lids. Add the green trellis between the flowers using ceramic or glass paint as before. You may need to apply two coats if using glass paint to achieve a strong colour.

PEACOCK SALT BOX

Crackle varnish creates an interesting 'antique' finish on a prettily decorated wooden salt box. Such boxes can be purchased from specialist craft suppliers at little cost. First, draw your design in pencil on to the pieces of the box. Go over the pencil marks using a fine paint brush and black acrylic paint.

Now fill in the design using brightly coloured acrylic paints, mixing and diluting them with a little water if necessary. Leave the paints to dry thoroughly before pinning the box pieces together.

Cover the box with a coat of patina varnish and leave it to dry for between 4-12 hours before applying a second coat. Once the second coat is dry to the touch (rather than completely dry), paint on a coat of crackle varnish. This should crackle in 15-20 minutes, leaving the box with a crazed, old appearance.

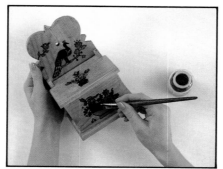

SUPER SCALES

With a design 'borrowed' from the turn of the century, new life has been breathed into some old kitchen scales. To transform your own scales you will need gold and black ceramic paints and some gold spray paint. Clean the surface of the scales with soapy water, then sand down with fine sandpaper. Now apply a coat of black paint; you may need two coats to cover the old finish.

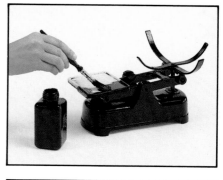

When the black ceramic paint has dried, paint your design in gold using a fine artist's brush. Create the outline first and then fill in with more gold paint. (You may wish to practise your design first on paper before actually applying paint to the scales.)

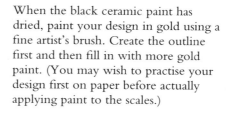

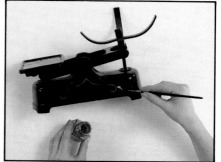

If the scales are purely for a decorative purpose, spray the old dish with gold paint. If they are going to be used for food it is probably better not to paint the dish. Remember always to use spray paints in a well ventilated area.

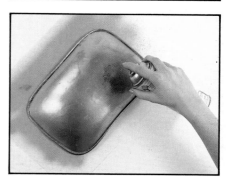

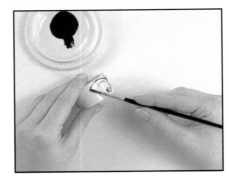

Decorate some napkin rings, and even some napkins, to match your tea or dinner service. You will need ceramic paints that match the colours of your china: in this case blue, green and pink. First, paint the outline of the design using a very fine brush and being careful to make a single sweeping movement with each stroke.

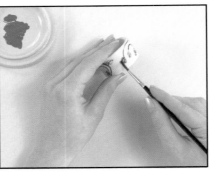

When the initial coat is dry, begin to fill in the outline with a second colour, carefully following the design on your plate.

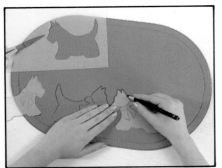

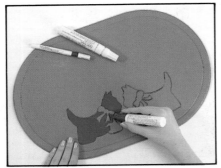

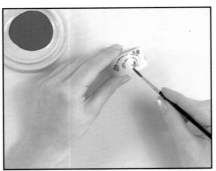

Finish off with a third and, if necessary, a fourth colour, allowing each coat to dry before applying a new one. Protect the design with a coat of ceramic varnish. If you wish to decorate your table napkins as well, follow the same procedure using fabric paints instead of ceramic ones.

Here's a design the children will love: personalized plate mats delightfully decorated with dogs, cats or even some cute woolly sheep. Look in cards, magazines and children's books for images to copy. Either trace your design or draw it free-hand on to some paper. Cut out and draw round your motif on to a plain mat with a chinagraph pencil.

Colour in your image using multi-purpose felt tip pens. If, after you have finished, you have left smudges on your mat, rub them out with lighter fuel. Finish off with a coloured border round the edge of the mat.

GIFTS & NOVELTIES

Why not have some fun restoring a battered old box and, rather than simply giving it a coat of paint, transform it with a striking black and white leopard skin design? As you can see, this cabinet was originally in a very sorry state with its chipped paint and peeling labels.

First sand the box down, then give it a coat of black ceramic paint. This paint is suitable for metals and gives a shiny finish. If your box is wooden, you can use acrylic paints instead.

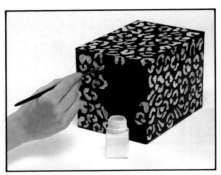

When the black paint has dried, paint the leopard skin markings in white ceramic paint. Look at pictures of leopards and other animals with interesting markings for inspiration. If your box is for stationery, you can even paint some black pens to match.

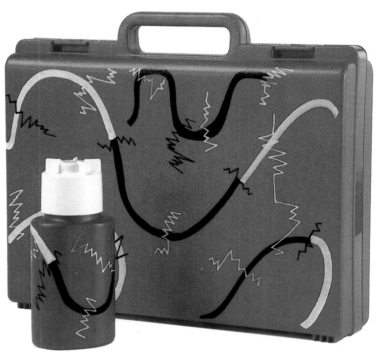

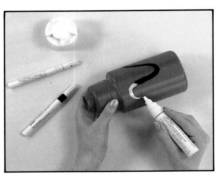

Here's another idea for the kids – a customized school bag and flask. All you need are the case and flask and some multi-purpose felt tip paint pens. Choose striking colour combinations such as the red, white and black used here. In a strong sweeping movement, paint a deep wavy line using a thick pen. Change pens and finish the curve in a contrasting colour.

Add more wavy lines, alternating colours as before. Then, using a fine pen, draw zig-zag lines cutting across the curved lines. Finally, change pens and draw more zig-zag lines in the second colour.

There is no excuse for mislaying letters with this smart letter rack. From thick mounting board cut a rectangle 24cm × 8cm (½in × 3¼in) for the front and 24cm × 10cm (9½ × 4in) for the back. Diagonally trim away the top corners and cover one side of each piece with giftwrap.

Cut giftwrap slightly smaller than the front and back sections and glue in position on the wrong side. Take a piece of wood 24cm (9½in) long by 3cm (1¼in) wide and 1cm (⅛in) thick. Cover the wood with coloured paper.

Cut a rectangle of mounting board 27cm × 7cm (10½in × 2¾in) for the base and cover with coloured paper. Use a strong glue to stick the front to one narrow edge of the wood keeping the lower edges level. Glue the back to the other side in the same way. Finish the letter rack by gluing this upper section centrally to the base.

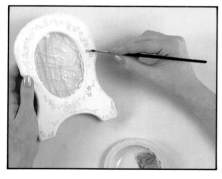

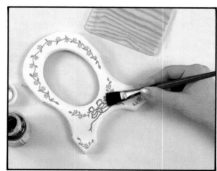

This pretty little frame is perfect for standing on a dressing table. Firstly, sand the frame until it is smooth and then give it a coat of white acrylic paint. Apply a second coat of paint if necessary and, when dry, draw the design with a soft pencil. Paint the design using acrylic paint in soft blues and greys with the flower centres in bright yellow.

Remove the backing and the glass and give the frame a protective coat of polyurethane varnish.

NOVELTY BLACKBOARD

Transform a pear-shaped chopping board into a novelty blackboard for the children. All you need is blackboard paint and some acrylic paint for the leaves. First draw the leaf design in pencil on to the board.

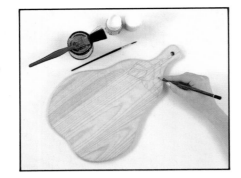

Now paint the board with the blackboard paint, using a fine brush to paint round the leaf design. The board may need more than one coat of blackboard paint, so allow the first coat to dry before applying the second.

When the paint is dry, apply the colour to the leaves with a fine brush. Finally, give the leaves a coat of varnish to make them shine. Do not varnish the black paint!

BRILLIANT BOXERS

Create a unique gift for the man in your life by decorating a pair of boxer shorts with fabric felt tip pens. Draw your design on to paper first, referring to the template on page 245 if your wish to create this busy design. Work out your colour scheme by colouring in your design with felt tip pens.

Place a piece of card between the front and the back of the shorts to stretch the waist band and stop the paint seeping through. Draw the design on to the fabric using a fine fabric felt tip pen. If you don't feel confident drawing the design straight on in pen, trace it on in pencil first.

Colour in the design in bright colours, using either fabric felt tip pens or fabric paint and a brush. To fix the paint, iron on the back of the fabric once your design is complete.

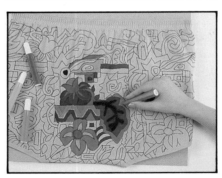

This colourful design is applied using transfer paints. As well as the paints, you will also need a piece of non-absorbent paper, such as tracing paper, and an iron. Draw your design on to the paper, referring to the template on page 245, and making sure it will fit on to the scarf you wish to decorate.

Colour in your design with the transfer paints in the same way as you would using any water-based paints. Mix the colours together and dilute them with water as you wish.

Leave the paints to dry for an hour then place the design face down on the scarf so that the paint is against the fabric. Set your iron to the cotton setting and iron on the back of the paper for one minute so that the colour is transferred. When the paper has cooled, remove it from the scarf.

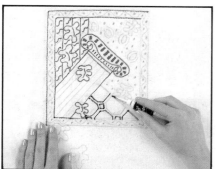

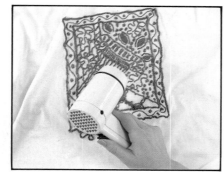

These Grecian-style tee shirts are decorated with a paint that expands upon heating, so that the design is raised above the surface of the fabric. First, draw your design on to a piece of paper. Then stick the design on to a piece of cardboard and stretch the tee shirt over the card, fastening the fabric down with masking tape. Trace the design on to the tee shirt using the 'expanding medium' paint.

Leave the paint to dry for 20 to 30 minutes before fixing it. This can be done by ironing the reverse of the design for 15 seconds (using a silk or wool setting). The other way to set and expand the paint is to use a hair dryer.

R elive the memories of peaceful holidays by the sea with this seascape collage. Tear strips of tissue paper – pale blue and white for the sky and pale green and turquoise for the sea. Cut out a circle of orange paper for the sun. Arrange the strips horizontally across a piece of white cardboard to get an idea of the finished picture.

Stick the top two strips across the cardboard with spray glue, leave a gap then apply the fourth strip. Glue the sun on top and then the third strip across the sun. Continue down the card. Cut straight across the strips that will meet at the horizon. Tear slithers of white frosted paper and glue across the bottom of the picture as surf.

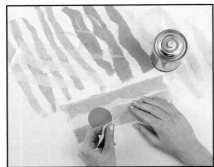

Cut a jagged cliff shape from brown crepe paper and glue to the collage. Glue a slither of green tissue paper on top for grass. Trim away the excess paper around the edges of the card. Cut out three seagulls from black paper and glue on the sky.

G ive your home a period touch with this classic decoration. You can use a clear profile sketch or a photograph as a basis for your picture. Make a tracing of the outline and place it face down on the back of a piece of black paper. Redraw the design to transfer it.

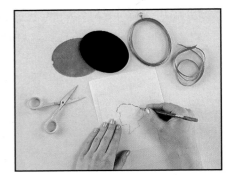

Cut out the motif with a pair of small, sharp scissors and glue the design to white paper. Trim the paper to fit your frame. Place the picture in the frame and glue a small ribbon bow to the top.

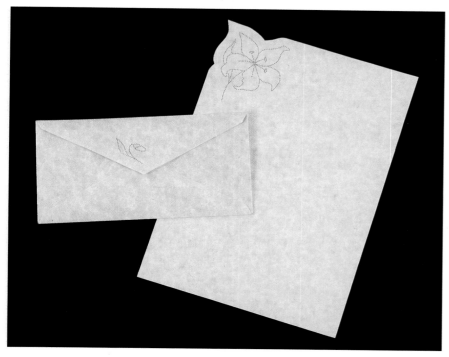

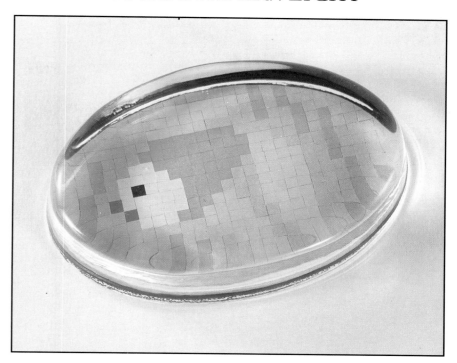

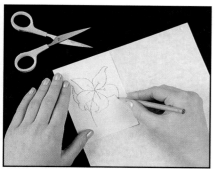

Stylish and original stationery is expensive to buy but this delicate design is cheap and easy to produce. Draw a simple motif on layout paper then retrace the design on the other side. Place your drawing on the top left-hand corner of a sheet of writing paper about 1cm (⅜in) inside the edges. Redraw the motif to transfer it to the writing paper.

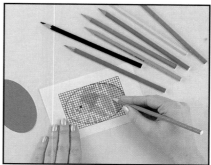

Glass paperweights such as these are available in kit form from craft shops. To work out a mosaic picture, draw a grid of squares about 4mm (³⁄₁₆in) apart. Trace around the paperweight template onto the grid and draw a design. Colour the picture as a guide for the finished mosaic.

Now prick along the lines with a needle or pin. You may find it helpful to practise on a scrap of paper first to judge how far apart the pinpricks should be.

Cut out tiny squares of coloured paper the same size as the grid squares. Draw a cross on a piece of paper to help keep the mosaic squares straight. Spread paper glue thinly along part of one line and press the squares in place. Nudge them into position with scissors or tweezers. Follow the grid design and glue on all the squares.

Rub out the pencil lines then trim away the corner of the paper to echo the shape of the design. Pinprick a co-ordinating motif on the matching envelope flap.

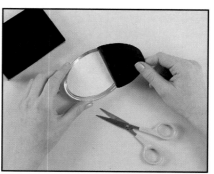

Use the paperweight template to cut the mosaic to fit the paperweight. Turn the paperweight upside down and lay the mosaic in the hollow. Peel the paper off the sticky-backed flock backing and carefully stick it over the back of the paperweight enclosing the mosaic.

The right mount can really enhance a picture. Buy a plain cardboard mount to fit your picture. Draw a 1cm (⅜in) wide border around the window with a pencil. Cut four 1cm (⅜in) wide strips of marbled paper. Spray the back of one strip with spray glue and place on the border. Cut off the ends diagonally at the corners with a craft knife.

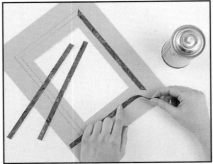

Apply the other strips to the mount, cutting the ends to meet diagonally in a mitred corner.

To make these smart frames, cut two pieces of mounting board 25cm × 19cm (10in × 7½in). Cut a window 17cm × 11cm (7in × 4½in) in the centre of one piece. Cut two pieces of giftwrap to cover the frames. Lay the window mount on the wrong side of one piece and cut a window in the giftwrap, leaving a 2cm (¾in) margin. Snip to the corners and glue the margins down.

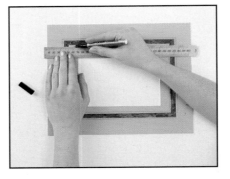

To complete the mount, draw a line each side of the border with a fine-tipped gold pen.

Cover the back of the frame with giftwrap, then cut two 1cm (⅜in) wide strips of mounting board 18cm (7¼in) long and one 22cm (8½in) long. Cover with paper and glue to the wrong side of the back just inside three of the edges. Spread glue on the strips and carefully place the front of the frame on top, checking that the outer edges are level.

Cut a rectangle of mounting board 18cm 6cm (7¼in × 2¼in) for the stand. Score across the stand 5cm (2in) from one end. Cover the stand with giftwrap and glue the second end to the back with the other end level with either a long or short side depending on whether your photo is in landscape or portrait form. Bend the stand outwards.

Papier-mâché is very durable and can be made in many ways. This traditional method uses a paste of flour and water. Tear up wallpaper lining paper into small pieces. Then grease the inside of a small bowl with Vaseline. Brush the paper pieces with paste and stick them inside the bowl, starting at the centre and working outwards.

Revive the Victorian hobby of découpage and decorate a box with pretty paper pictures. Cut out suitable pictures from greeting cards or magazines or use reproductions of Victorian prints.

Build up three layers of papier-mâché and leave to dry overnight. Apply at least four more layers. When the papier-mâché is completely dry, remove it from the bowl mould. Trim the top edge level with a pair of scissors. paint the bowl with a craft paint, sanding between coats. Cut coloured tissue paper into small triangles.

Arrange the pictures on the box and then stick them in place with spray glue. Smooth in place.

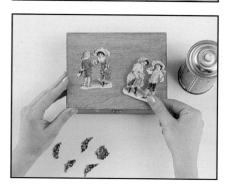

Stick the triangles to the bowl with a clear varnish such as PVA medium. Once the bowl is decorated, coat it inside and out with the varnish. Line the bowl with tissue paper and fill it with pretty bathroom accessories.

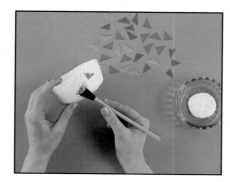

Apply a thin coat of clear gloss varnish all over the box and lid. Leave to dry and then sand lightly with fine sandpaper. Build up about six layers of varnish, sanding the box between each coat.

These amusing finger puppets are sure to entertain your friends. Use the template on page 244 to cut out the dancer in pale pink cardboard. Cut out the dress in shiny, deep pink cardboard and glue to the puppet. Next cut an 8cm (3in) diameter circle from the centre of a white paper doily for a petticoat and glue to the dress with spray glue.

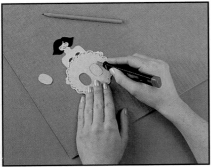

Colour the hair, draw the eyes and lightly mark the nose with a black felt-tipped pen. Draw the mouth with a red felt-tipped pen and rouge the cheeks with a red coloured pencil.

Mark the finger hole positions on the petticoat and carefully cut through all the layers with a craft knife.

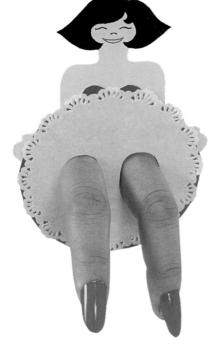

Quick and simple to make, this place mat will brighten up the supper table. Cut a wavy-edged rectangle of blue cardboard 35cm × 25cm (14in × 10in). Cut a row of wavy slits lengthwise across the mat with a craft knife.

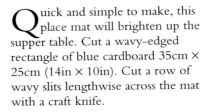

Cut wavy-edges strips 23cm (9in) long from green cardboard. Weave the first strip in and out of the slits close to one end. Weave in the remaining strips starting each alternate strip pat the next slit up.

On the back, lift up the ends of the strips and glue to the mat. Make a matching coaster from a small wavy-edged square of cardboard.

Using white glue and brown tape, sandwich the two front pieces and then the two back pieces together. Attach the support to the back of the frame, checking that the angle will be correct when the frame is standing, and that it will not lean too far back. Seal with thinned white glue to avoid warping.

Attach string to the front of the frame with epoxy glue. The three bobbles at the bottom edge are made from crumpled balls of masking tape.

Give the front and back each three layers of papier mâché, pushing the paper carefully around the string. To avoid warping, peg the front and back together when they are almost dry.

This attractive frame is designed to hold a standard 10 by 15cm (4 by 6in) print. From cardboard, cut pieces as shown in the diagram.

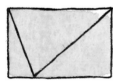

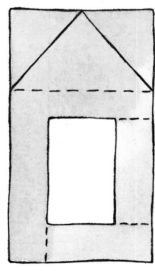

When both pieces are fully dry, sand the back and the back of the frame front, and give them two coats of emulsion. Joining the back and front together, apply two layers of papier mâché down the sides and along the lower edge.

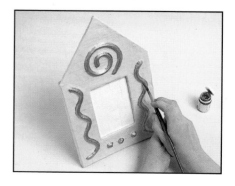

Sand, seal and emulsion the finished frame. Gold poster paint is used for the gilding, and the remainder of the frame is painted with gouache and then sealed with clear varnish designed for gouaches and watercolours.

The fixings for these can be bought at bead shops. The balls for the earrings are made from broadsheet newspaper, crumpled up and left in paste to soak overnight. The three sizes are made from a half, a quarter, and an eighth of a page respectively. When soaked, squeeze out excess paste and shape them into firm balls. Leave to dry.

Make indents for the glass jewels with a countersinking tool. Paint the dangly earrings with black emulsion and the gold ones with poster paint, finishing the latter with polyurethane varnish. Use a matchstick to put a drop of white glue in each indent, and push in a glass jewel. Connect up the dangling earrings and fit the ear wires. Attach clips to the other pair with epoxy glue.

Use a hat pin or similar sharp point to make holes for the connecting hooks of the dangling earrings: one hook for the largest ball, and one at both the top and bottom of the middle and small sizes. Use epoxy glue to secure the hooks. For the clip-on earrings, make one large ball, then cut it in half when dry.

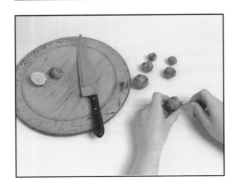

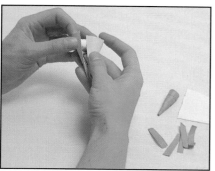

O n thin cardboard, draw a circle with a radius of 5cm (2in) and cut out a quarter circle. Bend this into a cone shape and tape over the join. Apply from two to three layers of papier mâché. When this has dried, attach a brooch pin along the length of the shape, using epoxy glue. Make sure that the pointed end of the pin lies at the pointed end of the shape.

T here are many sources you can use for animal badges, ranging from nature books to pastry cutters. When you have chosen your shapes, draw the outlines on cardboard. using a craft knife, cut out the shapes. Apply four layers of papier mâché to each side.

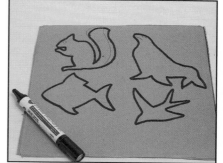

Apply two coats of emulsion, then paint with yellow gouache. Add blue spots, then attach a yellow bead to the pointed end of the cone, using epoxy glue. Varnish inside and out with two coats of semi-matt polyurethane varnish. To prolong the life of your flower and hold it in place, pack dampened tissue around the stem inside the cone.

Using epoxy glue, attach a brooch pin to the back of each shape. Apply two coats of emulsion, then paint the shapes with gouache colours. Add simple black eyes with white highlights. Finish with two coats of polyurethane varnish.

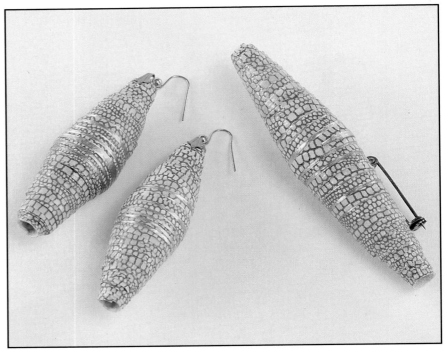

This bangle and matching necklace are made from papier mâché. You will need suitable moulds for each – a small washing-up liquid bottle is the right size for the bangle and a garden stick is ideal for the beads. Cover the stick and 5cm (2in) at the end of the bottle with Vaseline. This stops the papier mâché sticking to the mould.

Believe it or not, this jewellery is made of paper. For each earring cut a long triangle of snakeskin-effect paper (available from specialist art shops) 76cm (30in) long with a 6cm (2¼in) wide base and gold giftwrap 75cm (29in) long with a 5cm (2in) wide base. Using PVA medium stick the giftwrap centrally to the wide end of the snakeskin piece.

Tear paper into small strips. Wallpaper lining paper was used for the bangle and newspaper for the necklace. Mix PVA medium (available at art shops) with a little water to thin it. Dip a brush in the solution, pick up a strip with the brush and press it onto the mould. Cover the Vaseline overlapping the strips. Apply four layers and leave to dry.

Spread Vaseline on a length of wood dowel to stop the paper sticking to the wood. Starting at the wide end, roll the triangles tightly around the dowel, brushing with PVA medium as you go. Give the beads a final coat of the medium as a varnish, leave to dry, then gently remove the dowel.

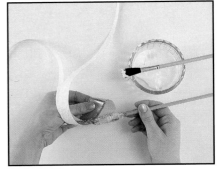

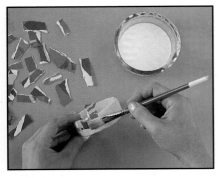

Build up the layers to about 5mm (¼in) thick and allow to dry overnight. Remove the jewellery, trim the bangle to 3cm (1¼in) wide with a craft knife and cut beads 3cm (1¼in) long. Tear giftwrap into small strips and apply to jewellery with the thinned PVA solution. Apply two coats of PVA medium as varnish. Thread beads onto cord.

Pierce a hole through the top of each earring and attach a triangle wire. Fix a small jump ring to the triangle wire with a pair of pliers. Attach an earring hook to the ring. The brooch is made in the same way with wider triangles of snakeskin and gold paper. Glue a brooch pin to the back of the brooch. Craft shops sell jewellery components.

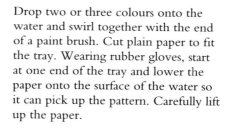

Drop two or three colours onto the water and swirl together with the end of a paint brush. Cut plain paper to fit the tray. Wearing rubber gloves, start at one end of the tray and lower the paper onto the surface of the water so it can pick up the pattern. Carefully lift up the paper.

Leave the paper to dry overnight on newspaper. You can remove the paint from the tray by drawing strips of newspaper across the surface of the water.

The marbled paper can be used in many ways. Here, a plain book takes on a sophisticated look when recovered. Cut a rectangle of marbled paper large enough to wrap around the book with a 2.5cm (1in) margin on all sides. Wrap the paper around the book, open the cover and glue the paper inside the opening edges.

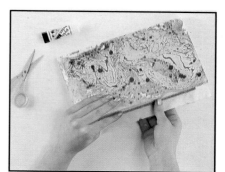

Prop up the book so the cover is open at a right angle. Snip the paper each side of the spine and stick the top and bottom margin inside the covers, folding under the corners.

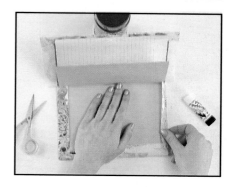

There are many methods for marbling paper but this way needs little equipment. Fill a shallow tray with water. Put spots of enamel paint on the water with a paint brush. If they sink the paint is too thick and needs thinning with a little white spirit. If they disperse into a faint film it is too thin and should be mixed with more paint.

Push the paper at the ends of the spine between the spine and the pages with the points of a pair of scissors. Arrange jewellery stones on the cover and use a strong glue to stick them in place. Cut two pieces of paper to fit inside the covers and glue inside.

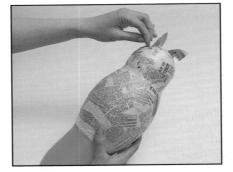

Blow up a long balloon, squeezing it so that you have a head-sized lump at one end. Apply six layers of papier mâché, as shown, and leave to dry. Cut two triangles from cardboard, curving the sides slightly to make ears. Tape these to the head end of the balloon and papier mâché over them. Burst and remove the balloon.

Each foot is made from a piece of papier mâché balloon offcut, perhaps left over from a previous project. Cut each foot to the shape of a lemon segment and tape it to the base, bending it to fit. Papier mâché over the joins.

Place the cat on cardboard and draw around the base, including the feet. Cut out the base and glue and tape it to the cat. Papier mâché over the join.

The tail is made from a piece of newspaper, rolled and crunched up and curled around the body. Tape in place and then papier mâché over the tail. When dry, apply two coats of emulsion.

Using gouache, paint the cat black, except for the tip of the tail, the inside ears, the paws and the tummy. Draw the details carefully in pencil, then paint them – eyes yellow with black pupils and white highlights, nose flesh pink, and cheeks white with tiny black dots in rows. Finish with two coats of semi-matt polyurethane varnish.

OCTOPUS

Take the large balloon. Mark and cut an oval on one side, as shown.

The larger round sits in the middle of the tangle of legs, to make the body. Tape it in position, and then papier mâché over the join.

Take the small balloon and cut it in half to make the two eyes. Tape them in position and again papier mâché over the joins.

Blow up a large balloon and apply up to eight layers of papier mâché. Also cover a small balloon. To make each leg, take a large sheet of newspaper and screw it into a long sausage. Now bend it into a loop and tape it to hold the shape. Make each leg slightly different from the others.

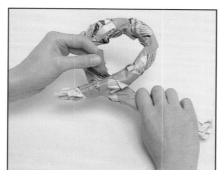

Apply two coats of emulsion, and then go wild with the colours. This octopus was stippled with green and orange household gloss paint, thinned with white spirit. The maroon suckers were painted with modellers' enamel. The eyes were carefully painted yellow and black, with a green rim.

Tape the eight legs together. You may use a lot of tape to achieve this, but it will all add to the strength of the finished octopus. Papier mâché over the legs, using long strips of newspaper, dipped in paste and then wound around the legs. You may need to support each leg a little, to prevent the loops from sagging.

Bend the sides to fit, and tape them together. Apply four layers of papier mâché and, when dry, two coats of emulsion.

Paint the banana with yellow gouache, blending in a tiny amount of green towards the ends. Paint the stalk and the tip brown. For realism, you might add very thin brown lines partway along the edges, and small spots on each side. Finish in the same way as the orange.

For the pineapple, apply eight layers of papier mâché to a balloon. Cut a long strip of card, about 10cm (4in) wide, and make tapering cuts along it. Curl each leaf shape individually, then tape the strip to the pointed end of the balloon. Start at the centre and work around until you have from four to five circles of leaves. If you need a second strip, make the leaves shorter.

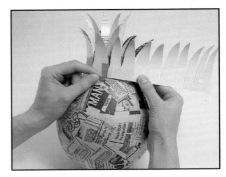

The oranges are the simplest of these colourful ornamental fruits – all you have to do is to papier mâché a small balloon in the normal way. Burst and remove the balloon, covering the end with more papier mâché. When dry, give the shape two coats of emulsion, then paint it with orange gouache. Finish with semi-matt polyurethane varnish.

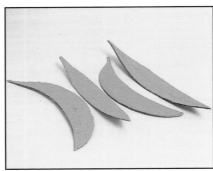

To make a banana, cut out four pieces of card, as shown. Two have curved sides and all are tapered at the top and bottom, and are longer at the stalk end. If in doubt, use a banana skin to make templates.

Papier mâché over the join, but not the individual leaves. Apply two coats of emulsion, then paint the leaves with green gouache, made by mixing yellow and blue, so that you can vary the tones from leaf to leaf. Paint the body with honey-coloured emulsion.

You may find it best to draw the segment lines in pencil before painting them, using a fine brush and light brown gouache. Build up the rest of the pattern with orange, sand and brown. It helps if you have a real pineapple to study as you work. The painting is repetitious but well worth the effort. Finish in the same way as the orange.

Apply eight layers of papier mâché, making sure that you push the pieces into the corners to maintain the shape. Use the blunt edge of kitchen scissors or something similar to help you to ease the pieces into position.

When the ark has dried, use a craft knife to cut it away from the cardboard. Cut around the boat, from one end to the other; use a craft knife for the papier mâché, then use a table knife to cut the modelling plastic. Remove the plastic, and glue and tape the two pieces together. Papier mâché over the join.

Place the boat on a fresh piece of card, and draw around the base. Cut this shape out and glue and tape it in position. Papier mâché over the join. Apply two coats of emulsion, then draw a large slot in the roof. Bear in mind that the slot must be large enough for the money to be shaken out as well as put in. Cut the slot with care, using a craft knife.

Y ou will require three fairly large pieces of modelling plastic for this, so that you can make a boat shape, a rectangular block for the boat house, and a roof.

Paint the boat with gouache colours, using brown for the hull, yellow for the deck house, red for the roof and pink for the deck. Give the deck house blue windows and a door, and add blues waves with little white crests around the hull.

Assemble the three pieces firmly together and place them on a piece of cardboard.

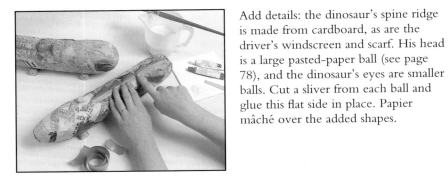

Add details: the dinosaur's spine ridge is made from cardboard, as are the driver's windscreen and scarf. His head is a large pasted-paper ball (see page 78), and the dinosaur's eyes are smaller balls. Cut a sliver from each ball and glue this flat side in place. Papier mâché over the added shapes.

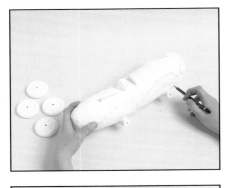

Sand and seal the shape(s), and then apply two coats of white emulsion. Also give the wheels, which can be bought from hobby shops, two coats of emulsion. When his has dried, draw the outlines of any painted pattern or details in pencil.

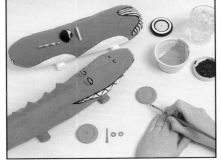

All the colours used here are gouache. Start with the palest, and work up to the darkest colours. It may be simplest to paint in sections, completing the top and then the underside.

Apply eight layers of papier mâché to a sausage balloon, drying between layers, then remove the balloon and paper over the hole. Cut two axles – long enough to hold the wheels clear of the body – from dowel. Drill screw holes for the wheels. At one end of the body, mark an outline to carry one axle. Cut, starting small and gradually enlarging the shape. Repeat at the other end.

Paint the edges of the holes and the axles with white glue. Insert the axles and hold them in place with masking tape. When the glue has set, remove the masking tape and cover the axles, where they touch the body, with at least four layers of papier mâché, using strips measuring about 4 by 7.5cm (1½ by 3in).

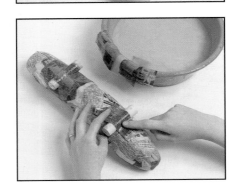

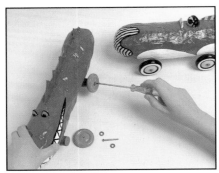

Finish with a coat of clear watercolour varnish, including the wheels. When dry, fix the wheels in position, using a metal washer on both sides. Take care not to make them so tight that they are unable to turn.

Papier mâché is a traditional material for a puppet head. First, mould pieces of modelling plastic to make the components for a Punch head. You will need the following: a large ball for the basic head shape, a large nose, two sausage shapes for eyebrows, another larger one for the mouth, a chin, a hat, and a ruff. You will also need a jam jar to sit him on.

Once you have prepared all the component parts, assemble them together, sitting the head on the jam jar. Do not worry about slight imperfections and joins – these will be concealed beneath the papier mâché.

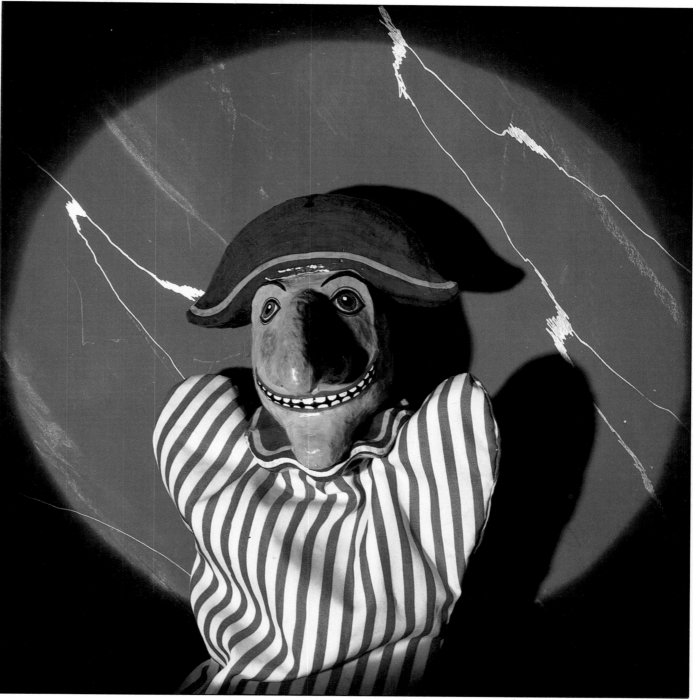

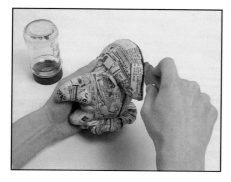

Using thin strips of paper, carefully papier mâché over the entire head. Make sure that it is well covered, giving it from six to ten layers. Leave it until it has dried out completely. Remove the head from the jar and carefully cut the front from the back, as shown. Cut through the papier mâché with a craft knife, and then through the modelling plastic with a table knife.

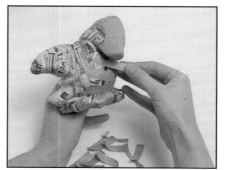

Tease the plastic out from the two halves, taking special care with the ruff and the nose. Tape the two halves back together again and papier mâché over the join. Give the finished head two coats of emulsion, then paint the face, hat and features with gouache. To make the flesh tint for the face, add a little red and a touch of yellow to white. Finish with a coat of varnish.

On cardboard, draw a grid of 2.5cm (1in) squares. Copying square for square from the diagram, draw and cut out one beak side, one feather shape and one beak base. Using the beak side as a template, mark and cut a second beak side to make a mirror image pair.

Paint white glue along the edges of the beak pieces and secure them with brown tape. Allow the beak to dry, then attach it to the face in the same way.

Using the feather already cut, mark and cut three more feathers from cardboard to make two mirror image pairs, as shown.

Using epoxy glue, attach the feather pieces to the mask, then apply from two to three layers of papier mâché to the entire mask and leave to dry. When dry, paint the mask with two successive coats of white emulsion.

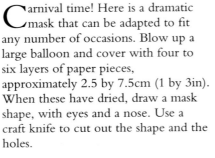

Carnival time! Here is a dramatic mask that can be adapted to fit any number of occasions. Blow up a large balloon and cover with four to six layers of paper pieces, approximately 2.5 by 7.5cm (1 by 3in). When these have dried, draw a mask shape, with eyes and a nose. Use a craft knife to cut out the shape and the holes.

When the emulsion is dry, coat the mask with red gloss house paint. Allow this to dry before adding either lines of yellow gloss or a decoration of your choice. To complete the mask, make a hole at either side and thread these with black elastic, securing this with knots at the back.

Cut out a 38cm (15In) square of craft paper and mark a diagonal line between two corners. Then, using a pencil, string and compass, or drawing pin (thumbtack), draw an arc between the other two corners as shown. Cut along the arc. Fold the piece along the diagonal and use it to mark out two pieces of sticky-backed plastic. Add a 1.5cm (½in) border to one straight edge of black plastic.

Cut out the pieces. Peel off the backing and stick the white plastic into position on the paper. Do the same with the black, leaving the backing only on the border. Form a cone, remove the border backing and stick the edges of the cone together. Make two holes along the front join and insert red pom-poms (see page 19). Secure ends on inside with tape.

Feel free to act the clown in this colourful hat. First of all, make a papier mâché mould using a pudding basin (small mixing bowl) or plastic microwave dish. When it is fully dry, remove the mould and paint it with white emulsion (water-based) paint. Sand down any rough edges and give it a second coat of paint.

Make the 'hair' from red crepe paper – you will need about six layers of paper, stapled together along the top. Cut the paper into even strips, stopping about 2.5cm (1in) from the stapled edge.

Cut out a brim from light cardboard, allowing about 5cm (2in) for the brim itself and an extra 2.5cm (1in) on the inside for attaching the brim to the crown. Make triangular cuts around the inside of the brim, fold the triangles up and glue them to the inside of the hat. Decorate with a crepe paper band and large coloured spots. Finally, glue the hair to the inside of the hat.

This glittery version of the medieval lady's hat, with its net veil, is sure to attract a knight errant. Cut out a 38cm (15in) square of black craft paper. Using a white pencil, string and compass, draw an arc from one corner to another. Cut along the arc.

The mould for this hat is a plastic flower pot. The one shown is for a child; an adult would need a much bigger one. Cover the flower pot in papier mâché. When it is dry, ease it off the pot and give it a coat of white emulsion (water-based paint), inside and out. When this is dry, sand down any rough edges on the outside and give it another coat.

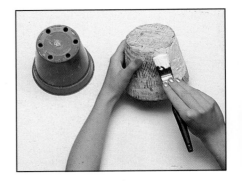

Peel the back off some sticky-backed plastic and stick the black paper down onto it. Cut out the shape, leaving a 1.5cm (½in) border on one straight edge. Use this to stick the hat together.

Next give the hat two coats of red paint, leaving it to dry after each coat. Make a little hole in the centre of the top of the hat.

Sew tinsel around the edge of a square of net, then attach this, with a little sticky tape, to the top of the hat. Make sure that the seam in the plastic is at the back. Finally decorate the hat with a few stick-on silver stars.

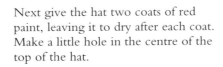

Now make a tassel of black yarn (see the instructions on page 19), and thread it through the top of the hat, fastening it on the inside with a little sticky tape.

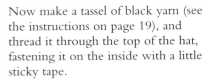

Although a bit more complicated to make than a cardboard mask, this mask will last much longer. The face is made from papier mâché (see page 18 for instructions); the mould is a balloon. Blow the balloon up as big as you can without bursting it, and build up the papier mâché over at least one half. When it is dry, gently let the air out of the balloon by piercing the knotted end.

Trim the mask down, cutting the pointed end into a forehead. Cut out circular eyes and a curved mouth. Now give the mould a coat of white emulsion (water-based paint), sand it down and give it another two coats to make it as smooth a surface as possible.

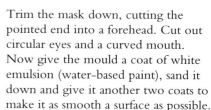

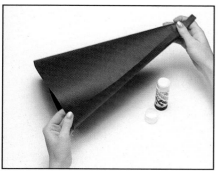

For this you need a large piece of black art paper, 38 by 39.5cm (15 by 15½in). Mark a 1.5cm (½in) border at one end of the longer side so that you have a 38cm (15in) square. Take a compass, string and a white pencil and mark an arc between two corners (see page 87 for details). Cut along the arc, spread glue on the border, and use this to join the edges of the cone together.

Use the cone to mark a circle on some black cardboard. Draw another line around the first, about 5cm (2in) from it, then another just 2.5cm (1in) inside the first line. Cut along the inner and outer lines, then make triangular cuts on the inside of the brim. Fold them up and glue them to the inside of the cone. Decorate with gold stars and moons cut from sticky-backed plastic.

Around each eye paint four slightly triangular stripes. Also paint large red lips and cheeks on either side. For the nose, paint a ping pong ball red and glue it in place. For the hair, cut short lengths of yarn and attach them to strips of sticky tape; stick these to the back of the mask. Finally, take a piece of elastic, staple it to either side, and paint over the staples with a touch more emulsion.

For a stunning party mask, buy a ready-moulded mask from a stationer's or toy shop. The half-mask shown here is coloured with oil stencil pencils. Start with the pink; apply a little to a piece of waxed paper, then pick it up on the stencil brush. Using a circular motion, cover about half the mask. Repeat with the blue, filling in the gaps and giving the eyes a semblance of eyeliner.

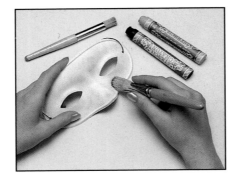

Next take a short length of lace and glue it to the back of the top half of the mask, down to where the elastic is attached. Glue some strands of curling gift wrap ribbon on either side. (Curl the ribbon by running the blunt edge of a pair of scissors along it.) Lastly, glue some large sequins over the tops of the ribbons to hide the ends, and glue another one in the centre of the forehead.

For the black mask, first sew some silver tinsel wire around the edge and around the eyes. Sew on some pearl beads either side, then sew two or three grey or white feathers under the edges for an owlish look.

The basic shape can, of course, be adapted in a wide variety of ways. Draw a mask shape on cardboard. If you want both sides to be exactly the same, draw one side only on stiff paper; cut this out, then draw around the eye and the outside, flipping it over to complete the mirror image. Cut the shape out, then gently curve it to fit the shape of the face.

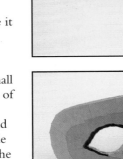

To make the big nose, blow up a small balloon and cover it with four layers of papier mâché. When this has dried, slice off the end with a craft knife and remove a curved notch from one side to make room for your nose. Tape the nose to the mask, with the notch at the bottom. Make a small hole at either side of the eyes to take the elastic at a later stage.

Give the entire mask three layers of papier mâché, and follow this with two coats of white emulsion. Using gouache colours, paint the nose red and the mask black, adding a fine red line around the edge. Finish with two coats of semi-matt polyurethane varnish. To complete the mask, thread black elastic through the holes; adjust to fit, and then make knots behind the holes.

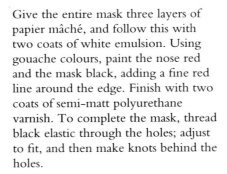

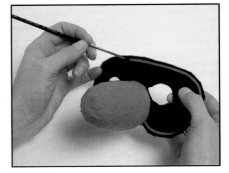

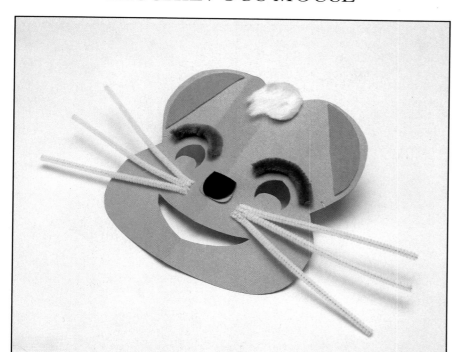

With this on, you are sure not to be recognized! First make the glasses shape from garden wire, then wind narrow ribbon all the way around them. Glue the ends in place to make sure it doesn't come undone.

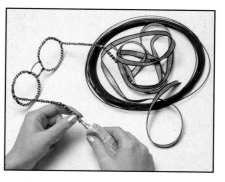

This mask is simple enough for small children to put together; the only tricky bit is drawing the pattern. First take a 20cm (8in) square of stiff paper. Fold it in half, and open it out, then fold it in half the other way. Now draw the shape of the face on one side as shown, including the mouth and nose.

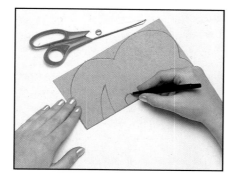

The nose is made from paper with a spongy finish. Cut a piece 9 by 10cm (3¾ by 4in). On the back, along one of the shorter sides, mark two lines, 3cm (1¼in) long and 3cm (1¼in) apart. Cut along these lines, so that you have three equal sections. Fold the two sides in and glue them on top of each other. Now glue the middle section over the others. Glue the edge of the nose to the glasses.

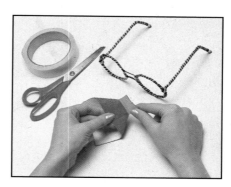

Cut around the outline, the mouth and the nose (notice that the nose isn't cut out completely). Turn back the folded edge a little way as shown; mark in an eye and cut it out. Open out the mask.

Finally, make the beard from a piece of white fake fur, cutting a hole for the mouth. Attach a narrow strip of paper to the inside of the nose and staple either end to the back of the beard. Finish off by sticking a silver star to the glasses, just over the nose.

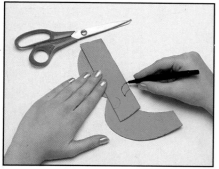

Cut out some pink felt ears and a black felt nose. Cut some white pipe cleaner whiskers and brown pipe cleaner eyebrows. Glue them all in place. Finally attach a piece of shirring elastic to either side, knotting it at the back.

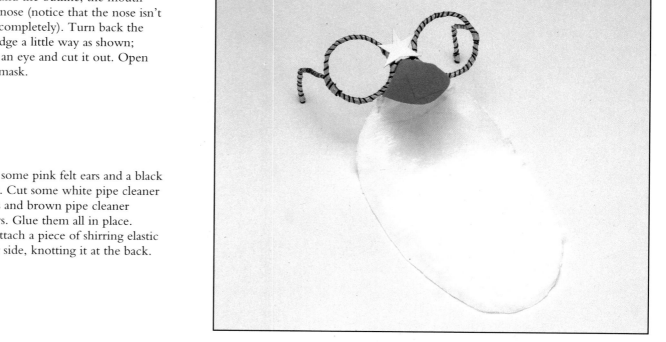

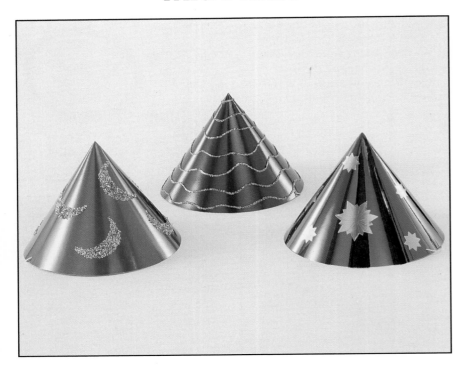

Here's a jaunty majorette's cap that is ideal for a fancy dress party. Cut a strip of coloured cardboard 60cm × 13cm (24 × 5in). Cut out a peak in silver cardboard. On the wrong side, score the peak along the broken lines and make snips in the cardboard to the scored line. Bend the snipped edge upwards.

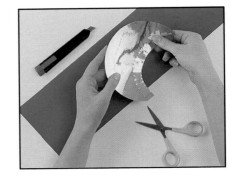

Stick an 18cm (7in) long strip of double-sided tape in the middle of one long edge of the hat on the wrong side. Overlap the ends of the strip and lightly hold together with masking tape. Press the snipped edge of the peak onto the sticky tape. Remove the masking tape.

These conical hats are so easy to make that you will want to make one for each of your party guests. Cut a 30cm (12in) diameter circle of shiny cardboard for each hat and cut to the centre. Cut a slice out of the circle so that the hat is not too bulky. Overlap the cut edges and glue together.

Wrap the hat around your head, overlapping the ends, and stick together with double-sided tape. Pleat a rectangle of foil giftwrap and bind the lower edge closed with clear sticky tape, forming a fan. Glue to the front of the hat. Finally, cut out a diamond shape from silver cardboard and glue it over the fan.

There are many ways to decorate the hats – stick on gold stars or use glitter pens to draw a pattern. Another idea is to spread glue in moon shapes on the hat and then sprinkle on glitter, shaking off the excess.

Make a hole with the points of a pair of scissors each side of the hat and thread with hat elastic. Adjust the elastic to fit under the chin and make a knot behind the holes.

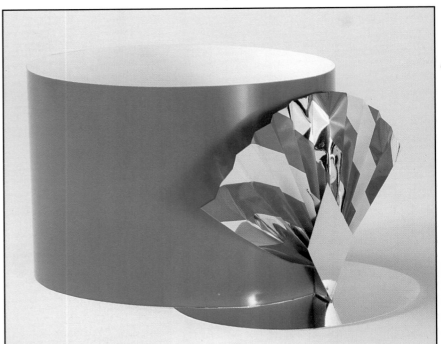

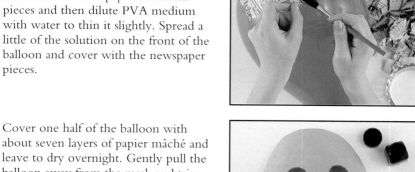

This lion mask is made from papier mâché moulded over a balloon. Blow up the balloon and tie a knot in the end. Tear newspaper into small pieces and then dilute PVA medium with water to thin it slightly. Spread a little of the solution on the front of the balloon and cover with the newspaper pieces.

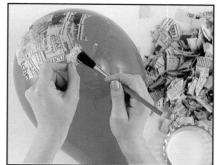

Cover one half of the balloon with about seven layers of papier mâché and leave to dry overnight. Gently pull the balloon away from the mask and trim the edges of the mask with a pair of scissors. Cut out two round holes for the eyes. Paint the mask with non-toxic ochre coloured paint and then paint a black nose and muzzle, as shown.

To make the mane, cut brown crepe paper 140cm × 16cm (55in × 6¼in) and fold lengthwise in half. Cut a fringe along the long edges. With a needle and long length of thread, gather up the mane close to the fold. Glue the mane around the lion's face. Finally, staple a length of thin elastic to each side of the back of the mask, to fit.

Make this colourful head-dress and join the tribe! Cut a 4cm (1½in) wide strip of red cardboard 60cm (24in) long. Cut out simple shapes from coloured papers and glue to the strip.

Overlap the ends of the strip and glue together. Stick three coloured quill feathers upright behind the strip with sticky tape.

Cut six 2.5cm (1in) wide strips of black crepe paper 40cm (16in) long. Spread paper glue along one edge and fold the strips in half. Staple three lengths together at one end and make a plait. Bind the end with embroidery thread and make another plait in the same way. Stick the plaits to each side of the head-dress with sticky tape.

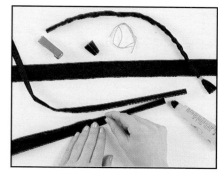

This appealing children's mask is covered in soft fake fur. Using the template on page 246, cut out the cat shape in thin cardboard, fake fur and white sticky-backed plastic. In all three, cut out the eyes.

These party bow ties lend a dashing look to a costume. For the flat tie, cut a bow tie shape in thin cardboard, using the template on page 246. Simply cover the shape with foil, sticky-backed plastic or felt, and attach shirring elastic to the back.

Glue the fur piece to the cardboard one. When the glue has dried, trim the edges, then cut a nose in black felt and two ears in pink felt. To make the whiskers, put some glue onto a piece of cardboard and pull black thread through it as shown. When the thread dries it will be stiff.

Or make a soft fabric tie by cutting a strip of felt or other material 18cm (7in) square. Fold it in half, right sides together, and sew the long edges together to make a tube. Turn it right side out, and finish the raw edges by turning them in and slip-stitching them.

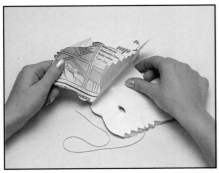

Glue the ears in place, then cut the thread into lengths of about 10cm (4in). Lay them where the nose is to be placed. Put some glue onto the nose and place it over the ends of the whiskers. Tape a piece of elastic to each side of the mask on the wrong side. Finally, peel the backing off the plastic and stick it to the underside of the mask.

Cut another strip of material 5 by 9cm (2 by 3½in). Fold the long edges in to meet at the back and glue them down. Wrap this piece around the middle of the tube and sew it in place at the back, folding in the raw edges to hide them. Sew on shirring elastic for wearing the bow.

Party &
Table
Decorations

Hang this traditional wreath on the front door to give a warm welcome to guests at Christmas. To begin, take a wire coathanger and pull it into a circle. Bend the hook down to form a loop.

Now wire together small bunches of holly, spruce and other foliage. Then attach each bunch to the circle. Be careful when handling the holly; you can get a bit scratched, and some people can come out in a rash from it. Keep going in one direction until the whole circle is covered.

This Christmas wreath is based on a child's plastic hoop, and makes a delightful decoration for the wall or mantelpiece. First of all you need a plastic hoop; any size will do. Cut long strips of wadding (batting) and wind them around the hoop, holding the edges in place with sticky tape. This one has two layers of medium-weight wadding.

On top of this add some wired pine cones and, for extra colour, some curly red ribbon. (Use curling gift wrap ribbon for this, running the blunt edge of a pair of scissors along it to make it curl.) Red holly berries look great if you can get hold of them, but they tend to drop very quickly, so they would need replacing often. Finish off with a big red satin bow.

Next take some 8cm- (3in)-wide ribbon and wind it firmly around the hoop, in the opposite direction to the wadding. Make sure the wadding is entirely covered. Take a contrasting ribbon, about 6cm (2in) wide, and wrap it over the first ribbon, leaving equal spaces between the loops. Repeat with a third ribbon, 4cm (1½in) wide.

Make sure each ribbon starts and finishes in the same place so that all the joins are together. This will be the top of the hoop. Wind tinsel around the hoop, over the ribbons. Pin or staple a wide piece of ribbon over all the joins at the top. Tape a cluster of ribbon, tinsel, baubles and bells at the top and add a large bow to finish off.

Add several sprigs of holly, again securing them with wire. If the holly is a bit short of berries, you can add some fake berries at this point.

To hang the wreath you will need two lengths of satin ribbon. Each piece should be twice the length of the drop from the ceiling to your hanging height, plus an extra 20cm (8in) for tying around the wreath. Tie each of the four ends opposite one another around the wreath so that the two lengths cross in the centre.

Make four bows from the same colour ribbon and pin them to the wreath over the four tying-on points.

Gently push a length of florist's wire through each of four red wax candles, approximately 1.5cm (½in) above the bases, as shown.

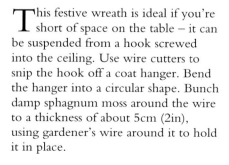

This festive wreath is ideal if you're short of space on the table – it can be suspended from a hook screwed into the ceiling. Use wire cutters to snip the hook off a coat hanger. Bend the hanger into a circular shape. Bunch damp sphagnum moss around the wire to a thickness of about 5cm (2in), using gardener's wire around it to hold it in place.

Take several bushy branches of evergreen, such as cypress, and arrange them to cover the circlet of moss, overlapping the pieces to cover any stalks. Tie the branches to the ring with gardener's twine or wire.

Position each candle halfway between two bows, and twist the wire around the wreath to hold it in place. To hang the wreath, tie another length of ribbon around the two main ribbons where they cross, make a loop to go over the hook, and tie the ends in a bow.

A large foil star like this can hang in the centre of the ceiling or over the fireplace. Try it out on a piece of ordinary paper first, as it is a little fiddly. Cut a piece of foil paper about 45cm (18in) square. Fold it in half from corner to corner, then in half twice again, making a small triangle.

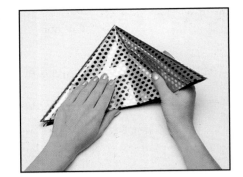

Bend the single-fold edge over to the edge with three folds. Open it out, and rule two lines from the corners at the base of the triangle to the centre crease. Cut along these two lines.

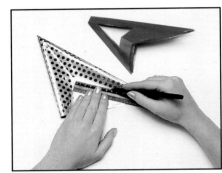

Refold the crease and rule two more lines, forming a small triangle as seen here. Cut this out. Now snip the point off and open the star out. Glue it to another piece of thicker foil paper for backing and cut the star out carefully when the glue has dried. Finish it off with a ribbon rosette in the centre.

This simple star can be hung on the wall or from the ceiling. First make the pattern for the star. Using a ruler and protractor, draw an equilateral triangle (each angle is 60°). Cut out the triangle and use it as a pattern to make another one. Then glue one triangle over the other to form the star. Use this pattern to cut a star from foil paper.

Fold the star in half three times between opposite points. Next fold it in half three times between opposite angles as shown. Every angle and point should now have a fold in it.

The star will now easily bend into its sculptured shape. Make a small hole in its top point with a hole punch or a skewer, then put some thread through the hole to hang it up.

GRACEFUL BELLS

This decoration can be made with tissue paper, coloured aluminium foil, thin cardboard or construction paper. Cut between six and twelve bell shapes (depending on the thickness of the paper you use). Fold each shape in half and then open it out again.

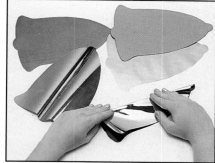

Lay the cut-outs carefully on top of each other with all the creases in the centre. Now take a needle and thread, and starting at the top, make three long stitches down the middle. Bring the needle up and over the bottom to secure the shapes in place. Next make a small stitch between each long stitch. At the top, knot the two ends together.

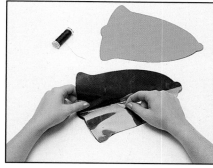

Ease the bell open, piece by piece, until it forms a rounded shape. You could easily do exactly the same thing with other shapes such as a heart, ball or tree.

FANCY FOIL

Make these shiny decorations from foil wrapping paper. Cut out eight circles in each of the following diameters: 9cm (3½in), 7.5cm (3in) and 6cm (2¼in). Then from cardboard cut out four circles 2cm (¾in) in diameter and two of 1.5cm (½in) for the centres. Fold the largest foil circles into quarters and staple four of them on to a large cardboard circle.

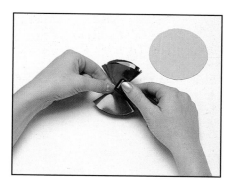

In the same way, staple the other four foil circles to another cardboard circle. Glue the two cardboard circles together with a string between them. Leave a long piece hanging below for the other two balls. Fluff out the edges of foil to make a good shape.

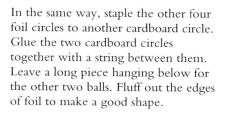

Now make the other two balls in the same way, using the smaller cardboard circles for the tiniest. Fix the balls to the string as you go.

PRETTY PLEATS

FANTASTIC

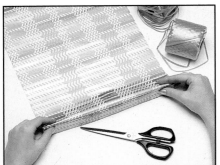

W hat could be simpler than these crisply-pleated paper fans, trimmed with curling ribbons? To begin, take a strip of printed wrapping paper and pleat it crosswise as shown.

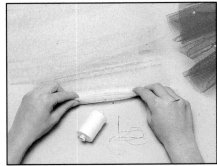

H ang these pretty net fans on the wall or on the corner of a mirror, or use them to decorate a tablecloth. They are made from strips of net about 30cm (12in) wide and 1 metre (40in) long. Cut two strips of each colour and concertina-fold them crosswise, treating the two layers as one. When you have finished pleating, make a few stitches through the net at one end to hold it together.

When you have finished the folding, hold the fan together by stapling it at one end. Cut some strips of gift wrap ribbon and run them along the edge of a ruler, or over a scissors blade, so that they curl.

Sew little pearl beads or silver sequins on to the net to decorate it. Trim away any rough edges on the outside of the fan.

Slip the ends of the ribbons between the folds of the fan and staple them in place. Finish by fixing a ribbon rosette over the stapled end.

Finish off by spraying some round wooden beads with silver paint and sewing them to the centre of the fan to cover the pleating.

PRETEND BALLOONS

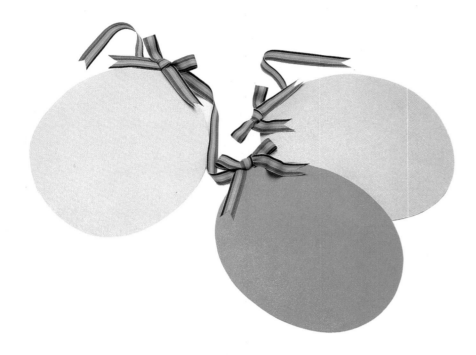

These are just as colourful as real balloons, but they won't pop, or even gently expire! Cut out balloon shapes from coloured cardboard or stiff paper, then cover them on one side with spray-on glitter.

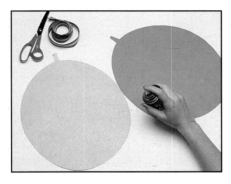

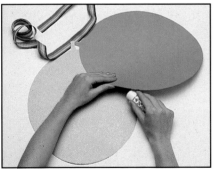

Two balloon shapes can be glued together at the edges, or they can all be strung up separately. Tape the balloons to a length of colourful striped ribbon.

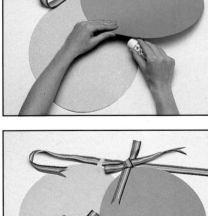

Lastly, use more of the same ribbon to make up some bows, and fix them to the balloons with some double-sided tape.

COLOURFUL KITE

The frame for this kite is made from garden sticks. Mark off the lengths specified, and stamp on them where you want them to break! Take one stick 60cm (24in) long and another 40cm (16in) long, and tie them together with twine so that the three upper arms are equal. Next add two top pieces, 28cm (11½in) long, and the two lower side pieces 45cm (18½in) long. Tie all these pieces in place.

Now take two large sheets of brightly coloured tissue paper. Tear one in half lengthwise and lay one half over the large sheet. Lightly glue it along the edges to keep it in place. Turn the paper over. Now lay the frame over the tissue, and cut around the shape, leaving a 5cm (2in) border all around.

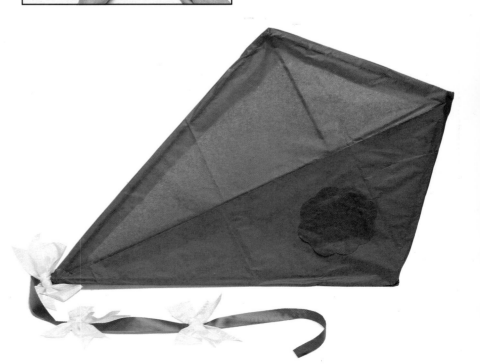

Apply glue to the outside frame of the kite, and fold the edges of the tissue over it. Finish by adding a red rosette and a paper ribbon tail with bows strung along it. After use on the big day, this can be transferred to the wall of the children's room. It has to be handled carefully, but once hung up will last for ages.

All you really need for this decoration is some garden wire, a little bit of tinsel and a couple of baubles; but a pair of pliers will make it easier to manipulate the wire. Bend the wire into the shape of a bell. (You could, of course, try much more complicated shapes once you get the hang of it.)

Luscious lips to show your sweetheart how much you love him on Valentine's Day or your anniversary. You will need a piece of fluorescent pink craft paper 76 by 12.5cm (30 by 5in). You should be able to get four strips this size out of a standard sheet of craft paper. Draw a lips shape (using folded paper will ensure symmetry) and cut it out in cardboard.

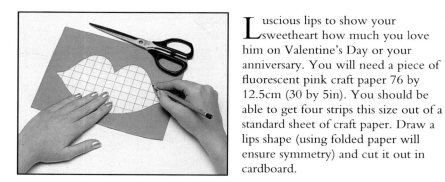

Now just wind tinsel around the wire until it is completely covered. A couple of layers will be sufficient.

Fold the paper in half from right to left, and then from right to left again. This will give you four sets of lips. Place the pattern on top and draw round it, making sure that the pattern meets each side; otherwise the lips won't hold together.

Finish off with a bauble, tied on to represent the clapper, and some bright red ribbon to tie the bells together.

Cut out the shape using sharp scissors. Join each set of lips together at the ends to make one long garland.

This makes an ideal Christmas wall hanging, particularly if you haven't room for a real tree. First make a paper pattern of a tree, about 75cm (30in) high and 59cm (23½in) wide at the widest point across the bottom branches. Also cut a pattern for the pot, about 25cm (10in) high. Make it about as wide as the base of the tree, with a slightly wider, 8cm (3in) deep 'rim' at the top as shown.

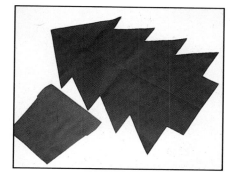

Cut out two pieces of green felt from the tree pattern and two pieces of red for the pot. Also cut out a piece of wadding (batting) for each. The wadding for the pot should be about 4.5cm (1¾in) shorter, since the rim of the pot will be turned down. On the front of the tree mark diagonal lines for the branches as shown.

Place the tree pieces together, with wadding on top. Pin, tack (baste), then stitch 1cm (3/8in) from the edge, leaving the lower edge open. Clip the corners and turn the tree right side out. Stitch along marked lines. Make up the pot, sewing up to 4cm (1½in) from the top. Turn it right side out and slip the tree inside; sew it in place. Sew the upper sides of the pot together and turn the rim down.

To decorate the tree cut out little pockets of red felt and sew them in place as shown. Insert little gifts – either real ones or gift-wrapped cardboard squares.

Finish off by adding plenty of ribbons and bells. Curtain rings also look good covered in ribbon and sewn on. Sew a loop to the top of the tree to hang it by.

This unusual decoration adds a festive touch to a mirror or favourite painting. Make it in separate sections, one to be horizontal, the other vertical. You need fake ivy, fern and other foliage, plus pine cones, gold baubles and gold curling gift wrap ribbon. Cut off the long stems and wire everything up as shown, using florist's wire.

Hanging up your Christmas cards always poses a problem. Here is a simple way to overcome it while making an interesting 'picture' for your wall at the same time. First take a piece of wooden garden trellis, extend it, and spray it with gold paint.

For the top section gradually lay pieces on top of one another, binding the wires and stems together with tape as you go along. The arrangement should be relatively long and narrow.

While the trellis is drying, lay out some ordinary wooden clothes pegs and spray them gold as well. You will have to turn them over a few times you that all sides are covered.

For the second section, use the same technique, but make the arrangement fuller. Hold the two pieces as you would like them to sit on the frame, and wire them together. Bend the stem wires back so that they will slip over the frame and hold the arrangement in place.

When the trellis is dry, take some thick strands of tinsel and wind them all around the edge of the trellis to make a frame. Now hang the trellis on the wall, and use the pegs to attach the Christmas cards as they arrive.

If the day outside is gloomy, try brightening the outlook with some 'stained glass window' pictures. These are cut from black art paper and backed with coloured tissue. First cut pieces of art paper 38 by 30cm (15 by 12in). Mark a 3.5cm (1½in) border all the way round. Now draw your design, taking care that it is always connected in some way to the outer border.

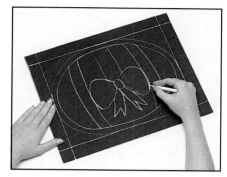

Next cut away any parts of the picture that you want to be coloured, taking care not to detach the black areas from the frame.

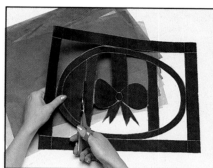

Now glue tissue paper to the back. For your first attempt use just one colour; then as you feel more confident, you can build up pictures using three or more different coloured tissues. When the picture is finished, affix it lightly to the windowpane, then watch what happens when the light shines through.

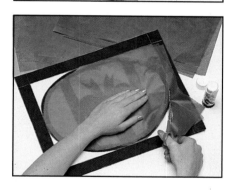

You can always have snow at Christmas, even when the sun is shining outside. Make this snow-flake in foil or in plain white paper and hang it over a window-pane. First take a square of paper, fold it into quarters, then in half diagonally, then lastly back on itself as shown.

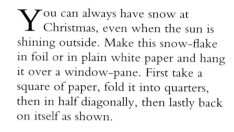
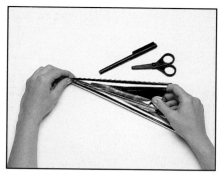

Make a pattern of the chosen design, then mark it on the folded paper with a black felt pen. Shade the areas that are to be cut away, then cut them out. Open out the snowflake. If you use a very flimsy foil, glue the snowflake on to a piece of paper, and cut out around it. This will make it easier to hang.

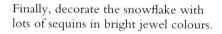

Finally, decorate the snowflake with lots of sequins in bright jewel colours.

This mobile is made from cardboard (or construction paper) bird shapes with tissue paper fanned wings and tails. For each bird cut two bird shapes, using the template on page 246. Glue the two pieces together, placing thread between them, in line with the wings, to hang the bird from. Mark where the wings will fit, and cut a slit.

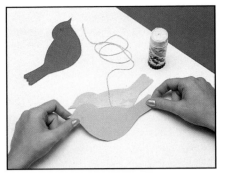

For the fanned wings take a piece of tissue paper 35 by 22cm (14 by 9in) and concertina-fold it lengthwise. Round off the edges and push the folded paper through the slit in the bird, so that there is an equal amount on each side. Glue the inside edges upward to the sides of the bird to make the wings fan out.

These little fluffy chicks make a charming mobile. For each chick you need two pom-poms (see page 19 for instructions). For the larger pom-pom use cardboard circles, 6cm (2½in) in diameter with 2.5cm (1in) holes. The small circles are 5cm (2in) across with the same size hole. When the larger one is ready to be cut away, put a pipe cleaner through the hole to form the legs and feet.

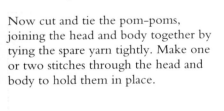

Now cut and tie the pom-poms, joining the head and body together by tying the spare yarn tightly. Make one or two stitches through the head and body to hold them in place.

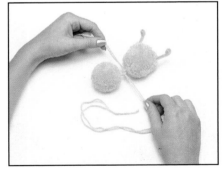

For the tail use a piece of tissue paper 35 by 12cm (14 by 5in), and concertina-fold it widthwise. Round off the edges, then slip one end over the tail of the cardboard bird; glue it in place as shown. Finish off with sequins for the eyes. Hang the birds from two crossed sticks, tied or glued together.

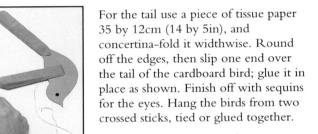

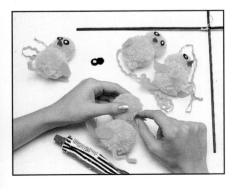

Trim each chick with a felt beak, eyes and wings, and a feather for the tail, sticking them on with a dab of glue. Tie a piece of shirring elastic around the neck, and use this to attach a piece of rickrack or ribbon to the chick. Then hang it on to two crossed sticks, tied together. Glue the rickrack in place to prevent the chicks from slipping off.

This tropical-style mobile is made of coloured modelling clay, the kind you can bake. You simply mould it, bake it in the oven, glue the pieces together and varnish it for a lovely shiny finish. You need eight palm trees for the mobile. Roll out the clay with a rolling pin and cut out the shape of the tree using the template on page 246.

If using more than one colour, cut the trunk and branches separately. Remember to make a hole in the top to hang each one. Also cut out a ring of clay about 15cm (6in) in diameter, with eight holes on the outer edge and four on the inner. Bake the shapes as instructed; when they are cool, glue the trunks and branches together. Varnish them on both sides.

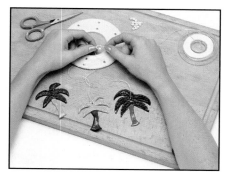

To string them, use a strong nylon or waxed cord. The first should be 5cm (2in) long, the second 10cm (4in) and so on, with 5cm (2in) added to each length. This will give the impression that the trees fall in a spiral. Slip them through the holes in the support and knot them on to a bead above. Knot four more strings through the inner edge, and attach them to a ring to hang the mobile.

For this mobile cut out 40 hearts in thin pink cardboard and 40 in blue. Glue one side of the blue heart, lay the end of a long piece of nylon thread on it, and place a pink heart on top; press them firmly together. Now glue another two hearts together, with the thread between them, leaving a gap of about 4cm (1½in) between this and the first heart.

Add three more hearts to the thread. Cut off the thread about 20cm (8in) above the top heart. Make seven more heart strings. Cut two circles of cardboard using a dessert plate as a pattern. In one make eight tiny holes, about 2.5cm (1in) from the edge. Insert the strings and tape them in place. In the other circle insert four threads and tie them to a curtain ring. Glue the two circles together.

CHRISTMAS TREE TREATS

These decorations are made from a basic recipe of 250g (8oz, 2 cups) plain (all-purpose) flour, 125g (4oz, 2 tablespoons) butter, 150g (5oz, ⅝cup) Caster (fine granulated) sugar and 2 egg yolks. Cream butter and sugar until fluffy, add egg yolks and flour, and mix them into a firm dough. Roll the pastry out until it is about 1cm (½in) thick, and cut out the chosen shapes.

Skewer a hole in each, so that you can push a thread through later. (This may close up during baking – in which case you will have to pierce another hole in them when they are cold – but very carefully, as the biscuits have a habit of breaking!) Put them on to a greased baking sheet, and bake them at 180°C (350°F), or gas mark 4, for 15 minutes.

When the biscuits are cool, make up some fairly stiff icing using icing (confectioner's) sugar and water, and ice them. Thread them on to some waxed thread – or ribbon if the hole is big enough – and hang them on the tree straight away; they won't stay there very long!

SUGAR BELLS

These ornaments are very easy to make; all you need are some bells from last year's tree. If you haven't got any, look for suitable moulds in the cake decorating section of a department store. Take some ordinary granulated sugar, put a few spoonfuls in a dish, and moisten it with food colouring.

When the colouring is thoroughly mixed in, push the sugar into a bell mould, pressing it in firmly to fill the entire cavity.

Now simply tap the sugar bell out of the mould. Leave the bells to dry out overnight. To hang them on the tree, cut out a little tissue paper flower, thread a loop through it and glue it to the top of the bell. (These ornaments are not edible, and should be placed out of the reach of small children).

These little boxes make charming tree decorations. If you haven't got any suitable ones that you can wrap for the tree, you can easily make your own from cardboard. For a cube, you need to mark out a Latin cross shape. The lower arm of the cross should be twice as long as the top and side arms. Also add a 1.5cm (½in) border to all arms except the top one for gluing the cube together.

Fold along all the lines as shown, then bring the cube together, gluing all the sides in place.

Now simply wrap the box in attractive paper, and tie it with ribbons and bows to look like a parcel. Pop it on or under the tree.

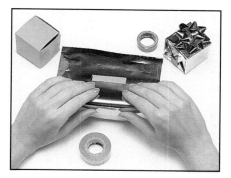

These pretty ornaments can be made any size. For a cube shape the pattern is a Latin cross (as shown), the long piece being twice the length of the others; all the other sides must be of equal length. Cut this shape out in satin, then cut a piece of iron-on interfacing, 1cm (½in) smaller all round. Iron on the interfacing. Also iron in creases to form the sides of the cube.

Placing right sides together, sew all the seams, using a small running stitch, cutting into the corners and using the interfacing edge as a seamline.

Leave one edge open so that you can turn the cube right side out. Stuff it with polyester filling, the slipstitch the opening edges together. Decorate the cube with ribbon and bows, then set it on a branch of your Christmas tree. For a rectangular box, simply widen the long section of the cross. The round box is a purchased box with satin glued on to it.

Another fun tree decoration that will last from year to year. Cut out the tree and pot in cardboard, using the templates on page 246. Now cut the shapes out in two different colours of felt, cutting two each of tree and pot. Place the two tree shapes together, and work buttonhole stitch around the edges, leaving the trunk end open.

These jolly Santa faces will add Christmas cheer to the tree. Cut out all the pieces in felt, using the template on page 246. Glue the main face piece to a piece of cardboard. When it is dry, cut around it.

Stuff the tree lightly with a little filling. Now buttonhole stitch around the pot, leaving the top open. Slip the trunk into the pot, and then lightly stuff the pot. Sew the tree and pot together at the sides.

All you have to do now is glue on all the other pieces. The nose and cheeks are affixed before the moustache, which goes on top.

Sew a little bow to the top of the pot, and decorate the tree with sequins and tinsel. Fix some gold or silver thread under the star on the top of the tree, so you can hang it up.

Place a loop of thread under the circle on the top of the hat, to hang up the face. Glue on two dark sequins to represent the eyes.

These miniature crackers can be hung on the Christmas tree or on the wall. First take a piece of cartridge (drawing) paper or light cardboard about 8cm (3in) wide and long enough to roll into a tube. Hold it together with a little sticky tape.

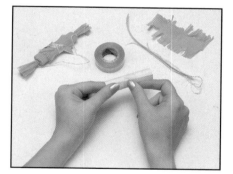

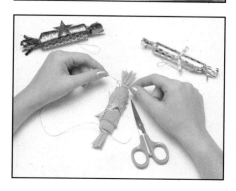

Cut a piece of crepe paper or foil twice as long as the tube, and roll the tube in it. Stick the edges together with double-sided tape. Squeeze the paper together at both ends, and tie some thread around them. Fluff out the ends and make small cuts in them to make a fringe.

To decorate the cracker, cut some extra, narrow pieces of crepe paper or foil, fringe them at the edges and wrap them around the tube as before. Alternatively, tie a bow round the cracker or stick a silver star in the middle. Tie a length of ribbon or sparkly twine to the ends by which to hang the cracker.

Make a pattern for a Christmas stocking using the template on page 246, and cut it out double in one piece by placing the pattern on the fold of the felt. Cut a strip of fake fur to fit the stocking, about 5cm (2in) deep. Catch the fur to the felt, top and bottom, by hand, with small stitches.

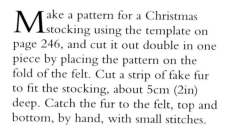

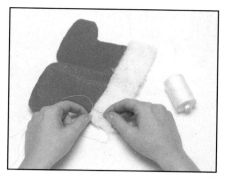

Now overcast the two sides of the stocking together, starting at the ankle and working around the foot and up the front. Turn the stocking right side out.

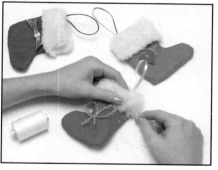

Turn the fur down about 2.5cm (1in) to the right side, catching it down around the edge. Decorate the stocking with sequins, bows, etc., and sew a loop of ribbon just inside the edge to hang it from the tree.

PING PONG PUDDINGS

Here is another cute tree decoration that is fun to make: tiny Christmas puddings. You start with ordinary ping pong balls. Spear each one into a fine knitting needle and paint it brown. After two or three coats, for a dark rich colour, finish off with a clear varnish to give the 'puddings' a lovely shine.

Now take some modelling clay, the sort you can bake in the oven, and roll it into a ball, the same size as the ping pong balls. Over this, mould a thick circle of white clay, to look like custard sauce. Bake this in the oven, and then remove it from the clay ball straight away, and pop it on to a pudding, so that it fits as it cools down and hardens. Don't forget to poke a hole in the top at this point.

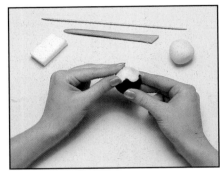

When the clay is cold, glue it to the pudding. Now take a double thread, knot the end and thread it through the pudding from the bottom upwards. Trim off the ends, then finish each pudding by gluing on foil holly leaves and red bead berries.

LET'S PRETEND

By the time Christmas arrives, you may not have much extra cash for Christmas tree baubles, so these colourful fakes are a great way of economizing. First cut some circles, with a little loop on the top, from some lightweight cardboard. Now mark out a pattern on each in pencil. Simple zigzags and curved lines are effective, but not too complicated to fill in.

Paint each bauble with several different colours, waiting for each to dry before painting the next. If you have some gold or silver paint, make good use of this, as it is very effective. Use black to make definite lines between colours.

When the baubles are dry, attach some thread, ribbon or some tinsel wire, so that you can hang them up.

If you haven't any shiny bells for the Christmas tree, it's not difficult to make some from foil, beads and a little string. First take a saucer and mark around it on to the back of some coloured foil. Cut out the circle, then fold it in half, and cut along the fold line. Fold each half of the circle into a cone and glue it in place.

For the clapper, string a bead on to a length of thread – preferably waxed – and tie a knot over the bead. Lay the thread against the bell so that the clapper is at the right level, then tie a knot level with the hole in the top. This prevents the string from being pulled through the hole when threaded. Pull the string through the hole from the inside and thread on a smaller bead at the top; knot in place.

Finish each bell by dabbing a little glue around the bottom edge and sprinkling on some glitter. When you have made three bells, string them together, and attach them to a ring so that they can be hung on the tree. Wind a little tinsel wire around the string, and tie a couple of bows for that final touch of glamour.

These miniature lanterns make attractive Christmas tree ornaments. First take a piece of foil-covered paper 11cm (5½in) square. Fold it in half, and rule a line 1.5cm (¾in) from the loose edges. Now rule lines 1cm (½in) apart, from the fold up to this first line. Cut along these lines and open out the sheet of paper.

Hold the paper with the cuts running vertically, and glue the two sides together. When this is firm, set the lantern on the table and gently push the top down to make the sides poke outwards.

Finally, cut a strip of matching paper 13cm (5in) long and 1cm (½in) wide. Dab some glue on each end, and glue the strip on to the inside of the lantern, at the top, for a handle.

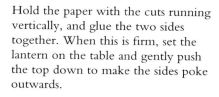

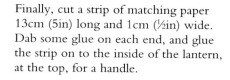

A shiny foil star makes a striking decoration for the top of the Christmas tree. Using the instructions on page 98, cut out a pattern in cardboard. Now cut two squares of cardboard, slightly larger than the star template, and cover each side with a different coloured foil. Next cut out two stars, one from each foil-covered squares.

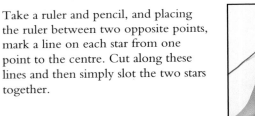

Take a ruler and pencil, and placing the ruler between two opposite points, mark a line on each star from one point to the centre. Cut along these lines and then simply slot the two stars together.

Use sticky tape and hold the points together and attach a piece of green garden wire to one set of points. You can then use the wire to attach the star to the tree. Finish the star by dabbing some glue on to the points and sprinkling glitter over them for an extra-sparkly effect.

This traditional English Christmas tree-top decoration makes a charming addition to the festivities. Using a saucer, cut a circle out of silver foil paper. Cut the circle in half and fold one half into a cone, tapping it in place.

Take a pink pipe cleaner and tape it to the back of the cone; then bend it into arms and hands. On top of this fix a triangle of doily to represent wings, using double-sided tape. For the head, take an ordinary ping pong ball and skewer it on to a wooden toothpick (or cocktail stick). Push the stick into the cone.

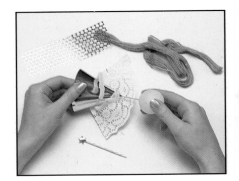

The hair is made from grey crewel or Persian wool, stuck on with double-sided tape, and the crown is a small piece of silver sequin waste. Draw the facial features with a fine-tipped silver pen. For the wand, spray a toothpick with silver paint and stick a small silver star on one end.

CANDLE CENTREPIECE

This sort of arrangement always looks very hard to achieve, but in fact it is very simple, provided you assemble everything you need before starting. What you need is a ring of florists' foam with a plastic base, which you can get from a florist. Also buy three plastic candle holders; stick these into the foam.

You will need holly, ivy and fern, all of them either real or fake, plus a selection of dried flowers. Daisy-like sunrays, yellow strawflowers or everlasting, yarrow, safflowers and sea lavender are used here. Simply break pieces off these and stick them into the foam. Try to space the flowers evenly in between the foliage.

When you have finished, stick three candles into the holders already placed. If any of the foliage is real, make sure to keep the foam damp.

CONE CANDLE STAND

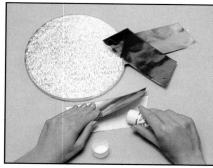

Believe it or not, this arrangement is quite simple once you get the hang of folding the cones. You need two colours of foil paper. Cut out lots of boat shapes 16.5cm (6½in) along the top and 12.5cm (5in) along the bottom and about 6cm (2½in) deep. Glue one colour to another, back-to-back.

Form each boat into a cone and glue it in place. The first few you make may not look too professional, but it doesn't matter; these can go on the outside of the stand and will be partially covered. You will soon get the hang of folding the cones. Bend the bottoms under; it helps to hold the shape and looks tidier.

When you have several cones made, start gluing them around the edge of a 20cm- (8in-) diameter silver cake board. Place another two layers inside the first, leaving room for a chunky candle in the middle.

The sideboard, as well as the table, needs a little dressing up at Christmas. This is bright and cheery, and the materials are quite easy to get hold of. If you don't have woodland nearby your florist should have small sections of bark for sale. Also buy a plastic candle holder. First put a large lump of green Plasticine (modelling clay) onto the bark, and stick your candle holder on the top.

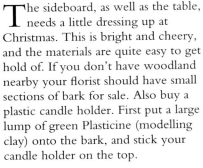

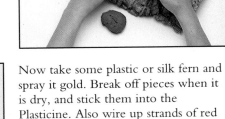

Now take some plastic or silk fern and spray it gold. Break off pieces when it is dry, and stick them into the Plasticine. Also wire up strands of red paper ribbon, pine cones and red baubles and stick these in.

What could be prettier than this profusion of ribbons and flowers? The one shown is pink and white, but you should choose whatever matches your décor. First of all you will need a biscuit or cake tin, Cover the outside with silver foil paper, allowing a little extra at the top to turn over and glue. (This will be easier if you snip down to the tin.) Decorate it with strips of ribbon.

Take a block of florists' foam and cut it to fit inside the tin, using the extra bits to fill in the gaps around it.

When the Plasticine is artistically concealed, place a red candle in the holder, and set the arrangement on the sideboard. Put a mat under it, though, or it will scratch the surface.

Now wire up pieces of gift wrap ribbon, little baubles, strips of crepe paper and silk flowers. Curl the ribbon by running the blunt edge of a pair of scissors along it. Push the wires into the foam, arranging them until the tin is totally full. Use strips of ribbon around the outside, and let them fall over the side of the tin.

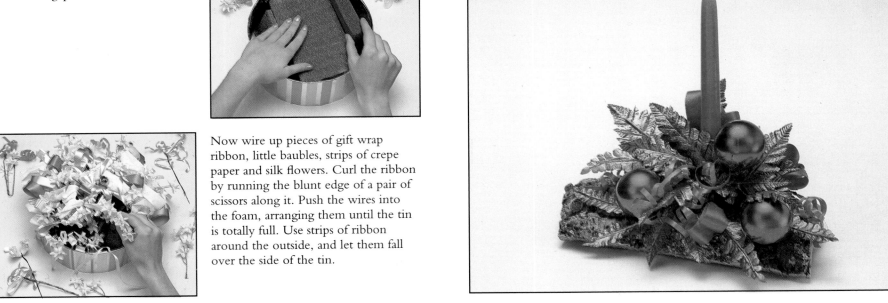

Spring is in the air, with a shiny silver pot plant, blossoming with pink silk flowers. You need a small plastic pot and a small, graceful tree branch. Spray them both with silver paint.

Now take a block of Plasticine (modelling clay), weighting the base with a stone if necessary. Push the silver branch into the middle and fix the Plasticine into the pot. For the 'earth' scrunch up a piece of silver foil and arrange it around the branch.

For the blossoms you need little pink silk flowers, scrunched up pink tissue, green tissue leaves and pink and green gift wrap ribbon. Glue these along the branch as shown, spacing them so as to look reasonably realistic.

Make some spring flowers that will bloom throughout the year. For the base of each daffodil head, cut a section from an egg box and trim it down to an even edge. Use a yellow one if you can, or else paint it yellow. Next take a flexible paper or plastic straw and roll it in a strip of green tissue, gluing both long and edges. Trim the ends and bend the straw without tearing the paper.

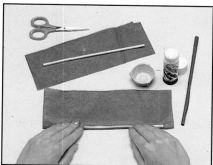

Cut out some yellow tissue petals and glue first one row, then a second, around the inside of the egg box base.

Finally, scrunch up a small piece of orange tissue paper and glue it to the centre of the flower.

If you have no room for a proper Christmas tree, this would be a good alternative – small but spectacular. First take a medium-sized plastic flower pot, about 15cm (6in) in diameter, and fill it, up to about 2.5cm (1in) from the rim, with fast-drying cement or wood filler. When this is just setting, insert a piece of 1.5cm (½in) dowelling about 40cm (16in) long.

When the filler is dry, spray paint the pot, the dowelling and the 'earth' surface gold. Lay it down to spray it, and when one side is dry, roll it over and spray the other side. The whole thing – especially the pot – will need a couple of coats.

When the paint is dry, take a ball of florists' foam at least 12cm (5in) in diameter and push it on top of the dowelling.

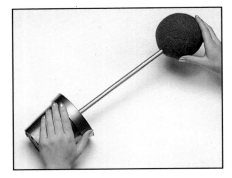

Now take short lengths of deep red and green satin ribbon, gold ribbon, shiny baubles and gold tinsel, and wire them all up, ready to push into the foam. Start with about a dozen of each; you can add to them as you go along, if necessary.

Start inserting the wires into the sphere, arranging the ribbons and baubles until it is covered, with no foam showing through. Finally wire up some curling gift wrap ribbon and insert it into the bottom of the ball. (Curl the ribbon by running the blunt edge of a pair of scissors along it.) Wind gold tinsel around the 'trunk' of the tree, and tie a large bow around the pot as a finishing touch.

These small fir trees are fun to decorate and add a festive touch to any Christmas sideboard or buffet table. For the gold tree, make small bows of fine gold ribbon. Drape a string of gold beads in a spiral over the tree, starting at the top, then fix the bows in between the loops of beads.

Wrap some tartan ribbon around the pot and secure the ends with fabric glue. Make a separate bow and attach it with glue or pins.

For the red tree, cut fine ribbon into 15cm (6in) lengths, tie them into bows and position them on the tree as shown.

Tie some tiny red ornaments to the branches; or, if the tree is dense enough, simply place them in the spaces between the bows. Add a wide red ribbon sash around the terracotta pot, tying it in a big bow.

A mound of luscious apricots, flowers and leaves makes a pretty centrepiece for a summer buffet or dinner party. Place a white doily on a glass or china cake stand. Carefully push ivy leaves underneath the edge of the doily. The leaves should be washed and can be wiped with cooking oil for extra shine.

Holding the doily in place with one hand, arrange the apricots in a pile. (If the apricots are to be eaten, do not allow them to touch the ivy leaves, which are poisonous.) Then arrange a few sprays of cream-coloured freesias around the pile of apricots.

Finally, slot flowers into the gaps between the apricots – any small cream or white flowers will do; those used here are narcissi. Check with your florist that the flowers you choose are not poisonous.

For an unusual Easter centre-piece fill a rustic basket with a selection of different eggs. The basket shown contains a mixture of hen's eggs, tiny speckled quail's eggs (which can be eaten as an hors d'oeuvre), and carved wooden eggs. Half fill the basket with paper to form a base for the eggs, then add a layer of packing straw.

Arrange your selection of eggs in the packing straw to show off their different colours and patterns. Tie a ribbon around the handle of the basket to provide a finishing touch.

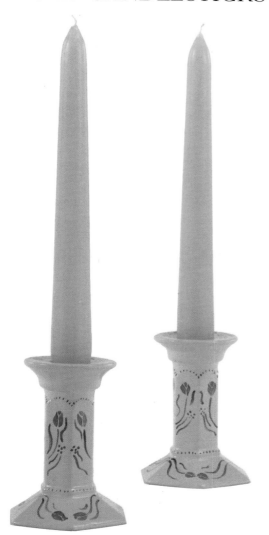

A touch of gold gives this platter of fruit and nuts extra richness. Begin by spraying ivy, clementines, bay leaves and fir cones with gold paint. (If the fruit will be eaten make sure that the paint you are using is non-toxic.)

Place the ivy leaves around the edge of a plain oval platter. The flatter the plate, the better, for this will allow the ivy leaves to hang over the edge.

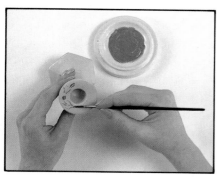

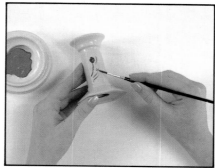

A simple motif such as a tulip can add style to the plainest of candlesticks. For this design you will need a pair of pink candlesticks, a fine paint brush and some garnet red and green ceramic paints. Decorate the top first, firmly holding the candlestick by the stem as you do so. Begin by painting the red flowers and clusters of tiny red dots, then fill in with green foliage.

Paint the stem and finally the base of the candlestick after the top has dried. Finish with lines of tiny red dots at the top and bottom of the stem, following the shape of the candlestick. Finally, when the paint is completely dry, apply a coat of ceramic varnish.

Arrange the clementines on the platter, surround them with dates and nuts, and place a bunch of shiny black grapes on top. Add the gold leaves and fir cones for a luxurious finishing touch.

This elegant candle-ring is the ideal centrepiece for a special dinner party at any time of the year. A circular cake base serves as the foundation for the arrangement. Begin by attaching strands of ivy to the edge of the base, securing them with drawing pins.

This stunning centrepiece looks grand enough to grace the most formal dinner party, and yet is very simple to make. Using a pastry brush, coat each piece of fruit with egg white.

Build up the ring by adding more stands and bunches of leaves until only a small space remains in the centre. Push stems of freesia among the ivy leaves to provide colour contrast.

Working over a large plate, sprinkle granulated sugar over the fruit so that it adheres to the coating of egg. Alternatively, the fruit can be dipped into a bowl of sugar, although this tends to make the sugar lumpy.

Use a mixture of white and green candles of varying heights to form the centre of the arrangement. Secure each candle to the base with a blob of glue or Plasticine (modelling clay).

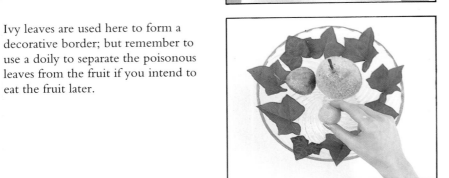

Ivy leaves are used here to form a decorative border; but remember to use a doily to separate the poisonous leaves from the fruit if you intend to eat the fruit later.

HOLIDAY CENTREPIECE

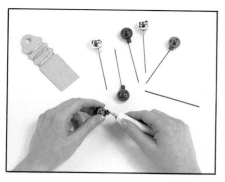

For a bright party centrepiece – ideal for Christmas or New Year's Eve – fill a glass bowl with a mixture of shiny glass baubles, foil crackers, feathers and streamers. To make clusters of small baubles, first remove the hanging string. Put a dab of glue inside the neck of each bauble and push in a short length of florist's wire. Leave them to dry.

Hold the wired baubles in a cluster and wind fine fuse wire around the stems to hold them together.

Wrap a piece of shiny giftwrap ribbon around the stems and tie it into a bow. Arrange the baubles and other ornaments in the bowl as shown.

FLOWERS AND FRILLS

This pretty centrepiece is a good wintertime alternative to a vase of real flowers. Lay a sheet of coloured tissue between two different-coloured layers of net. Place a vase in the centre of the net and tissue, and gather the three layers up around the neck of the vase.

Secure the net and tissue in place with a piece of twine or an elastic band. Tie a length of contrasting wide satin ribbon in a bow around the neck of the vase.

Fluff out the layers of net and tissue to create a frilled effect. Fill the vase with artificial flowers – such as the tulips shown here – or with real flowers, if you prefer.

MARZIPAN FRUIT PARCELS

Exquisite marzipan fruits deserve special presentation. Nestling in little tissue 'parcels' and piled into a cake stand, they make a colourful centrepiece. All you need is several different colours of tissue paper and some pinking shears. Instead of marzipan fruits, you could use chocolates or marrons glacés.

From a double layer of one colour of tissue, cut a 10cm (4in) square. Pinking shears give an attractive serrated edge. From another colour of tissue, also double, cut a smaller square, measuring about 6cm (2½in).

Lay the smaller square on top of the larger one. Place the marzipan fruit in the centre and gather the tissue around it. Hold it in place for a few seconds and then let go; the crumpled tissue will retain its rosette shape. Place several of the parcels on a doily-lined glass or china cake stand.

FUN FAIRY CAKES

These individual cakes, each with its own candle, make an unusual alternative to a large birthday cake for a children's party and form an attractive centrepiece. Decorate each cake with a pattern, or pipe a child's name on to it.

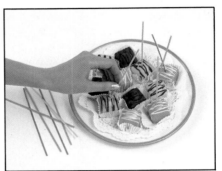

Stick a long taper candle into each cake and arrange the cakes on a large plate. Once lit, the candles should not be allowed to burn for too long, as the hot wax will begin to drop on to the cakes.

For a summer table centrepiece nothing can surpass the beauty of flowers. The secret of successful flower arranging is a careful choice of containers and a harmonious colour scheme. When using several containers, try to get a variety of shapes. The jugs used here have contrasting forms but similar colours; the flowers include shades of pink, white and red.

The tall jug contains a mixture of anemones, ranunculus, kaffir lily (schizostylis) and white September flowers, the mixture of shapes providing variety. The smallest vase contains a tiny narcissi, ranunculus and anemones with a few sprigs of love-in-a-mist (nigella). The deep red anemone at the front serves as a focal point.

This fat, rounded jug has a fairly wide neck and is therefore ideal for full-blown roses, which look good clustered together to form a close, rounded shape. Delicate stalks of white September flowers (aster) and a few heads of love-in-a-mist show up well against the pale pink roses and give more definition to the arrangement.

Although flowers are most often arranged in vases, it is just as easy to create a pretty centrepiece using ordinary containers you may have around the house. This natural, yet graceful, arrangement uses a mixture of spring flowers in jam jars. A few coloured glass bottles are added for contrast.

Here a squat clear jar is used for a mixture of white flowers and silvery-green foliage, forming a cool two-colour arrangement.

A single hyacinth is enough to fill the smaller jar, and the twisted stem of an anemone fits perfectly into a thin blue glass bottle. A colourful bunch of anemones in another jam jar completes the centrepiece.

This cute little rabbit can be popped over a soft-boiled egg to keep it warm. First cut out two rabbit shapes in white felt, using the template on page 246. Cut the ears from pink felt, the waistcoat from yellow, and the nose and eyes from black. Glue them in place. Embroider the mouth and whiskers in black thread. Glue on sequins for the buttons and for the whites of eyes.

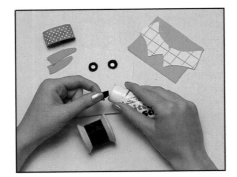

Take a piece of ribbon 5cm (2in) long and glue the ends together to form a loop. Tie a piece of thread tightly around the middle of the ribbon to form a bow, and sew it to the rabbit between the mouth and the top of the waistcoat.

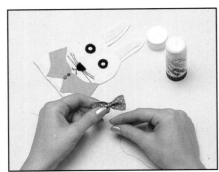

With wrong sides facing, sew the front and back together along the edge, using blanket stitch.

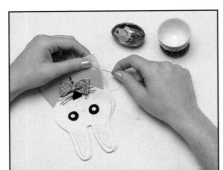

To break the ice at a kids' party – iced cupcake name badges. The template for the pieces is on page 246. Cut each cake shape from thin cardboard as a base for the felt. Then cut out the top and bottom pieces, again in cardboard.

Glue the latter pieces to different colours of felt and cut around them. Now glue these separate pieces to the base card.

Finish off by sticking a name label to the front of the bun and a little double-sided tape to the back. When the little guests arrive simply tear off the backing from the tape and label them!

POTATO PRINT 'PLACEMAT'

Why not decorate a plain white tablecloth with a placemat outline to match your china? All you need is a raw potato and some paint. First cut the potato into a cube about the size of your chosen motif. The leaf shape shown here is about 3cm (1½in) square. Using a sharp knife, cut the motif on one side of the cube as shown.

Use a paint suitable for fabric, or a water-based paint if you are printing on a paper tablecloth. Spread the paint evenly over the raised motif.

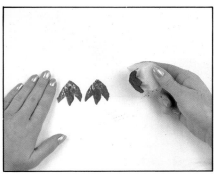

On a piece of stiff paper, draw the outline of the 'placemat' in black felt-tip pen. Place this under the cloth as a guide when printing. Press the potato down on to the cloth, taking care not to smudge it. Practice first on a spare piece of paper. The same technique can be used to print a border design around the edge of the napkin.

RIBBON-TRIMMED TABLECLOTH

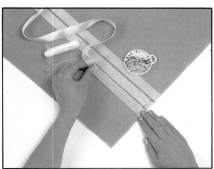

This pretty tablecloth isn't hard to make but requires a bit of patience. You can make the cloth yourself or buy one ready-made. Buy enough ribbon in each colour to run along four sides of the cloth, plus 24cm (8in) if using a ready-made cloth. Position the ribbons as shown, with fusible webbing underneath (omitting the area where they will cross), and pin them in place.

Continue to pin the ribbons in place along all the edges, making sure that you keep them straight. Thread the ribbons underneath one another to create a lattice effect, as shown. If you are using a ready-made cloth, allow the ribbons to overlap the edge by 3cm (1in); this will be folded under later.

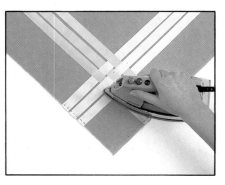

Replace the corner pins with tacking (basting) stitches, if you are working on an un-hemmed cloth; this provides extra stability. Press the ribbons in place with a warm iron, removing pins as you go and stopping just short of the tacking. Finally, hem the edges. On a ready-made cloth, sew the ribbon ends to the wrong side by hand.

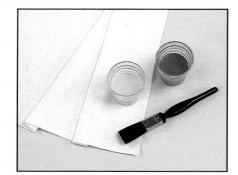

Transform a plain tablecloth with this eyecatching design. Choose a brush the correct size for your design, and use a paint suitable for fabrics. (Because the paint is applied quite thickly, a paper tablecloth is not suitable.)

Practice first on a spare piece of cloth or paper, dipping the brush into the paint for each new stroke. Then paint the cloth, applying the lighter colour first; allow it to dry thoroughly.

Paint on the second colour in broad sweeps, allowing the paint to fade off towards the end of each brushstroke. Follow the manufacturer's instructions for fixing the fabric.

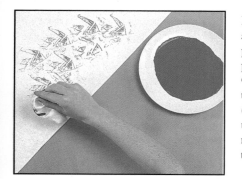

Rag-rolling, or ragging, is a quick and easy way to transform a plain fabric or paper tablecloth. Pour a water-based paint or fabric dye on to a plate, and dip a crumpled piece of cloth in it. Blot the cloth on some waste paper or fabric to remove excess paint.

Lightly press the crumpled fabric on to a spare piece of paper or cloth to practice getting an even amount of paint over the area to be covered. Once you feel confident, rag the tablecloth, adding a second colour (once the first had dried) if desired. If using fabric dye, follow the manufacturer's instructions for fixing the colour.

FLEUR-DE-LYS TABLECLOTH

FLOWER-STREWN TABLECLOTH

Add a touch of luxury to a dinner party by decorating your own tablecloth in gold. First choose a simple image, such as the fleur-de-lys motif shown here. You can either decorate an existing cloth or buy a length of wide inexpensive cotton fabric. Draw the shape in pencil first, and then go over it in gold paint.

This simple idea can transform an ordinary tablecloth into something special. Choose a plain white or pastel-coloured tablecloth and artificial flowers with small blossoms. You will also need some green sewing thread and a needle.

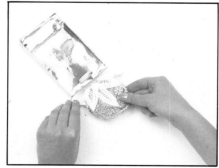

If the flowers you have chosen have several blooms to a stem, trim them into individual sprigs. Set aside the remaining leaves.

To echo the shape of the fleur-de-lys symbol you can dress up your table napkins as shown. A napkin with a lacy edge will look best. Fold the napkin into a square. Keeping the lacy edge nearest to you, fold the left- and right-hand corners in to overlap one another. Fold the remaining point in to meet them.

Slide the napkin, lacy edge towards you, into a shining foil gift bag. Because both napkin and china are white, a lacy gold coaster was inserted into the bag, underneath the lace detail on the napkin to give it more definition.

Sew the flower sprigs to the cloth. You can use as many or as few sprigs as you wish; you could sew one or two by each place setting or, for a stunning effect, cover the whole cloth with them – leaving room for place settings and serving dishes. Place the leftover leaves with a single flower sprig on each guest's plate.

This unusual placemat is easily made from cardboard and a wallpaper border. A black and white border has been chosen to co-ordinate with the table setting on pages 96-97. Cut a 30cm (12in) square from a sheet of thick cardboard, using a steel rule and craft knife to ensure precision.

Cut the border into four strips, allowing a little extra on each strip for trimming. Apply double-sided tape to the back of each strip, but do not peel off the protective backing strip yet. Lay two adjacent strips in place; where they meet at the corners, try to match the pattern repeat. Holding one strip on top of the other, cut diagonally across the corner.

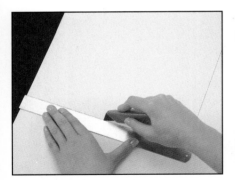

Holding each strip in place along its inner edge, begin to peel back the protective paper from the double-sided tape, as shown. Rub a soft cloth along the border as you peel to stick it in place.

Give a touch of luxury to plain white china by using a larger gold plate underneath each dinner plate. You will need some old white china plates, about 1.5 to 2.5cm (½ to 1in) wider all around than your dinner plates, a few ivy leaves (at Christmas use holly and mistletoe as well), gold spray paint and a few gold or silver dragées.

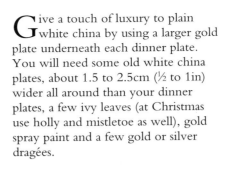

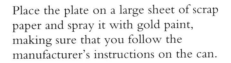

Place the plate on a large sheet of scrap paper and spray it with gold paint, making sure that you follow the manufacturer's instructions on the can.

Lay the holly and ivy leaves on a sheet of scrap paper and coat them with gold paint. Leave them to dry for 10 to 15 minutes, and then arrange the painted leaves on the smaller white plate with an unsprayed sprig of mistletoe for contrast. Add a few silver dragées for the finishing touch.

PRETTY PVC PLACEMAT

Attractive and simple to make these PVC (vinyl) placemats will also readily wipe clean. Cut a 30cm (12in) square from a sheet of thick cardboard. Take the diagonal measurement of the square – 42.5cm (17in) for this size mat – and mark a square of that size on the wrong side of the PVC; cut it out.

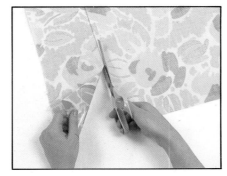

Place the cardboard square diagonally on the larger square of PVC. Spread a strong glue all over the cardboard and also on the exposed triangle of PVC. Allow them to dry until tacky.

Fold each triangle of PVC into the centre of the cardboard square so that they all meet. Press them firmly in place on the surface with a soft cloth to ensure that there are no air bubbles.

LACE-TRIMMED PLACEMAT

Delicate lace edging and pastel ribbon give a pretty, feminine look to a place setting. Use a plain white handkerchief, or hem a piece of fabric about 30cm (12in) square. Cut a length of lace trimming approximately 130cm (50in) long, and sew it around the edge of the fabric, gathering it at each corner and joining the ends neatly.

Cut four lengths of 1cm- (⅜in)-wide ribbon and stick them down along the join with double-sided tape. (See page 132 for instruction on mitring corners.)

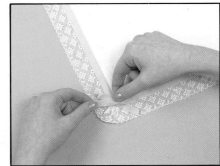

Cut a 20cm (8in) length of ribbon and tie it in a bow; trim the ends neatly. Attach it to the corner of the mat with double-sided tape, or sew it on with a few stitches. The ribbon can easily be removed when the mat needs washing.

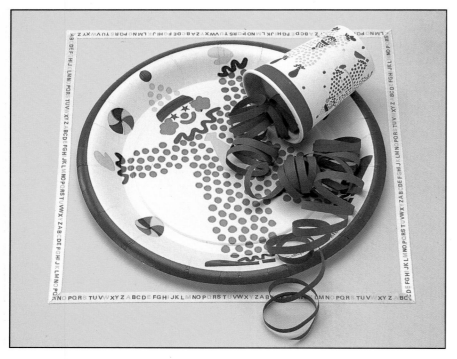

This sparkling placemat is an obvious winner for Christmas. First draw a Christmas tree on the reverse (matt) side of a piece of shiny green cardboard. The length should be about 10cm (4in) longer than the diameter of your dinner plate and the width about 20cm (8in) wider. Cut out the mat using a craft knife and a steel ruler.

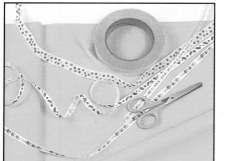

Jolly up a plastic or paper tablecloth for a children's party by using colourful strips of ribbon to mark out individual place settings. All you need, besides the tablecloth, is 1.3m (50in) of patterned ribbon for each setting and some double-sided tape.

Add 'ornaments' by sticking tiny baubles to the tips of the tree using strong glue.

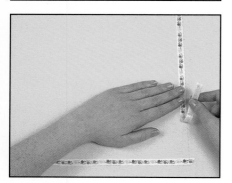

For each setting draw a 30cm (12in) square on the tablecloth. Use a ruler and set square (right-angled triangle) for accuracy. Cut the ribbon into four equal lengths. Stick tape on to the back of each ribbon and remove the backing. Stick the ribbon on to the cloth, overlapping it at the corners as shown and smoothing it just enough to hold it in place.

Cut out or buy a star shape to put at the top of the tree. Finally, stick small silver stars over the mat. Or, if you prefer, just scatter the stars freely over the mat, first positioning each mat on the table.

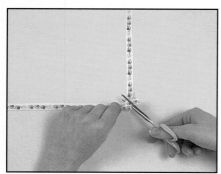

Where the ribbons overlap, at the corners, lift them gently and cut diagonally across them to give you neatly mitred corner. When you have trimmed each corner, run a finger along the ribbons, sticking them firmly in place.

COLOUR-FLECKED PLACEMAT

The perfect solution if you can't find tablemats in the right colour – paint your own, using plain cork tablemats and two colours of water-based paint. For applying the paint you will need an artist's paintbrush and a natural sponge.

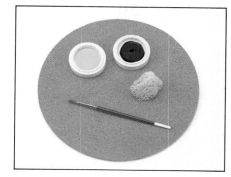

Paint the cork mat all over with the lighter-coloured paint. Allow it to dry. If the colour is very pale you may need to apply a second coat.

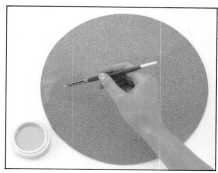

Dip the sponge into a saucer containing the colour; dab it a few times on a piece of scrap paper to remove any excess paint. Sponge the mat all over, allowing the first paint colour to show through. When the paint is dry apply a coat of clear polyurethane varnish for protection.

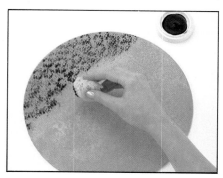

PICNIC TRÈS CHIC

Convenient and stylish, too, this placemat roll wraps up each person's cutlery and napkin until needed. For each roll you will need a quilted cotton placemat and matching napkin and three co-ordinating ribbons, about 55cm (22in) long.

Lay the placemat flat, wrong side up. Lay the napkin and cutlery on top, then roll them up together as shown.

Trim the ends of the ribbons diagonally. Lay the roll on top of the ribbons and tie them around it into a bow.

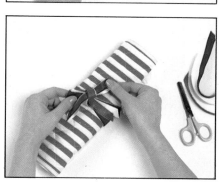

This pretty design is not as difficult to create as it may appear. The technique is similar to that used in folding the origami 'fortune cookies' so popular with children. Lay the napkin flat, and begin by folding each of the four corners into the centre.

Here's a quick and simple way to dress up a plain napkin for afternoon tea. All you need is a square paper doily, preferably in a colour contrasting with the napkin, and a floral motif. Begin by folding the napkin into a triangle.

Repeat this same procedure, drawing the corners inwards to make an even smaller square. Then turn the napkin over and repeat for the third time, holding the corners down in the centre to keep them in place.

Fold the doily diagonally. To create a 'spine' to allow for the thickness of the napkin, unfold the doily and make another crease about 1cm (⅜in) from the first fold.

Still keeping your finger on the centre, reach behind the napkin to one of the corners tucked underneath and draw this gently outwards as shown until it peaks out beyond the corner of the square. Repeat the process with all four flaps to form the petals. Finally, reaching underneath again, pull out the four single flaps to make the sepals.

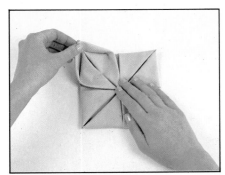

Cut out a Victorian scrap or other floral motif and glue it to the centre of the small (top) side of the doily. Insert the napkin.

This elegant napkin fold is easier to produce than it looks. First fold the napkin in half diagonally, then bring the left- and right-hand corners up to meet at the apex.

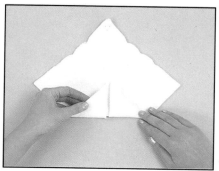

Turn the napkin over, and fold the lower corner up slightly as shown.

Fold the left- and right-hand corners underneath the napkin on a slight diagonal, pressing the folds lightly in place.

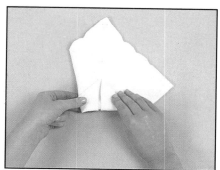

A crisply starched napkin is required for this pretty fold. Lay the napkin flat. Fold two edges to meet in the centre as shown. Then fold the half nearest you across the centre line and over on the top of the other half, to form a long, thin rectangle.

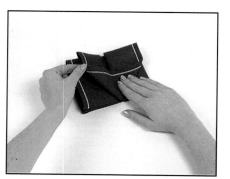

Fold the right-hand end of the rectangle in towards the centre, and with another fold double it back on itself as shown. Repeat with the left-hand side so that the double folds meet in the centre.

Pull the right-hand back corner across to the left, bringing the front edge across the centre line to form a triangle. Anchoring the right hand side of the triangle with one hand, use the other hand to fold the corner back to its original position, thus creating the 'wings' of the arrangement. Repeat the process on the left-hand side.

Fold the napkin twice to form a square and position it with the loose corners at the top right. Fold the top corner back diagonally to meet the lower left corner, then turn it back on itself as shown. Continue to fold the corner back and forth to create a 'concertina' effect along the diagonal strip of napkin.

Lift the next layer of fabric from the top right-hand corner and repeat the process described above to create two parallel strips with zigzag edges.

Pick the napkin up in both hands with the zigzag folds in the centre. Fold it in half diagonally to form a triangle, keeping the pleats on the outside. Take the right-hand and left-hand corners of the triangle and curl them back, tucking one into the other to secure them. Stand the napkin upright on a plate as shown.

For best results use a crisply starched napkin to make this attractive fold. First fold the napkin lengthwise into three to form a long rectangle. Lay it horizontally with the free edge away from you, and fold the left- and right-hand ends in to meet in the centre.

Fold down the top right- and left-hand corners to meet in the centre forming a point. Take the napkin in both hands and flip it over towards you so that the point is facing you and the flat side of the napkin is uppermost.

Lift the sides and pull them over towards one another to form a cone shape. Tuck the left-hand corner into the right-hand corner to secure it. Turn the napkin around and place it on a plate as shown in the main picture.

Fold the napkin in half to form a crease along the centre line. Then open the napkin out again. Fold one half of the napkin lengthwise into three by bringing the top edge of the square inwards to the centre line and then folding it back on itself as shown. Repeat with the second half.

Fold the napkin in half lengthwise by tucking one half under the other along the centre line. Lay the resulting strip flat with the three folded edges facing you. Mark the centre of this strip with a finger and fold the right-hand edge in towards the centre and back on itself as shown. Repeat with the left-hand side.

Pull the top left-hand corner across towards the top right-hand corner to create a triangle, pressing down gently along the folds to hold them in place. Repeat with the remaining left-hand folds, and then do the same with all the right-hand folds. Ease the folds open slightly and display the napkin with the centre point facing the guest.

This mitre-shaped fold can be displayed either on a flat surface (as above) or in a glass, cup or soup bowl, which allows the flaps to drape gracefully over the sides. Begin by folding the napkin diagonally to form a triangle, then pull each corner up to the apex as shown to form a square.

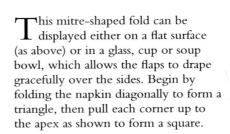

Turn the napkin over so that the free edges lie towards you. Pull the two top flaps up and away from you; then fold the remaining two flaps back in the same way to form a triangle.

Carefully turn the napkin over once more, and pull the two outer corners together so that they overlap; tuck one flap into the folds of the other to hold them in place. Finally, turn the front of the 'hat' to face you, position the napkin upright and pull the loose flaps down as shown in the main picture.

This design looks best in a conical glass but can be adapted for a wider-based container. Although it takes a little more practice than most, it is worth the effort. First lay the napkin flat and fold it in three lengthwise. Position it as shown, with the free edge on top.

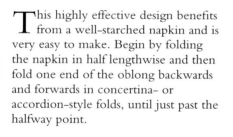

This highly effective design benefits from a well-starched napkin and is very easy to make. Begin by folding the napkin in half lengthwise and then fold one end of the oblong backwards and forwards in concertina- or accordion-style folds, until just past the halfway point.

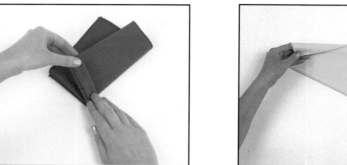

Holding the folds firmly together, fold the napkin lengthwise down the middle to bring both ends of the 'concertina' together. Keeping the folds in position in one hand, fold the loose flap of the napkin over across the diagonal.

Take hold of the top left-hand and right-hand corners of the napkin with the index finger and thumb of each hand. Roll the corners diagonally towards you as shown.

Push the flap underneath the support as shown to balance the napkin, and, letting go of the pleats, allow the fan to fall into position.

Without releasing your hold on the napkin, continue to roll the corners inwards in one sweeping movement by swivelling both hands and napkin down, up and over until your hands are together palms uppermost. By now the napkin should be rolled into two adjacent flutes. Release your hands and place the napkin in a glass, arranging it neatly.

FLEUR-DE-LYS

LADY'S SLIPPER

This pretty design is ideally suited to teatime settings. Begin by folding the napkin into four – left to right, top to bottom – to form a small square. Then fold the four loose corners back across the diagonal to form a triangle.

Holding the napkin firmly at the apex, fold one of the outer corners over and towards you as shown, so that it overlaps the base of the triangle. Repeat with the second corner so that the edges of both flaps meet down the centre of the napkin.

Turn the napkin over and fold the protruding flaps back over the base of the triangle. Then fold the triangle in half by pulling one of the corners over to meet the other. Finally, holding both corners firmly together, turn the napkin upright and pull the four loose corners upwards as shown in the main picture.

This graceful fold is easier than it looks. Lay the napkin flat and fold it in half diagonally to form a triangle. Position it with the folded edge towards you. Bring the top corner towards you, so that the point overlaps the folded edge slightly. Carefully turn the napkin over and repeat with the other corner.

Pleat the napkin evenly across from left to right, in accordion- or concertina-style, folds. Holding the straight edge of the 'concertina' firmly in position, arrange the napkin in a glass. Pull the front layer of the top point towards you, creating a pointed flap over the front of the glass.

FOUR FEATHERS

This simple fold looks elegant placed in a wineglass. Open the napkin flat. Fold it in half diagonally to form a triangle, and place the folded edge towards you. Place your index finger on the centre of this edge. Using the top layer of fabric only, bring the apex down to meet the left-hand corner.

Again working with the top layer only, bring the far corner down and across to the bottom left-hand corner.

Bring the remaining top corner down and across to the lower left corner as before, forming a triangle once more. Splay the folds slightly, then turn the napkin over so that the folds are underneath. Lift the edge and roll the napkin into a loose cone shape as shown, stopping about halfway across. Fold up the bottom point and insert the napkin in the glass.

CANDLE FOLD

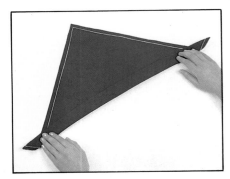

This tall candle-shade fold looks especially good if the napkin has a contrasting border. Begin by laying the napkin flat. Fold it in half diagonally to form a triangle. Turn up the folded edge about 3cm (1¼in), then turn the napkin over so that the fold is underneath.

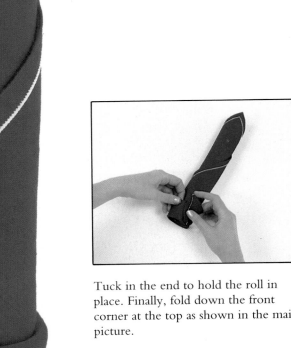

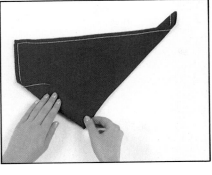

Starting at the left-hand corner, roll the napkin to form a cylindrical shape.

Tuck in the end to hold the roll in place. Finally, fold down the front corner at the top as shown in the main picture.

BUFFET ENVELOPE

This design is perfect for a smart buffet. Fold the napkin in half, and then fold it again to form a square. Take one layer of fabric from the 'open' corner, and fold it diagonally over three times, with the final crease across the centre. Fold the second layer of fabric in the same way, making slightly shallower folds, and tuck it under the first fold.

Fold the left- and right-hand sides to the underside, leaving a central panel in which to place the cutlery. Or use the napkin as it is (without the cutlery inside) for a sit-down meal.

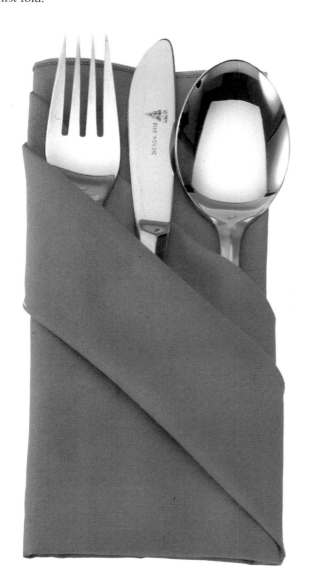

POCKET NAPKIN

This simple napkin fold is embellished with a few artificial flowers tucked into the pocket. Fold the napkin in half and then in half again to form a square; then fold it across the diagonal to form a triangle.

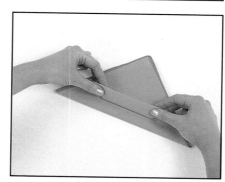

Position the napkin as shown with the four loose corners uppermost. Working with the top layer only, fold it down several times to make a cuff at the bottom.

Fold the next (single) corner over so that the tip touches the top edge of the cuff. Fold the next two corners over to form three tiers. Finally, turn the right and left corners of the triangle to the underside and overlap them. Position the napkin as shown in the main picture and insert the flowers.

THANKSGIVING NAPKIN

T his simple place setting is perfect for a Thanksgiving or Harvest Festival dinner. Use a sisal or straw placemat and a plain white napkin. For the decoration you will need a selection of dried flowers and grasses and three lengths of beige or wheat-coloured ribbon, each about 50cm (20in) long.

Tie the lengths of ribbon together at one end. Plait them until the plait is long enough to tie around the napkin twice with a little left over.

Group the bunch of dried flowers and grasses together, securing them with thread or twine. Fold the napkin in half twice to form a long, thin rectangle. Lay the flowers on top of the napkin. Wind the plaited ribbon around the napkin and flowers twice and tie the ends under the napkin.

LACY NAPKIN BOW

I deal for a wedding or anniversary dinner, this lacy napkin bow is not only pretty but also easy to make. The napkins themselves should be pretty, preferably with a lace detail around the edge. For each napkin you will need about 90cm (1yd) of wide satin ribbon and the same amount of insertion lace.

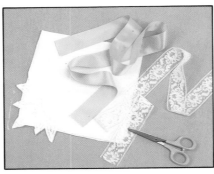

For best results, the napkin should be starched and well ironed and folded into quarters. To cut decorative points for the ribbons and lace, fold the ends as shown and cut them diagonally.

Fold under two corners of the napkin to overlap in the centre, forming the shape shown here. Iron the folds flat. Lay the ribbon and lace flat, wrong side up, with the ribbon on top. Place the napkin on top and tie the ribbon and lace around it in a bow.

CIRCULAR NAPKIN

This original napkin fold makes a pretty circular shape and is embellished with a bead and ribbon trimming. Paint a plain 25mm (1in) wooden bead with a water-based paint to match your napkin. Then paint on a pattern with a harmonizing or contrasting colour. Allow the paint to dry between coats.

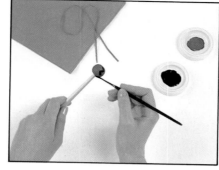

Fold the napkin in half once along its length, and then pleat it accordion-fashion along its length, making sure the folds are the same size.

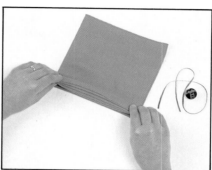

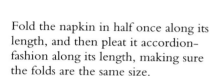

Thread a length of thin ribbon through the bead and tie it to hold the bead in place. Wrap the ribbon around the centre of the napkin, and tie it in a neat bow just below the bead. Fan the napkin out so that it forms a full circle.

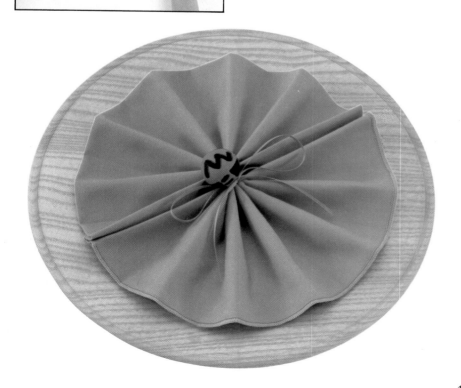

TASSEL NAPKIN RING

This tasselled napkin ring is ideal for a special occasion. You will need two tassels and approximately 40cm (16in) of cord per napkin, and a strong fabric glue. Attach the tassels to the cord by wrapping the loop around the cord and pulling the tassels through it.

Make the ring by feeding the cord through both loops of the tassels twice more. Make sure that the ring is large enough to slip easily over the napkin.

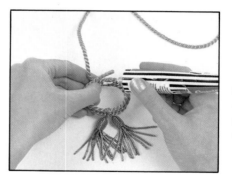

Using a strong glue, secure the ends of the cord to the back of the ring. Lay one end along the back and trim it. Having applied the glue to the inside of the ring as shown, wrap the remaining end over the cords, covering the trimmed end. Cut the remaining piece of cord on the inside, and clamp it in position until it is dry.

FLORAL NAPKIN RING

This charming flower-trimmed napkin ring adds a touch of elegance to a table setting and is very easy to make. Bend a short length of florist's wire into a circle; twist the ends together to secure them.

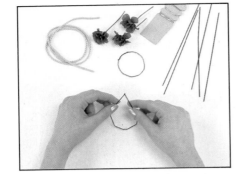

Wind some fine fuse wire around one or two small silk flowers – chosen to co-ordinate with your china and table linen. Then twist the ends of the fuse wire around the circle of florist's wire to hold the flowers in place.

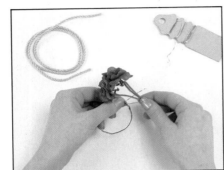

For covering the ring choose a fine ribbon or decorative braid. Hold one end in place with one hand, and use the other hand to twist the braid around the circle to cover it completely, beginning and ending underneath the flowers. Secure the ends with glue. Insert the napkin and add a fresh flower for the finishing touch.

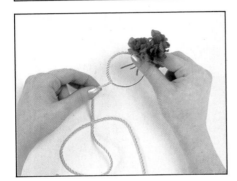

NET NAPKIN RING

For a touch of frivolity, tie your table napkins in several shades of net. For each napkin cut three different-coloured rectangles of net, 45 by 35cm (18in by 13in). Fold each piece crosswise into three equal sections.

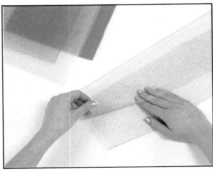

Fold the napkin twice to form a square, and then fold it diagonally to form a triangle. Now roll it lengthwise.

Place the lengths of net on top of each other; tie them around the napkin and fan out the ends.

This is a lovely decoration for a wedding table and makes the most of a crisp white tablecloth. Begin by taking some large white wooden rings – the kind used on curtain poles – and winding ribbon around them as shown.

Tie a bow at the top to hide the little metal ring, then pin each one to the front overhang of the tablecloth, spacing them evenly. Thread through a length of net, bunching it between the rings to make a good swag.

When the net is evenly arranged, attach strips of curling gift wrap ribbon to the lower edge of each ring as a finishing touch. Curl the ribbon by running the blunt edge of a pair of scissors along it.

The paper used for these crackers is similar in texture to curling gift wrap ribbon and has a lovely shiny satin finish. Cover empty toilet paper rolls or cardboard tubes with white sticky-backed plastic, which prevents the colour from showing through. Now cut pieces of shiny paper, twice as long as the tubes, and wide enough to go easily around them.

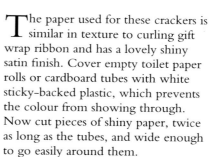

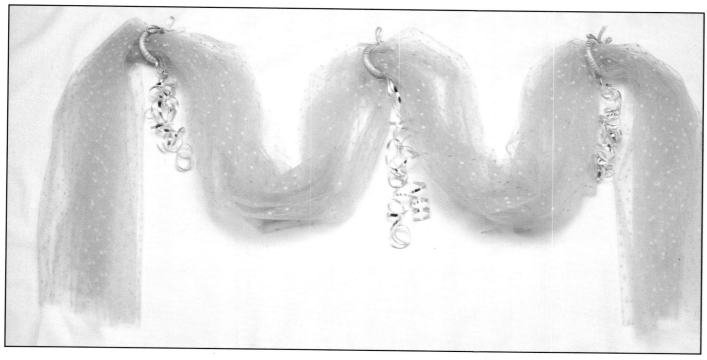

Wrap the tube in the paper and fix in place with double-sided tape. Don't twist the ends; scrunch them in with elastic bands, which you can then cover with strips of curling ribbon. Decorate the crackers with boiled sweets, stuck on with double-sided tape. Staple the crackers on to a strip of tinsel and trim with sweets and baubles.

Here are a couple of ideas for jazzing up ordinary paper napkins. For the blue napkin, cut a star shape from a piece of cardboard – the cardboard must be slightly wider than the folded napkin. Hold the cardboard firmly in place over the napkin and spray silver or gold paint over the area. Let the paint dry for several minutes before you allow anything else to touch it.

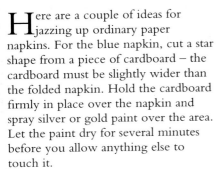

The white napkins have a design stencilled on them with oil-based stencil crayons. You buy these separately or in packs, with ready-cut stencils. Choose your design, then place it over the area you want to stencil – in this case the corner of the napkin. Rub the crayon over a spare area of stencil, then take the colour up on to the brush and paint it over the stencil, in a circular motion.

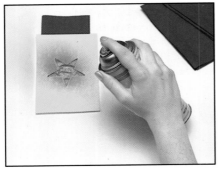

Use the brush only over the parts you wish to show up in that colour. Now switch to the next colour. It is best to use a different brush for each colour if you want clear colour definition.

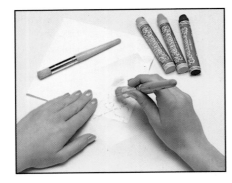

For a bit of fun at Christmastime, make some especially festive napkin rings. Each is made from a piece of cardboard tubing. The leaf sprig ring is first covered with a strip of sticky-backed plastic. Cut the plastic wide enough to go over to the inside of the ring, and cover the inside with a thinner strip of ribbon. The leaf design is a Christmas cake decoration.

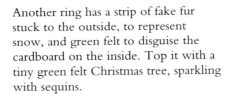

Another ring has a strip of fake fur stuck to the outside, to represent snow, and green felt to disguise the cardboard on the inside. Top it with a tiny green felt Christmas tree, sparkling with sequins.

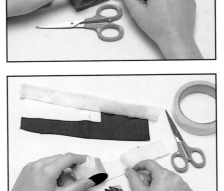

Still another idea is to cover the ring with a small strip of wide satin ribbon. Glue a piece of narrower toning ribbon to the inside, folding the edges of the wide ribbon under as you go. Lastly, tie a strand of tinsel wire around the ring and finish with a bow.

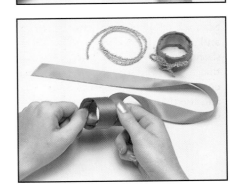

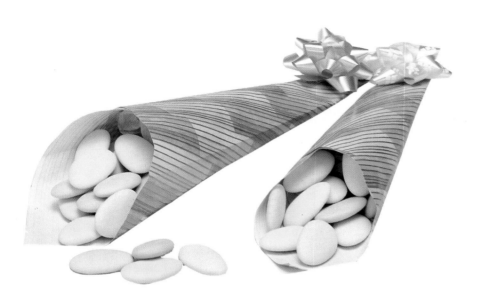

To make this simple gift for the table, fill a paper cone with chocolate drops or sweets for a children's party or with sugared almonds for grown-ups. All you need is a small square of brightly coloured wrapping paper, a ribbon rosette, and some tissue paper. Simply roll the paper into a cone from corner to corner, taping it into a nice rounded shape.

These are cute little gifts to place beside each setting on the table. Begin by cutting out a circle of net, using a standard sized dinner plate as a guide.

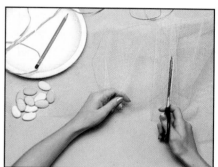

Flatten the cone slightly, positioning the top point in the centre; then fold up the bottom and stick on the ribbon rosette.

Place a few pastel-coloured sugared almonds into the net, and bunch it into a parcel with an elastic band to hold it together.

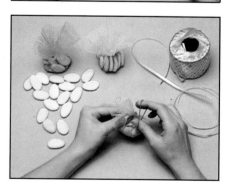

Scrunch up a little bit of tissue paper and slip it inside the cone to hold it in shape, then fill the top with sweets so that they spill out on to the point. You could attach a place card to each cone and use the cones to mark place settings at a large party.

Now just trim the parcel with curling gift wrap ribbon. (Curl the ribbon by running the blunt edge of a pair of scissors along it.) You could slip a name tag over the ribbon before tying it and use the parcel as an unusual place marker.

This method of decorating is known as resist painting. To create this primitive design you will need a mixture of glass and ceramic paints. Using a chinagraph pencil, draw the design on to the plate. Remember that whatever areas you cover with the chinagraph will appear white on the finished plate.

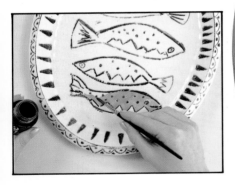

Carefully paint the fish using contrasting ceramic paints. These fish are coloured in deep blue and yellow, but you can try other colour combinations such as purple and orange or black and gold. Now paint the border pattern in bright colours – red looks particularly attractive.

Paint the water surrounding the fish in emerald green glass paint, applying it in an undulating wave pattern to represent water currents. Use glass paint for the water as it is more translucent than ceramic paint. When the paint is completely dry, rub away the chinagraph with a soft dry cloth to reveal the white china.

You may need to use a cloth soaked in turpentine to tidy up the edges of the pattern. Finally, protect your design with a coat of ceramic varnish.

148

FASHION FLOWERS

These most unusual flowers are made from coloured nylon stockings or tights. First cut some pieces of copper wire 20cm (8in) long. Bend each into a petal shape with pliers. You need five petals for each flower. Cut the nylons into pieces and stretch them over the wire very tightly, binding them on with green tape.

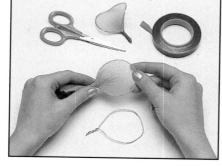

Take five stamens (obtainable from craft shops), bend them in half and use pliers to attach them to the end of a long piece of copper wire, again binding them with green tape.

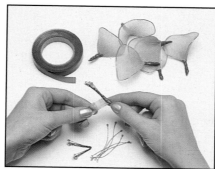

Now arrange the petals around the stamens. Start by placing the middle two opposite each other. Bind them, then add the other three around them. When all the petals are in place, tape around the top of the stem and continue down it to the end. When you have made several blooms, wrap them in shiny paper and tie a net bow around the outside.

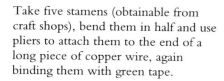
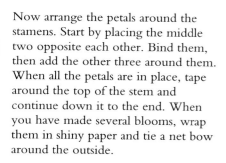
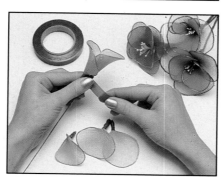

GLAMOUR CRACKER

This beautiful cracker is not designed to be pulled but to be taken home as a memento. First take a tube of cardboard and wrap white crepe paper around it. Insert short cardboard tubes into each end, leaving gaps of 5cm (2in) between the main and end sections. Cover the central and end sections on the outside with silver foil paper, and stick pink foil paper to the inside of the end sections.

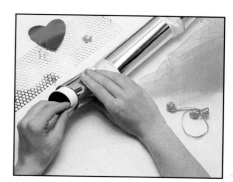

Wind a length of silver sequin waste around the centre. Next take two strips of pink net and draw a piece of thread through the centre of each to gather it. Tie them at each end with a strip of curling gift wrap ribbon. (Curl the ribbon by running the blunt edge of a pair of scissors along it).

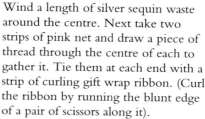

Finish by decorating the cracker with large sequins and a pink foil heart, or with some other shape if you prefer. If you like, pop a little gift inside – a hand-made chocolate, perhaps, or even a diamond ring!

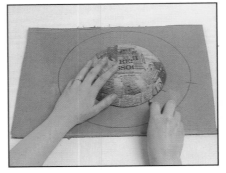

This fruit bowl is based on a wok shape, with a second bowl placed inside. Coat the inside of a wok with petroleum jelly and apply eight layers of papier mâché all at one time. When this has dried, cut around the edge to neaten. Separate the papier mâché shape from the wok.

Repeat the process on a smaller bowl of a similar shape. When dry, mark a line partway down this papier mâché bowl, as shown. Cut, making a shallow bowl.

Apply two layers of papier mâché to the edges of both bowls. When dry, mark the wok outline on cardboard, making a register mark on the bowl and the card. Repeat with the small bowl, centring it as shown. Cut out the ring and glue and tape the pieces together, aligning register marks. Apply four layers of papier mâché to the rim and leave to dry.

Next apply a layer of tissue paper. This will wrinkle, adding texture. When dry, sand, seal and emulsion the bowl. Using blue and green children's chalks, scribble all over the surface. Brush over the surface with clear water and repeat three more times, to create a greater depth of colour. Finish with a coat of matt polyurethane varnish.

GIFT WRAPPING

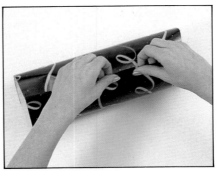

When wrapping a cylinder, avoid using very thick or textured paper as it will be difficult to fold neatly. Cut the paper longer than the cylinder, allowing for extra paper at each end to cover half the cylinder's diameter, and just wider than the gift's circumference. Roll the paper around the parcel and secure with a little tape.

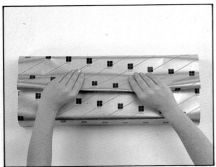

Wrapping square or rectangular presents isn't difficult – but perhaps your technique needs brushing up. Wrap the gift wrap tightly around the box. You can simply stick down the free edge with tape or, for a smarter effect, fold over the top edge of the paper and stick double-sided tape underneath it, leaving a neat fold visible at the join.

Begin folding the ends of the paper in a series of small triangles as shown here. Continue around the whole circumference, making sure that the 'triangles' are neatly folded into the centre.

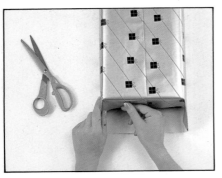

If your paper has a linear design, try to align the design so that the join is not too obvious. Fold the join section of paper down over the end of the box to make a flap; crease the fold neatly. Trim off any excess paper so there is no unnecessary bulk.

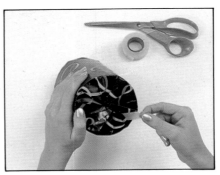

Use a single piece of tape at the centre to fix all the folds in place. If the finished folds are not even, you could cheat a little by sticking a circle of matching paper gift wrap over each end of the cylinder.

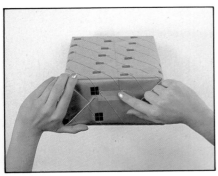

Crease the side flaps firmly, and fold them over the ends of the gift. Smoothing your hand along the side of the box and round on to the end ensure that each flap fits tightly. Fold up the remaining triangular flap, pulling it firmly along the edge of the box, and stick down; use invisible tape (its matt surface is scarcely discernible) or double-sided for the best results.

The usual method of wrapping a sphere is to gather the paper around the gift and bunch it all together at the top. Here is a more stylish method. Put your circular gift in the centre of a square of paper, checking that the two sides of paper just meet at the top when wrapped around the gift. Cut off the corners of the square to form a circle of paper.

Bring one section of the paper to the top of the gift and begin to pleat it to fit the object as shown. The paper pleats at the top of the gift will end up at more or less the same point; hold them in place every three or four pleats with a tiny piece of sticky tape.

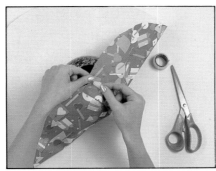

Continue pleating neatly and tightly all the way round the circle. It isn't as complicated or as time-consuming as it sounds once you've got the knack! When you have finished, the pile of pleats on top of the gift should look small and neat. Then you can either cover them with a small circle of paper stuck in place or, more attractively, add a bunch of colourful ribbons.

Wrapping awkward-shaped presents is just that – awkward. The gift wrap always looks creased and untidy around the angles of the gift. The solution is not to use paper – instead, use brightly-coloured cellophane which doesn't crumple. Cut a square of cellophane a great deal large than your gift.

Gather the cellophane up and tie it into a bunch above the present. Fan out the excess and add some curled ribbon as a finishing touch. Alternatively, if your gift is cylindrical, roll it in cellophane somewhat longer than the parcel and gather the ends with ribbon.

Stylish, expensive-looking wrapping paper can be achieved very quickly with this method of spray stencilling. Choose some plain coloured paper for a base, and make your stencils from plain cardboard or paper. Cut the stencils into squares of two different sizes; alternatively you could use any kind of basic shape – stars, circles or whatever.

Lay some of the shapes in a random pattern across the plain paper, holding them in place with a spot of Plasticine or modelling clay. Cover the whole paper with paint spray. Use car paint or craft spray paint, but do carry it out in a well-ventilated room.

Once the paint is dry take off the sprayed squares and put a new random pattern of fresh squares across the paper. Overlap some of the original square with the new ones to create interesting effects, then spray the entire sheet with a second colour of paint. Remove the squares and leave the wrapping paper to dry before using it.

Stencilling is great fun to do – and so easy. Design a simple motif then make a trace of it. With a soft pencil, scribble over the back of the trace and put the tracing paper face up on stencil cardboard. Draw round the design again, pressing hard so that the lines are transferred on to the cardboard beneath. Repeat the motif several times and cut out the shapes with a craft knife.

Position the cut-out stencil on plain paper, and either hold it or use masking tape to keep it in place. Mix up some poster paint, keeping the consistency quite thick. Apply the paint through the stencil, using a stiff brush. When you have finished a row of motifs, lift the stencil carefully and blot it on newspaper so that it is ready to use again. Leave the design to dry.

Keep repeating the process until you have covered enough paper to wrap your gift. To help you keep the spacing even between beach run of motifs, add some 'markers' to the stencil. Cut half a motif at the end of the run and another one above the run to mark the position of the next row. Paint the markers along with the other motifs, then use this image for re-positioning the next row.

DESIGN WITH A SPONGE

All kinds of effects can be achieved with a sponge and some paint. You'll need a piece of natural sponge as man-made sponge doesn't produce the right effect. Choose some plain paper and mix up some poster paint to a fairly runny consistency. Test the paint on a spare piece of paper until you're happy with the colour.

Dab the sponge into the paint and pat it evenly over the paper. The sponge should hold sufficient paint for about four 'dabs' before you need to dip it into the paint again. You'll need to mix up a lot of paint as the sponge absorbs a considerable amount.

Rinse the sponge out well and squeeze dry. When the paper has dried, repeat the process with another colour — you can use as many colours as you wish. Match the ribbon to one of the colours; see page 169 for instructions on how to create the ribbon trim shown here.

SPATTER PATTERNS

This method makes striking wrapping paper — with apologies to artist Jackson Pollock! Creating the pattern is great fun, but rather messy; cover your work area well with an old cloth or waste paper before you start. Begin by mixing up two or more colours in fairly runny poster pant.

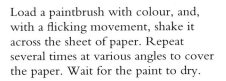

Load a paintbrush with colour, and, with a flicking movement, shake it across the sheet of paper. Repeat several times at various angles to cover the paper. Wait for the paint to dry.

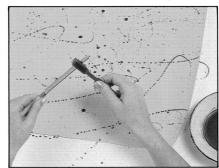

Dip an old toothbrush in another colour paint, avoiding getting the brush too full of liquid. Rub the toothbrush across the blade of a knife to cause the paint to spatter over the paper. Repeat until the spattering is as dense as you like.

Here is a novel way to disguise two lightweight presents. Put each gift in a rectangular box and wrap with giftwrap. Apply double-sided tape to the end of one box (the smallest, if they vary in size). Peel off the tape backing and press the gift against the other one making an 'L' shape.

From mounting board, cut two large circles for the back wheels and two smaller ones for the front. Cut a circle for each wheel in giftwrap with 1.5cm (⅝in) added all around. Stick the wheel on the wrong side and snip into the edge all around. Apply double-sided tape to the circumference of the wheel and stick the snipped edge over on to the tape.

Cut giftwrap circles slightly smaller than the wheels and stick to the wrong side. Use a craft knife to cut a slice from a cardboard tube for the funnel. Apply double-sided tape in a cross shape over one end and remove the backing tape. Roll the funnel in a strip of giftwrap, snip the excess at the top and tuck it inside.

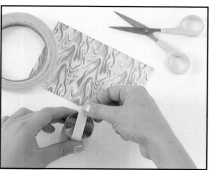

Use a strong glue to stick the wheels to the sides of the train, then press the funnel on to the 'engine'. Stick three lengths of narrow giftwrapping ribbon together at one end. To coil the ribbon, pull the lengths smoothly over the blades of a pair of scissors. Stick the ribbon inside the funnel for the 'smoke'.

A GIFT IN A GIFT

PAPER DUET

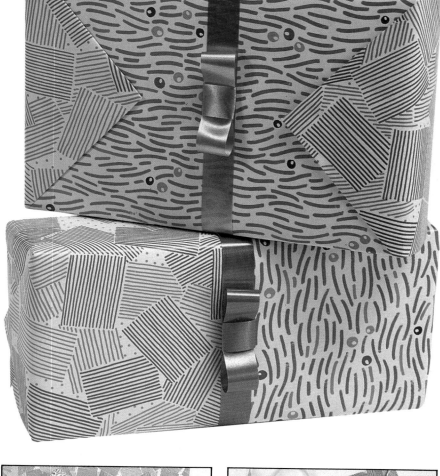

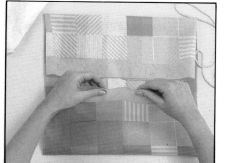

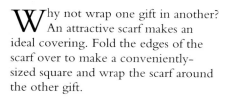

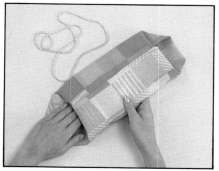

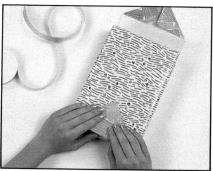

Why not wrap one gift in another? An attractive scarf makes an ideal covering. Fold the edges of the scarf over to make a conveniently-sized square and wrap the scarf around the other gift.

Tuck the top layer of each end of the scarf under the other present as shown, then fold up the end flaps. Use a ribbon or string of beads to hold the flaps in place. Alternatively, a couple of pretty handkerchiefs make a good wrapping for a small gift such as soap. Gather the hankies around the gift and secure in a bunch with a length of lace.

It is very annoying if the gift wrap you have bought is just too small to cover your present. The answer is to use two pieces of contrasting paper — the result can be very chic! Wrap your gift with one of the pieces of paper, using a strip of scrap paper to protect the gift from the tape. Fold in the ends neatly.

Cut the contrasting gift wrap into a strip the exact width of your parcel, long enough to cover the back and both ends plus two flaps. Use this strip to hide the uncovered back of the gift and fold it over the two ends. Make two flaps on the front of the parcel as shown and secure with double-sided tape. Alternatively, wrap each end of the parcel in different paper, hiding the join with a ribbon.

Employ a humble potato to create simple yet beautiful designs. Begin by cutting a large potato in half and draw a simple design on it. Use a sharp knife or craft knife to sculpt the potato, leaving the design raised from the surface.

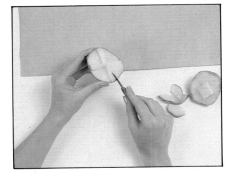

To ensure a regular print, draw a grid lightly in pencil on a sheet of plain paper. Then mix up fairly thick poster paint and apply it to the potato-cut with a paintbrush. Print the design in the middle of each square of the grid. You should be able to do two or three prints before the colour fades and needs replenishing.

Glittering wrapping paper is always glamorous, and with glitter available in such a variety of colours your creativity need know no bounds! Spread out a sheet of plain coloured paper and, using a bottle of glue with a fine nozzle, draw a series of simple patterns across it.

Cover the whole sheet with one design. Cut another design on another potato half; repeat the whole process, this time printing on the cross of the grid. When the paint is thoroughly dry, rub out the grid lines still visible and wrap up your present.

Sprinkle a line of glitter across the paper. Tip up the sheet and gently shake all the glitter from one side of the paper to the other, across the glued designs, making sure that all the patterns have been well covered. Tip the excess glitter off the page on to a sheet of newspaper; the glitter can then be used again.

Now use the glue to make more designs and coat these in glitter of a different colour. Localize the sprinkling of the glitter over the new patterns to be covered and leave to dry. Tip off the excess glitter and return it to its container.

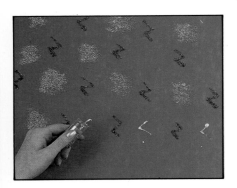

Wallpaper borders can look very effective on any square- or rectangular-shaped gift. Cut a strip of border the length of one side of your wrapped gift; glue it in place along the edge.

Cut another border strip for an adjacent edge. Apply glue, and position the strip so that the end of it overlaps the first strip. Now mitre the overlapped corners by trimming the top strip at an angle. Do this by ruling a line between the corner of the gift and the point at which the strips overlap, as shown here.

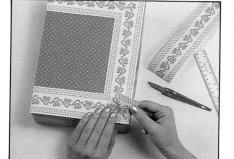

Cut off the excess triangle of wallpaper border with a craft knife. Don't press too hard or you could damage the gift underneath. Cut two matching border strips for the other edges of the gift and repeat with mitring process with the remaining three corners.

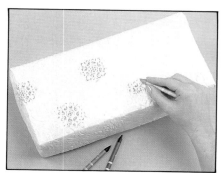

Wallpaper is often useful as a gift covering – particularly if your present is very large. Here we have used thick wallpaper with an embossed pattern and given it a touch of style and individuality. Wrap your gift, and choose some wax crayons in contrasting shades. Rub a colour over the raised surface of the wallpaper to highlight one of the motifs in the design.

Choose another colour, and use it to pick out another section in the pattern. (Instead of wax crayons, you could use coloured pencils or chalk; the latter would need to be rubbed with a tissue afterwards to remove loose dust. The medium you choose must slide over the embossing without colouring in the whole design – paint is therefore not suitable.)

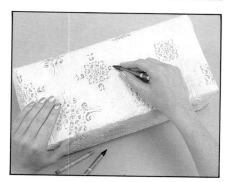

Repeat the process using a third colour and continue with as many shades as you like. A tip while wrapping your gift – you'll probably find that ordinary tape will not stick to the surface of wallpaper; double-sided tape used between two folds will be more effective.

The delicate silhouette of a doily against a contrasting background colour looks attractive on a gift. Wrap your present up in plain paper and glue the doilies wherever you like. To decorate the corners of a large gift, fold a doily in half, then in half again.

Unfold the doily carefully and spread it out. Cut off one of the quarters of the doily; the folds along which you should cut will be clearly visible.

Paste the doily over one corner of the gift as shown. Repeat with alternate corners, unless your gift has enough space to take a doily over each corner without overlap. The doilies don't have to be white: silver or gold is also effective. Nor do they have to be circular – square ones would be smart on a square-sided present.

B rightly-coloured adhesive tape can give any plain wrapping paper a touch of style. A geometric design is easiest to create with tape, and the most effective; curves are rather difficult! Work out your design first and measure it out accurately on the parcel in pencil.

Stick the tapes in place along the pencil marks. Take care that the tapes don't stretch at all during application or they will cause the paper to pucker slightly. Sticky tapes are available in an enormous variety of colours, textures and patterns; choose a strong contrast with your paper.

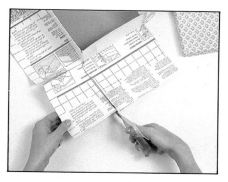

When re-covered in plastic, a shoe box makes a great container for a present. Put the box in the centre of a piece of self-adhesive plastic and draw around it. Then draw around the shape of the sides and ends of the box so you end up with a diagram of the 'exploded' box. Allow extra plastic all round for overlaps. Cut out the pattern you have just created.

Peel the backing off the plastic and position the box carefully in the middle of the covering. Smooth the rest of the plastic up over the box, starting with the ends. Wrap the small overlap around the corners as shown.

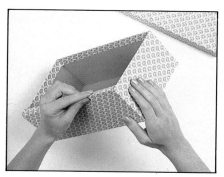

Smooth the plastic up over the sides, trimming off the edges to make the pieces the exact size of the sides. Fold over the overlaps around the rim. Cover the lid in the same way. For complete co-ordination, you could cover the inside of the box to match. Alternatively, you could line the box with co-ordinating tissue paper or net.

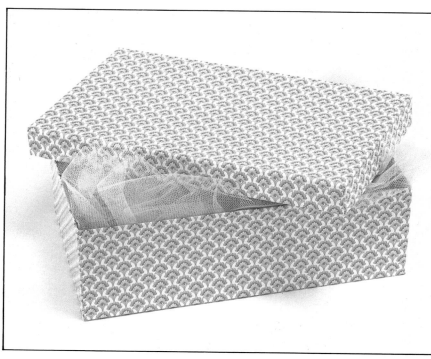

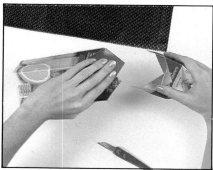

A handy gift container, ideal for home-made sweets, can be made from a well-washed juice carton. Draw V-shapes in each side of the carton. These should be inverted on two opposite sides, and pointing towards the top of the carton on the other two sides. Cut cleanly along the drawn lines with a craft knife as shown.

Cover the carton with gift wrap; adhesive in spray form achieves the best results. Make sure the join lies neatly down one corner of the box. Trim the overlap at the top of the carton so that it is even and fold the paper over the edges, taking care that the corners are neat. Punch a hole at the apex of both the pointed sides and thread ribbon through.

This cube-shaped box is ideal for containing any kind of gift and it can be made to any size. Measure out the shape of the box on to thin cardboard, following the template on page 124. It's very important that all the squares are exactly the same size and that all the angles are right angles. Cut out the shape, and score along the fold lines – the back of a craft knife is useful for doing this.

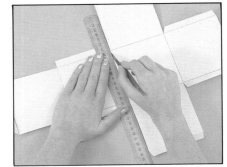

Bend the card carefully along the score lines, making a neat crease along each fold. Crease the flaps on the lid and base and fold the four sides into the shape of the box.

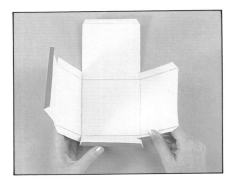

Stick the side flap to its opposite side as shown. You can glue this, or alternatively, use double-sided tape. Fold in the base flap – it should fit precisely and thus give the box rigidity. Finally close the lid flap.

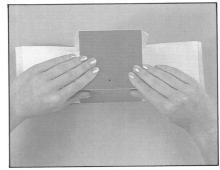

Making a box from scratch can be a little complicated, so why not start with an empty cereal packet? Take your cereal packet and careful open it out flat. Separating the joins needs care – if necessary slide a knife between the seams to part the glue, rather than tear the packet.

Draw the box you want, using the template on page 252 as a reference. Make sure the lid measures the same as the width of the side panels. Cut to the new shape with a pair of scissors, and cover it with your chosen gift wrap. Spray adhesive is best, since this gives a very smooth finish, however glue in a stick form will do. When the glue has dried, cut neatly around the cardboard shape.

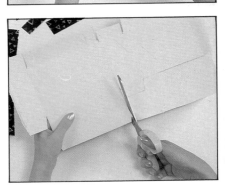

Score along the new fold lines of the box using the back of a craft knife or the blunt edge of a pair of scissors. Fold the box into shape. Stick the side flap in place as shown: you can use double-sided tape or glue. Fix the two flaps on the bottom (either glue or tape them). Put in some shredded tissue as padding, slot in your gift and tuck the lid neatly into place.

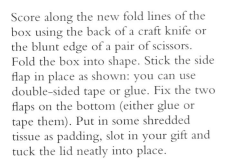

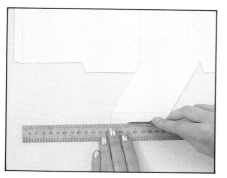

A variation on the cube gives this box an unusual diamond shape. Draw the template on page 252 on to thin coloured cardboard. Check that all the sides are the same size, and that their angles measure 90°; the angles of the lid and base should measure about 60° and 120°. Cut out the shape with a craft knife.

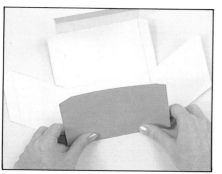

Score along the fold lines on the sides and flaps of the box with the back of a craft knife or the blunt edge of a pair of scissors. Fold the scored edges over, making sure that they are well creased for a crisp shape.

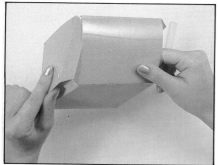

Fit the box together, sticking down the side flap with glue or double-sided tape. Fold in the base and the lid; it is the shape of these which converts the box from being an ordinary cube into the more exotic diamond shape.

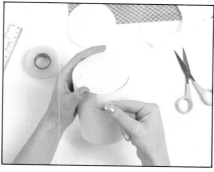

A cylindrical box looks much more difficult to make than it is. Wrap a piece of thin cardboard around the gift to determine the measurement of the box. Cut out the cardboard, roll it up and stick down the edge with a length of tape. Draw and cut out a circular base, and a slightly larger circle for the lid. Attach the base with small bits of tape.

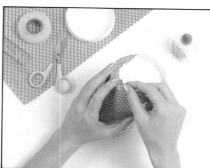

Cut a strip of cardboard slightly longer than the circumference of the cylinder. To make the lid, stick the edge of the strip to the edge of the circle with tape. Next, spread glue on some gift wrap and roll the cylinder in it. Cut the paper to fit, allowing an overlap each end. Tuck the overlap into the open end; secure. Fold the base overlap in a series of small triangles and stick to the base.

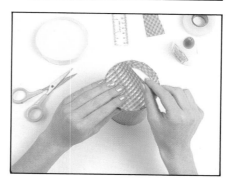

Draw a circle of gift wrap slightly smaller than the base. Cut it out and glue in position, hiding all the folds, and bits of tape. Cover the lid in the same way. If you like, you can punch two holes in each side of the container and thread through short lengths of decorative braid.

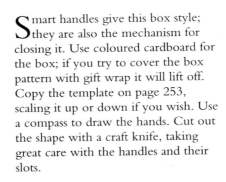

S mart handles give this box style; they are also the mechanism for closing it. Use coloured cardboard for the box; if you try to cover the box pattern with gift wrap it will lift off. Copy the template on page 253, scaling it up or down if you wish. Use a compass to draw the hands. Cut out the shape with a craft knife, taking great care with the handles and their slots.

Score along all the fold lines using the back of a craft knife; crease them well. Fold the carton into shape, and stick down the side flap with double-sided tape or glue. Fold the base down, pushing the flap inside the box to secure it.

T his attractive and unusual bag will add prestige to any present. Draw the template featured on page 252 on to a sheet of thin cardboard with the aid of a compass and a protractor; use a pencil as some of the design will need to be erased later. Cut out the circle and score along the lines of the 'star' and the central octagon with a sharp edge – the back of a craft knife will do.

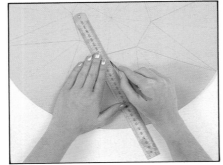

Close the first two flaps of the lid, folding the handles up to fit. Pinch the handles together and fold the two top flaps of the lid over them, fitting the handles through the slots.

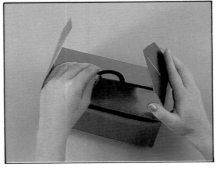

Take care not to overscore along the intersections of the lines, as the cardboard could eventually tear. Rub out any line not scored. Bend along the edges of the octagon, being careful not to crease the sides. Then fold along the arms of the 'star', to form a series of triangles (these will come together to form the container for your gift).

Folding the box needs patience, but it's not as complicated as it looks! When the folding is complete, punch holes in either side of the top of each triangle (see the template) and thread the ribbon through the holes as shown. Arrange the curved edges so that they radiate out from the centre. You can made the bag any size you want; as a guide, though, ours had a diameter of 40cm (16in).

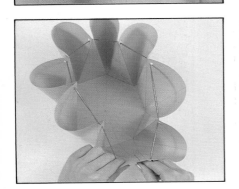

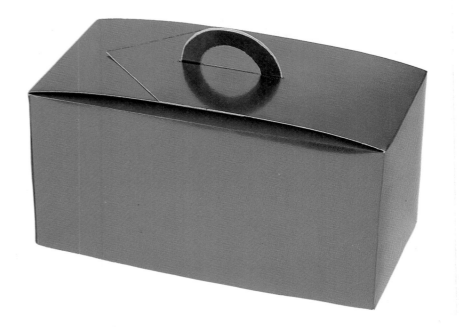

A plant is a notoriously difficult item to wrap; here's a smart solution. Measure an equilateral triangle on some coloured cardboard. The length of each side should be twice the height of the plant; use a protractor to ensure all the angles measure 60°.

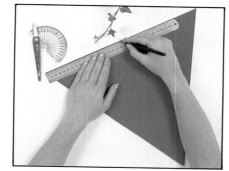

Divide each of the three sides of the triangle in half. Join all the half marks together to form an inner equilateral triangle; this will form the base. Bend the card along a ruler at each inner line as shown and bring up the sides to form a three-dimensional triangle. Punch a hole in each apex and thread ribbon through to close the parcel; double length ribbon gives a pretty finishing touch.

These rigid little boxes are ideal for presenting jewellery but you can make them to fit anything you like. Choose thin cardboard, either in the colour you want the finished box to be, or white so that you can cover it later with gift wrap. Measure out the template on page 253. The size of the triangular sides doesn't matter, as long as they are all the same, and the base is a true square.

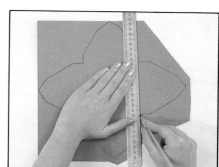

Cut out along the exterior lines with a craft knife. If you're covering the cardboard shape with gift wrap, do it at this stage, cutting the paper to fit. Score along all the fold lines carefully, using the back of the craft knife, then bend the box along the score marks, creasing firmly.

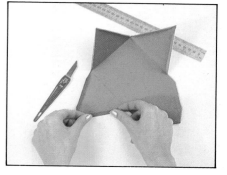

Punch holes in each apex and fold the box into its pyramidal shape. Thread the ribbon in and out of the four holes and, making sure all the side-folds are tucked inside the box, tie the loose ends together with a bow.

These sachets are ideal for ties, soaps, scarves, jewellery, hankies, socks and so forth. On to thin cardboard, trace the template on page 253. It's probably more interesting to cover the shape with gift wrap as shown here, but you can use plain cardboard if you wish. If using gift wrap, cut out the shape and paste it on to your chosen wrapping paper.

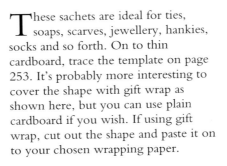

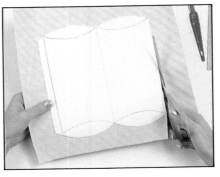

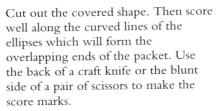

Cut out the covered shape. Then score well along the curved lines of the ellipses which will form the overlapping ends of the packet. Use the back of a craft knife or the blunt side of a pair of scissors to make the score marks.

Stick the side flaps together with either double-sided tape or glue. Fold in the ends; if you've scored the lines sufficiently they should pop in easily with just a little guidance. They can be re-opened with no difficulty, but make sure the covering gift wrap doesn't begin to lift off the cardboard.

This method is best suited to a small box as the end result is not particularly strong. From thin cardboard, cut out a cross-shaped piece as shown, made up of four sides and a base, all the same size and all absolutely square. The lid will also be a square measuring 5mm (¼in) larger than the base, with sides about 2cm (¾in) deep.

Paste both shapes on to gift wrap and when dry cut off the gift wrap around the box and lid, leaving a small turning or flap around each edge. Fold in the flap on the left of each side of the box and glue it down as shown. Score along the edges of what will be the base, to form fold lines for the sides of the box.

Bend the sides upwards. Put glue on the patterned side of the flaps of gift wrap left unfolded on each side; stick these flaps inside the box to the adjacent sides as illustrated. Crease down the sides firmly and leave to dry. Finally, fold in and glue the top lip. Treat the lid in exactly the same way.

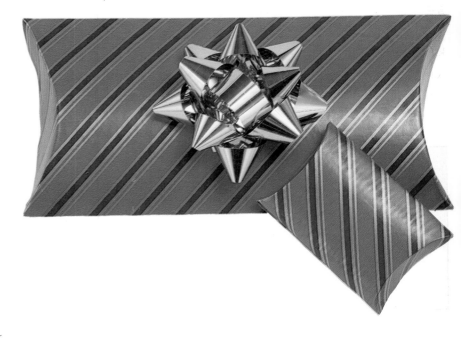

Gift bags are very useful as containers for awkwardly-shaped presents and they can be made to any size. Find something with the required dimensions of the finished bag to serve as a mould – a pile of books should suffice. Choose a good quality, strong gift wrap for making the bag. Cut a strip of gift wrap long enough to wrap round the 'mould' and fold over the top edge.

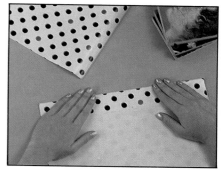

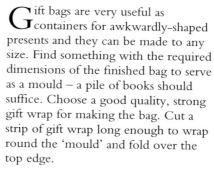

Wrap the paper round the mould; glue or use double-sided tape to join the seam at the back. Fold over the end flaps in the usual way of wrapping any parcel to make the base of the bag; be sure to attach sufficient tape to make the base strong.

This small narrow box would be ideal for giving someone a watch or a piece of jewellery – unless, of course, you make it bigger! Trace off the template on page 253 on to thin cardboard. Cut it out, and either cover it in gift wrap or, if you like the colour of the cardboard, just leave it plain.

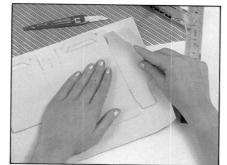

Cut around the template with small sharp scissors to trim away the excess gift wrap; take extra care with the slots and handles. Then score along all the fold lines, using the back of the craft knife or the blunt edge of the scissors.

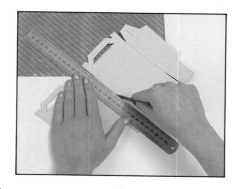

Slip the mould out. Fold in the sides of the bag, creasing them in half at the top; fold the base up over the back of the bag. Punch two holes, spaced apart, at the top of the front and back of the bag as shown. Thread through a length of cord to form a handle; knot each end inside the bag. Repeat on the other side. Alternatively, you could thread the bag with ribbon.

Crease all the folds properly. Fold the box into shape and stick the side flap to the inside of the opposite side. Close the top section, being sure to fold the lid sections upright as shown, halfway across at the point where the two handles meet. Fold over the end flaps and slot them in position to close the box. Finally close the base.

A few pretty soaps are a double welcome gift when wrapped in one of these pretty fabric draw-string bags. Cut a strip of cotton fabric about 5cm (2in) wider than you want the finished bag to be, and about 10cm (4in) longer. Turn in about 5cm (2in) at the top of each edge and run a double line of stitching along it to form a channel for the draw-strings.

A flat gift can be slipped into this pretty and useful fabric envelope. Make a paper pattern measuring about 5cm (2in) wider than your gift and two and a half times its depth, cutting a shallow V-shape at one end for the flap. Fold your fabric in half and position the paper pattern with the straight edge opposite the pointed end on the fold. Pin it on and cut the fabric out.

Pin the side seams with the right sides of the fabric together, making sure the tops of both sides match. Sew the seams, leaving a gap at each end of the draw-string channel. If you don't have a sewing machine, the sewing can be done easily by hand.

With right sides of the fabric together, pin and sew around the edges, leaving a small opening of about 7.5cm (3in); this is to enable the bag to be turned inside out. Turn the bag and press it. Then sew up the gap which was left. You can of course sew all this by hand if you prefer.

Turn the bag right side out and press it. Get some ribbon four times longer than the width of the bag and cut it in half. Attach a safety pin to the end of one half; thread it and the ribbon through the channels around the top of the bag so that both ends come out of one side. Knot the ends. Thread the other ribbon through both channels too, so the ends come from the other side; knot these too.

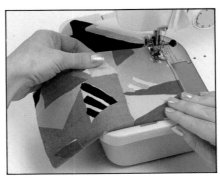

Fold the strip into an envelope shape, with the pointed flap at the top. Pin up the edges carefully and sew them in position with a double row of stitching as shown. Sew a length of ribbon on to the back of the bag with a couple of smaller stitches, pop in the present and tie the ribbon in a bow at the front.

Apom-pom bow adds a cheerful touch to a present of any shape or size. Use the kind of ribbon which will stick to itself when moistened. Cut seven strips; four measuring about 30cm (12in), the other three about 23cm (8in). You'll also need a small piece of ribbon about 5cm (2in), for the central loop.

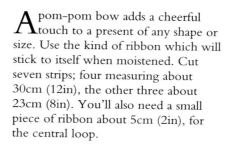

Overlap the ends of each of the long strips and moisten them; stick them together to form a loop. Moisten the centre of each loop and stick it together as shown. Cross two of the looped strips, joining them at the central point. Repeat with the other two loops. Join both crosses together so the loops are evenly spaced apart.

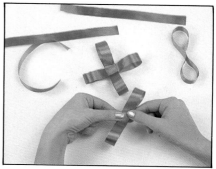

Here is an easy way to achieve a very pretty effect. Choose three colours of narrow ribbon which co-ordinate with your gift wrap. Using one ribbon, tie it around your parcel in the usual way, crossing it underneath the parcel and knotting it tightly on top; leave long ends. Tie a length of different coloured ribbon to the centre point, then do the same with a third colour.

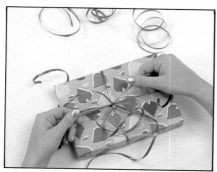

Continue tying on lengths of ribbon so that you end up with two lengths. (that is, four ends) of each colour. Tie the central knots tightly to keep them as small as possible. Pull the ribbon length gently along the open blade of a pair of scissors; this will cause it to curl into ringlets. Repeat with each length until they are as curly as you want.

Loop the three shorter lengths, and cross them over each other, fixing them together at the centre. Stick the resulting star in the middle of the large rosette. Fill in the centre with the tiny loop. Obviously, the length and width of ribbon can be varied, according to the size you want the finished pom-pom to be.

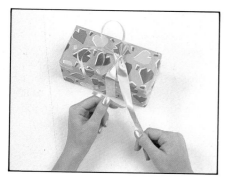

An alternative is to use wide gift ribbon. Tie it round the parcel once, make sure that the knot is as neat as possible and leave long ends. Cut two small nicks in the ribbon, divide it evenly into three; pull it to split the ribbon up to the knot. Run each of these lengths along the blade of a pair of scissors until they form ringlets.

ELIZABETHAN BOW

The scrolled shapes of this decoration are reminiscent of the curlicues embellishing Queen Elizabeth I's signature. Wrap up your present, and choose some gift wrapping ribbon to match or contrast with the colours of the gift wrap. Hold the end of the ribbon in one hand, and form a loop as shown, leaving a small tail.

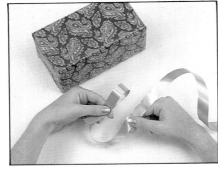

Make a corresponding loop below, forming a figure-of-eight shape. This will be the size of the finished bow; adjust the proportion of the loops at this stage if you want a bigger or smaller bow. Continue folding loops of the same size until you have as many as you want – seven at each end is usually enough.

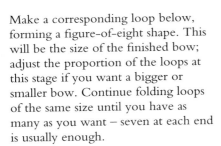

Check that all the loops are the same size, and pinch them all together by wrapping a piece of sticky tape around the middle. You can then hide this by wrapping a small piece of matching ribbon over it. Attach it to the present with double-sided tape.

FLOPPY BOW

This bow, with its floppy loops, gives a soft, casual effect. You'll need about 2m (6ft) of acetate or craft ribbon, 2.5cm (1in) wide. Cut off about 30cm (12in) ribbon; wind the rest round your fingers. Holding the ribbon firmly, make a notch in both edges with a pair of scissors as shown, cutting through all the layers of ribbon.

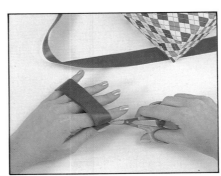

Take the ribbon off your hand and notch the edges of the opposite side of the loops. Flatten the loops so that the notches match in the centre and loops are formed either side. Take the 30cm (12in) length of ribbon and tie it tightly around the notches as shown.

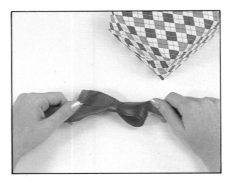

Starting with the innermost loop on one side of the folded bow, gently pull each loop away from the other loops and into the centre of the bow. You'll end up with each loop being visible, thus forming the shape of the finished rosette.

TWISTED TRIM

This trimming can be made to match or contrast with the wrapping. You will need the type of ribbon which sticks to itself when dampened. The smallest strip of ribbon measures about 20cm (8in); cut it out and twist it into the shape of a figure '8'.

Twist the ribbon shape to form a point at each end as shown, then secure it in position by dampening the tape. Cut the next strip, about 7.5cm (3in) bigger; repeat the process. Put the small shape on top and in the centre of the new shape; fix it in place.

Make four other figures-of-eight cutting each one about 7.5cm (3in) longer than the last. Pile them all up and fix them together in the centre. Put the decoration on your gift and attach it by wrapping ribbon round it and the parcel. Finally, arrange it so that each loop is raised above the others and not overlapping as they're inclined to do!

A POINT TO REMEMBER

You couldn't distinguish this pointed pom-pom from a shop-bought version – yet it's a fraction of the price! Use ribbon which sticks to itself when moistened. Make a small loop by wrapping the ribbon round your thumb; moisten the ribbon and fix it in place. Now twist the ribbon back on itself to form a pointed loop, as shown; stick it in position.

Go on looping the ribbon in twists, spacing them evenly as you go. It is fairly fiddly but keep trying – you'll soon master the technique. You'll probably need to wait a minute between each fixing for the ribbon's glue to dry before turning the next loop.

Continue winding outwards in a circle until the bow is as big as you want; cut off the ribbon, leaving a small tail just visible. Attach the pom-pom to the present with double-sided tape.

I t's hard to believe that these pretty flowers and the butterfly are made from tights and fuse wire. Cut up a pair of discarded tights or stockings. Cut some 15 amp fuse wire into lengths, some shorter than others, suitable for making petals. Make a circular shape out of each length and twist the ends together.

Put a piece of stocking material over a wire circle and pull it tight, making sure that the whole circle is covered. Fix it in position by firmly winding matching cotton around the twisted stem of the wire. Cut off the excess fabric.

Take seven petals, smaller ones in the centre, and bind them all tightly with thread. Bend the petals around until you're happy with the look of the flower. Tie up your parcel with ribbon and attach the flower with double-sided tape. The butterfly is made in just the same way: the two pairs of 'petals' are bound together with thread, then bent into the shape of wings.

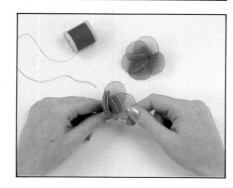

H ow to give a tall thin present even more presence! Take a spool of gift ribbon – the sort that sticks to itself when moistened. Roll a length round your thumb to form a small circle; moisten and stick in position.

Make another ring, larger than the first; stick that down too. Make another circle, and another, ensuring that their increase in size is in the same proportion each time. Four circles is about the maximum the ribbon can take before flopping slightly and thus losing the crispness of the decoration.

172

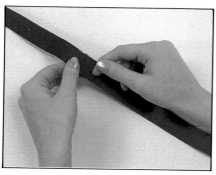

This decoration looks best on a rectangular gift. Take 66cm (26in) of woven ribbon; lay it flat. Measure 13cm (5in) from one end of the ribbon and mark both edges. Then mark along the ribbon's length a further 10cm (4in), 7.5cm (3in), 5cm (2in), 7.5cm (3in), 10cm (4in). Using one piece of thread, pick up tiny stitches at each mark along one edge.

Run a similar gathering thread up the other edge of ribbon, making sure that the stitches are exactly level on both sides. Gather up the loops as shown; it's easiest to knot the two threads together at one end of the gathers and ease the loops along.

Pull the thread tight to make properly-formed loops; sew the joins in place and cut off the excess thread. Tie the ribbon around the gift and use double-sided tape to attach the loops in the centre of the long side of the gift. Snip a diagonal cut at the ends of the ribbon tails.

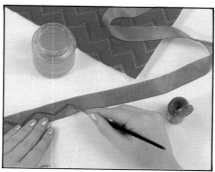

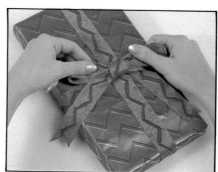

It is quite easy to paint wide ribbon to co-ordinate with your wrapping paper. And the results are stunning! Choose a gift wrap with a simple design. Decide whether you want the ribbon to be a positive version of the paper's design, like the blue example shown here, or a negative one, like the black and white suggestions. Experiment with poster paint on your chosen ribbon.

Keep the design very simple and stylized. When you're happy with your pattern, paint enough ribbon to wrap up the gift, allowing sufficient for a fairly large bow. Leave the ribbon to dry thoroughly before tying it around the parcel. If the paint does crack a little when tying up the ribbon, simply touch it up and leave it to dry again.

CREPE PAPER RUFFLE

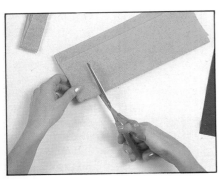

Crepe paper is the ideal material to make a stylish ruffle. There's such a range of colours to choose from, too. For each ruffle, cut two strips of crepe paper, one a little wider than the other. They should both be half as long again as the circumference of the parcel.

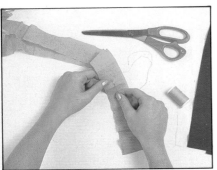

Lay the two strips flat, with the narrower one on top. Sew them both together with matching thread, running a gathering thread down the centre. Gather the strips slightly.

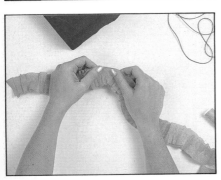

Gently stretch the crepe between both hands along the entire length of the strip; this will create a more ruffled effect. Do each strip separately, then make another ruffle. Wrap the ruffles around the gift, sticking the ends with tape. Tie narrow cord in the middle of the strips to hide the gathering stitches; fluff up the crepe ruffles either side.

RIC-RAC ROSETTE

This elegant two-tone cord with its matching rosette is made of twisted ric-rac. Choose two colours of ric-rac braid to co-ordinate with your wrapping paper; buy about 1m (3ft) of both colours. Wrap one piece of braid around the zig-zags of the other, twisting them so that they fit snugly together. Do enough to wrap around your gift and press the braid with a cool iron.

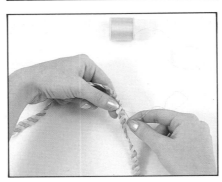

Twist some more braid together to make the rosette – the length you need depends on the size of the rosette. Take a needle and thread through each point of one side of the twisted ric-rac.

Having threaded about 45cm (18in), gently pull the thread, easing it along the ric-rac. This will cause the ric-rac to coil up on itself; arrange it into a flat circle, sewing it together as you go. When you have a large enough rosette, cut the braid and sew the edges neatly under. Tie the long length of braid around the parcel and sew in position; sew on the rosette.

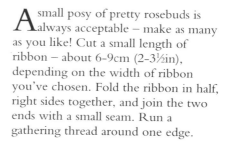

A small posy of pretty rosebuds is always acceptable – make as many as you like! Cut a small length of ribbon – about 6-9cm (2-3½in), depending on the width of ribbon you've chosen. Fold the ribbon in half, right sides together, and join the two ends with a small seam. Run a gathering thread around one edge.

Pull the gathering thread tight to form the rosebud; sew it firmly across the base. Make another two or three buds and sew them all together at the base; you may need to add the occasional supporting stitch at the top edges to hold the buds close together.

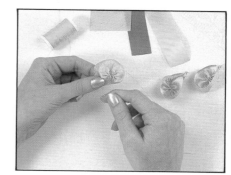

The leaves add an attractive contrast. They are made from a strip of green ribbon, two corners from which have been folded over to form a point. Fix with double-sided tape since glue can leave a mark on ribbon. The illustration below shows the rosebuds grouped on a length of ribbon twice the width of the flowers, set off with narrow green ribbon.

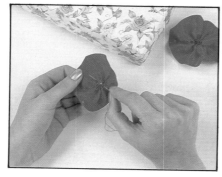

A winning idea for any gift! Cut a length of fairly wide ribbon; you'll need about 30cm (12in) for each rosette. Fold it in half with the right sides of the ribbon together; sew up the two ends to form a seam.

Using tiny stitches, gather up one edge of the ribbon. Pull the gathering thread tight, arranging the rosette into a neat circle. Finish it off by sewing across the base. Make as many rosettes as you need and attach them to your parcel with double-sided tape.

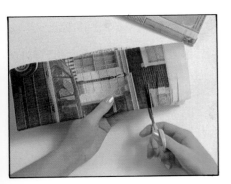

Whaven't any gift wrap and the shops are shut? You use newspaper! The flower on top give the parcel a stunning and stylish finish. To create the flower cut several lengths of newspaper, some about 15cm (6in) wide, some a little narrower. Fold one strip in half lengthways, and make a series of cuts along its folded edge as shown here.

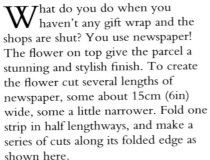

When you've cut along the whole length, roll up the resulting looped fringe. Secure it at the base by winding a piece of sticky tape round it. Fluff out the 'petals' of the flower.

Use up all the strips of paper in the same way. Gather the sections together, smaller ones on the outside. Join them all with tape; leave the ends unstuck and use them to attach the flower to the gift. You can even match the paper to the recipient, for example a financial newspaper for a businessman, a comic for a child.

Ya single colour, but they look more effective if you choose several. For each twist, you need three squares of tissue for the outer colour, two for the middle colour and two for the inner (most visible) section. The squares needed for the inner section are smaller than those for the outside; the middle leaves must be of a size in between.

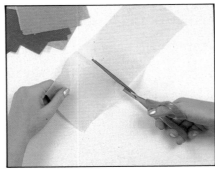

Pick up the squares in order, putting one on top of the other; outer colour first, then the middle, then the inner squares. Position them so that the corners of each square are at a different angle, as shown. Put a couple of stitches through the centre point to secure all the squares together and leave some thread hanging.

Fold the whole thing in half and half again, twisting the folded point at the base to form the shape of the 'flower'. Pull the thread out at the point, and wind it tightly around the twisted base to secure it; 'fluff' out the finished decoration. Make several 'flowers' and group them together on your present.

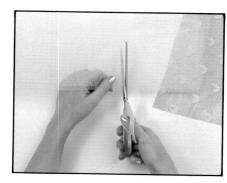

Frothy net is a very attractive decorative feature, and silver glitter adds a sparkle and a touch of glamour. Cut a strip of net long enough to wrap twice around the perimeter of the gift; make its breadth about 15cm (6in) wider than the length of the parcel.

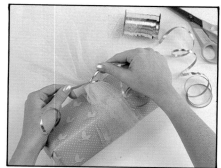

Gather the net in small pleats and wrap it around the middle of the parcel, as shown. Tie the net with narrow gift ribbon and leave the ends of the ribbon trailing. Gently pull apart the net tails. Cut another piece of net the same width as the first piece and twice the height of the existing 'frill'; thread it underneath the frill and secure it with ribbon as before.

Put some silver glitter in a bowl and dab glue along the raw edges of the net. Dip the net in to the glitter (this involves holding the parcel upside down). Shake off the excess glitter and allow the glue to dry. Curl up the trailing lengths of ribbon by pulling them against a scissor blade.

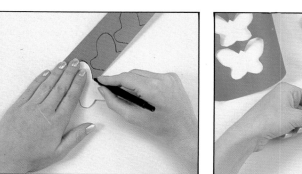

An interesting effect is achieved by attaching three-dimensional decorations all over your parcel. Wrap your gift in plain coloured paper. For the butterflies, take a strip of contrasting plain paper and fold it in half. Draw a butterfly shape on thin cardboard; cut it out and trace round half of it as shown on to the coloured paper. Draw as many as you want to cover the gift.

Cut out the butterfly shapes and fold them on both sides of the half-way fold, to give them bodies. Use glue or thin strips of double-sided tape to attach them in a random pattern to the parcel. Alternatively, tie lots of little bows of the same size using contrasting ribbon; scatter them over your gift using double-sided tape.

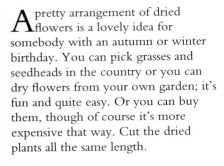

A pretty arrangement of dried flowers is a lovely idea for somebody with an autumn or winter birthday. You can pick grasses and seedheads in the country or you can dry flowers from your own garden; it's fun and quite easy. Or you can buy them, though of course it's more expensive that way. Cut the dried plants all the same length.

Bunch the flowers together; when you're happy with them, wrap sticky tape around the stalks. Hide the tape by winding ribbon over it. Tie ribbon round the parcel, finish off with a knot, and attach the little bouquet by tying its trailing ribbons over the knot; trim the ends of the bouquet ribbon away. Using the ends of the other ribbon, finish off by making a pretty bow over the bouquet.

What a lovely bonus to receive with a gift – a beautiful fresh flower. This works most effectively with a long, thin present, showing off a single bloom to perfection. First choose your flower. Trim off any excess leaves and, in the case of roses, thorns. You should end up with just one sprig of leaves.

To prevent the flower from staining the gift wrap or making it damp, wrap the end of the stalk with cling film. Then cut a narrow strip of matching gift wrap; wrap it around the length of the stalk, fixing it at the back with tape. Cut a small 'V' shape at the top of the paper tube, and attach the bloom to the parcel with double-sided tape.

Craft foil is the perfect material for creating this decoration. Use a compass to draw four circles; the ones shown here measure 8cm (3in), 6.5cm (2½in) 5cm (2in) and 4cm (1½in) in diameter. Draw an inner ring of 2cm (¾in) in the centre of each circle. Rule lines to divide the circles evenly into eighths; cut along the lines to the inner circle to make eight segments.

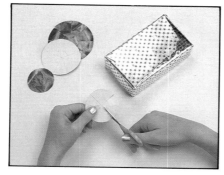

Roll each segment of the circle into a cone; use a dab of glue to secure it. Make sure that each cone shape has a good sharp point by rolling it fairly tightly. The process is a bit fiddly; you may find it easier to roll each cone around the point of a stencil to give it shape. Repeat with the other circles.

Starting with the largest star shape, glue all the stars inside each other, positioning the points of each star between those of the preceding ones. When the glue is dry, gently bend each cone of the middle two stars towards the centre, to fill in the central space, so forming a semi-circular three-dimensional star.

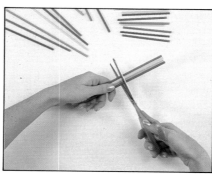

Brightly-coloured drinking straws lend themselves to decorating presents. Look for colours to co-ordinate with your gift wrap. The straws can be made of paper or plastic; both work well. Select the colours you want and cut four straws in half; discard one of each half. Cut another four straws in two, leaving one section slightly longer than the other; retain both pieces.

Place four halves, one of each colour, together over a central point in a star shape and staple them together. Do the same with the other slightly longer straws and their shorter counterparts so that you end up with three stars of slightly different sizes. With the smallest on top and largest on the bottom, staple all three together. Attach the triple star to the parcel with double-sided tape.

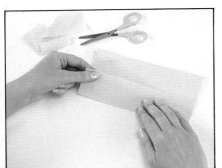

These flowers will pretty up any parcel at very little cost – they're made from tissues. Open out a tissue, and fold it in half lengthwise. Trim away half of the top layer (that is, a quarter of the tissue) along the whole length as shown – this prevents the 'stalk' of the finished flower from being too bulky.

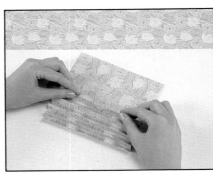

Paper fans are simple to make but can look stunning, used either singly or in a row to create a ruffle around your gift. Cut a strip of paper the width you'd like the fan to be when opened, and three times the length. Fold it in half widthways, then fold it up in small even pleats, starting with the folded end. Create a sharp crease along the pleats by running them firmly between your fingers.

Tuck in the top corner of one end very slightly and gather up the tissue in very small pleats, gradually turning the 'flower' round as you go. When the gathering is completed, fold in the top corner of the end of the tissue as before.

When you have pleated the entire length, hold the pleats together with the folded edge of the strip on top. Bend the fan in half and stick the two folded edges together with sticky tape along their length as shown. Make sure that the tape continues right to the outer edge so that the join cannot be seen when the fan is open.

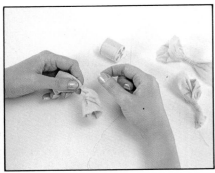

Give the 'stalk' a couple of twists to make it firm. Bind it tightly with thread and tie it securely. Make as many flowers as you need for your gift – you can make an entire bouquet if you like and wrap it up in a paper doily. Tie the flowers together with a ribbon, make a bow and attach the bouquet to your present.

Open out the fan and apply double-sided tape to its flat side; stick the fan in position on your gift. Care is needed in deciding how big to make the fan – too big and the present will be swamped, too small and it will look insignificant. It might be worthwhile experimenting with rough fans cut from newspaper first, to get the scale right before cutting your gift wrap.

A sweet treat for children of all ages! Boiled sweets with plain cellophane wrappers look best because of their clear colours, but you can use alternatives such as toffees or peppermints. Select five or six of the chosen sweets, and hold them in a bunch by one end of their wrappers.

Take a narrow piece of ribbon and tie all the sweets together tightly; if the wrappers are a little short it may help to bind them first with sewing thread. Leave a reasonably long piece of ribbon on each side of the bunch of sweets so that you can attach it easily to the parcel.

An added bonus on this gift is the sweet-smelling pouch of pot-pourri. Select some fabric which will tone with your gift wrapping paper. The fabric should be fine, but not loosely woven; the scent of the pot-pourri can then easily diffuse through the material, but the petals and dust cannot. Cut out a piece of fabric measuring about 15-20cm (6-8in) square.

Tie the same ribbon around the parcel, leaving the ends long, then tie the sweets to the centre point as shown. Curl up each ribbon end by pulling it gently along the open blade of a pair of scissors. Try to co-ordinate your gift wrap with the chosen confectionery – black and white paper with humbugs, for example, would look very attractive.

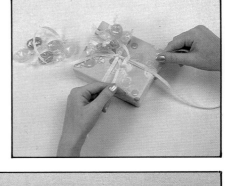

Put enough pot-pourri in the centre of the fabric to make a generous sachet – a good handful should be just right. If you can, choose a perfume which will match your present – rose pot-pourri would be ideal for a rose bowl, lavender for lavender-scented soaps. You could even use dried herbs to create a bouquet garni for a cookery book!

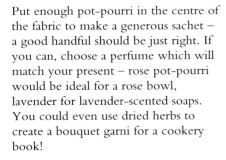

Pick up the four corners of the fabric to form a bundle. Wind sewing thread tightly around the neck of the bundle, and knot the thread securely. Tie the pot-pourri bunch very firmly in case the recipient uses the bag later in her wardrobe. Hide the thread by tying a piece of ribbon around it to match the ribbon on the parcel. Tie the pot-pourri to the gift using a little more matching ribbon.

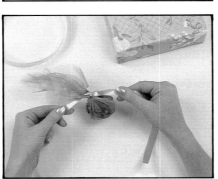

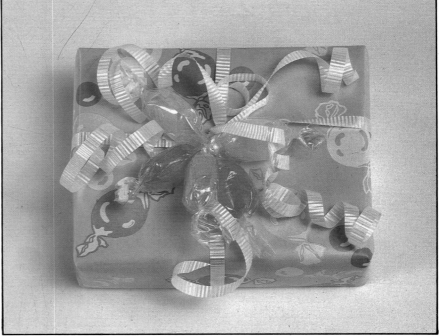

Silky tassels give a luxurious look to a gift, especially if they are made of sparkling Lurex yarn. Cut a piece of thin cardboard the length you'd like the tassels to be. Wind yarn around the cardboard until it's the density you had in mind for the finished tassel.

Thread a length of yarn through all the strands. Tie it firmly at the top of the cardboard as shown, leaving the ends long. Cut through the strands of yarn at the opposite end of the cardboard.

Tie some yarn around the tassel, about 1cm (1/2in) from the top; trim the ends to the length of the tassel fringe. Make another tassel. Twist together four long lengths of yarn and tie them round the parcel in the usual way; tie the tassels at each end. Ordinary yarn or thick rug yarn woud look just effective.

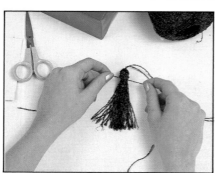

The metallic sheen of sequins, and the strip of metallic plastic from which they are pressed, looks rather chic. Sequin waste – that is, the strip of metallic plastic – can be bought by the metre or yard from good craft shops. This idea looks best on rectangular flat parcels. Wrap a piece of sequin waste around the length of the present; fix it with tape.

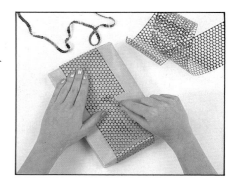

Take another strip of sequin waste and join the two ends to make a large loop. Use sticky tape to fix them, making sure the holes overlap so that the join is almost invisible.

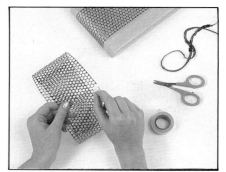

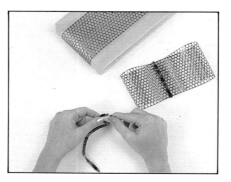

Put a strip of threaded sequin trim of the same colour across the middle of the loop. Remove a few loose sequins so that you can tie the trim in position. Repeat with another length of trim; space the two evenly apart in the centre of the loop to form a bow. Attach the bow to the parcel with double-sided tape. Sequin trim as a gift tie in its own right gives a glamorous finish to any gift.

Pick out the colours of your gift wrap to make your own pretty plaits. From narrow fabric ribbon – 2mm (½in) wide – choose either three colours which feature in your wrapping paper or, if you prefer, three lengths of the same shade. Knot them together at one end, leaving small tails.

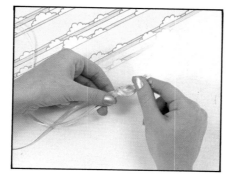

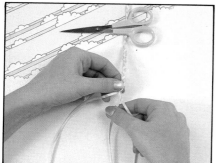

Start plaiting the ribbon. This is easier if you weigh down the knot with something; the scissors will do fine. Keep plaiting as evenly as possible, moving the weight along the growing length of plait as necessary.

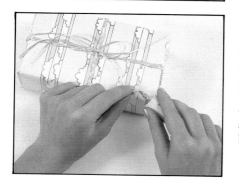

When you've finished, tie the plait round your gift in the usual way. Before knotting it, undo the knot you made when you began plaiting; tie a single tight knot to keep both ends of the plait in place. Loop each tail back on itself, dabbing on a tiny spot of glue and fixing it in the centre beside the knot.

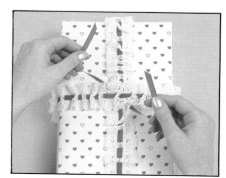

For an elaborate and slightly saucy effect for your present, select some slotted lace and some ribbon to co-ordinate with your gift wrap. Measure the amount of ribbon needed to tie up the parcel; you will need twice as much lace. Thread the ribbon through the slots.

Gather the lace up on the ribbon. Wrap it round the length of the parcel and sew it together at the back. Then wrap the width; sew that too. Finish by tying an extra bow at the intersection of the two laces. Any present looks pretty simply tied with lace, even if the lace can prove a little expensive. Look out for remnants in haberdashery departments or market stalls.

Windmills are cheerful and fun for people of all ages – not just children! Cut out a square of plain coloured paper which complements your wrapping paper. Measure a square of about 23cm (9in), depending on the size of windmill you want; make sure the corners are right angles. Cut out the square and draw straight lines between the opposite corners.

Cut along these lines, starting from the corners and leaving about 2.5cm (1in) uncut in the centre. Bend up one side of each cut corner to the centre, as shown, anchoring it with double-sided tape.

To attach the windmill to a 'pole', take a coloured plastic drinking straw and insert a two-pronged paper fastener in the end; open the prongs out a little so the fastener stays firm. Pierce the centre of the windmill with another paper fastener; pass its prongs through the one inserted in the straw before opening them out. Attach the straw and windmill to the parcel with double-sided tape.

A smartly-dressed present for a smartly-dressed man – or woman! This is suitable for a tall thin gift. Wrap it up in paper of a colour and design that is plausible for a shirt. Cut out a 'collar' shape as shown from stiff white paper; fix it in position around the top of the parcel with glue or double-sided tape.

Using patterned ribbon for the tie (such as this elegant paisley design), wrap it around the collar and knot it like a tie. Before pulling it tight, put some glue or double-sided tape on the collar where the tie should sit; position the tie correctly and tighten the knot. Finally, fold over the two corners of the collar shape to make an elegantly formal shirt.

Victorian ladies created beautiful pictures using pressed flowers. Why not make a miniature version for a pretty gift tag? Pick up a selection of flowers and leaves and lay them face down on blotting paper. Press another layer of blotting paper on top, keeping the flowers as flat as possible. Place the flowers between the pages of a heavy book and leave them for at least a week.

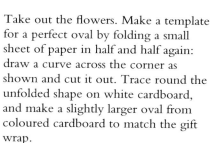

Take out the flowers. Make a template for a perfect oval by folding a small sheet of paper in half and half again: draw a curve across the corner as shown and cut it out. Trace round the unfolded shape on white cardboard, and make a slightly larger oval from coloured cardboard to match the gift wrap.

Gift wrapping can prove so expensive these days, so why not make your own gift boxes? Here, some plain cardboard boxes have been covered in hand-marbled paper. Fill a large bowl with water, then mix some solvent-based paint such as ceramic paint, or some artist's oil colours, with a little white spirit. Use a paint brush to drop successive colours on to the surface of the water.

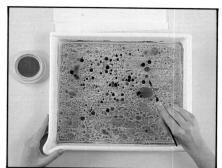

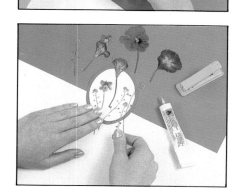

Stick the two ovals together, so that the larger one forms a frame for the tag. Arrange the pressed flowers on the white oval to your satisfaction. Glue the flowers in position, using a tube with a very fine nozzle; leave the arrangement to dry thoroughly. Punch a hole in the top of the tag, write the message on the back and tie it to the gift.

Stir the mixture with the handle of your paint brush or an old stick until you have a pleasant swirling pattern. An alternative way to form a pattern is to blow the paint across the surface of the water.

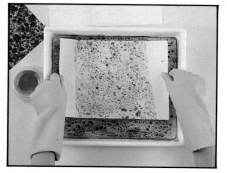

Wearing rubber gloves to protect your hands, put the paper on to the surface of the water, then lift it off immediately. The swirls of paint on the paper will create a marbled effect. When the paper is dry, neatly cover a small box, carefully folding the paper round the corners and sticking it down with glue or double-sided tape.

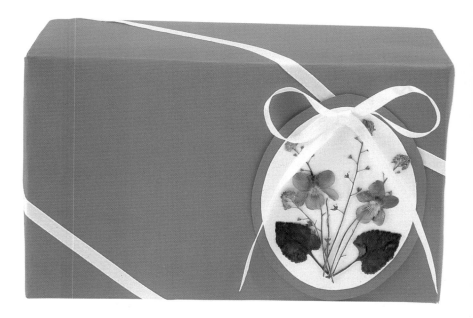

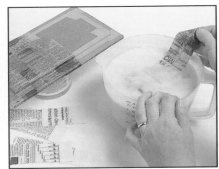

Using 5 by 10cm (2 by 4in) pieces, papier mâché both the box and lid, applying three layers. Dry the pieces on a cake stand in the airing cupboard. Lightly sand them and then apply two coats of white emulsion.

This durable, papier mâché chocolate box would make a lovely gift. Using a ruler and set square, mark and cut the following pieces from cardboard: four 27 by 15cm (10¾ by 6in), and two each measuring 23.5 by 11.5cm (9¼ by 4½in), 5 by 25cm (2 by 10in), and 5 by 12.5cm (2 by 5in). Glue and tape the largest pieces into two pairs and the narrow strips into a rectangle.

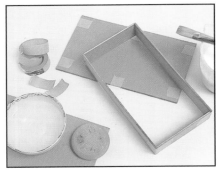

Glue the walls of the box to the base. Hold them with masking tape until the glue has set, then remove the masking tape and reinforce all joins with brown tape. Join the remaining two pieces with glue and tape, then centre them on the lid. Use the blunt end of a pair of kitchen scissors to ease the brown tape into the joins.

Paint the insides of the box and lid with blue gouache, made up to the consistency of thick pouring cream. Draw the outer lines in pencil first, then go over them with a waterproof black felt-tip pen. Do not worry about slight irregularities – they add to the effect. Apply one coat of polyurethane varnish.

Apply a further three coats, this time of gloss acrylic varnish (painted directly over gouache, it would make the colours run). When this has dried, the ribbon can be fixed in place with epoxy glue. Cover the join with heart shapes cut from adhesive-backed silver paper strip.

Stencil your own wooden presentation boxes to add a little extra to a small gift. Choose single motifs and use either quick-drying stencil paints or stencil crayons. Mask off a small motif from a large stencil and tape the acetate in position to complement the box shape. Stencil the box top and sides, mixing designs to create an attractive arrangement.

Make a coloured border on the lid by cutting a piece of cardboard slightly smaller than the box top, placing it centrally and stencilling around the edge. Finish off the box by gluing on lengths of satin ribbon, bows or self-adhesive parcel ribbon. You could also line the box with coloured tissue paper.

Making your own wrapping paper is great fun for a beginner at stencilling. Choose small, all-over motifs (see pages 37 and 247) and stencil with one or two different coloured stencil crayons. Use plain art paper and work across it, lining up the motifs as shown. Rub the crayon on the corner of the acetate and then collect the colour on to a stencil brush for stencilling.

Gold spray on dark paper makes a rich, dramatic gift wrap ideal for a man's Christmas present. Use the same stencil design but tape lining paper around the edge to act as a mask. Spray lightly through each motif, wait a few moments for it to dry, then move on to the next area. Matching gift tags can easily be made by cutting out one motif and gluing it on to folded cardboard.

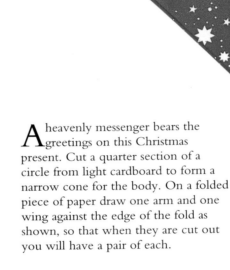

A heavenly messenger bears the greetings on this Christmas present. Cut a quarter section of a circle from light cardboard to form a narrow cone for the body. On a folded piece of paper draw one arm and one wing against the edge of the fold as shown, so that when they are cut out you will have a pair of each.

Make the cone and cover it with silver paper (aluminium foil would do). Trace the arm and wings on to silver paper; cut them out and glue them in their relevant positions on the body.

A three-dimensional Santa Claus tag, complete with fluffy beard, provides a jolly festive decoration on a gift. Draw a fairly large rectangle on thin red cardboard; make sure that all the corners are right angles. Score down the middle and fold the cardboard, creasing it well. Draw an inverted 'V' for Santa's hat, and a curve for his chin; cut them out with a craft knife.

Curve the hat and chin outward to give them a three-dimensional look, then draw in the eyes and mouth. Form a beard from a small piece of cotton wool, and stick it in position with a dab of glue. Do the same with the fur trim on the edge of the hat and the pom-pom on its tip. Punch a hole in the back of the label, write your message and tie the tag on the parcel.

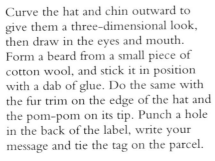

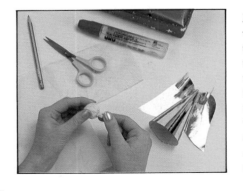

Make the head by rolling up some white tissue paper into a firm ball, twisting the ends of the tissue tightly to form a 'neck'. Glue the head into the top of the cone. Tie a scrap of tinsel into a loose knot and stick it on the head as a halo. Make a scroll from white paper, write on your message and stick it between the angel's hands. Attach the angel to the gift with double-side tape.

Draw any festive shape you like on to thin cardboard; this one is a Christmas stocking. Cut out the shape and cover it with bright paper; try to co-ordinate the colours with those in the gift wrap you use for your present.

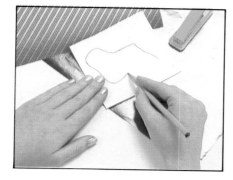

If your wrapping paper has a particular theme in its design make a tag to echo it. To ensure that your design is symmetrical, fold a piece of paper in half and draw on half the design against the outline through both layers of paper; open out and use this as a template for the design. Cover a piece of light cardboard with gift wrap and trace around the template.

Cut around the outline and punch a hole at the top of the tag. Write your message and tie the tag on to the parcel. You could cheat a little when designing the shape of your tag by tracing an illustration from a magazine or by using the outline of a pastry cutter.

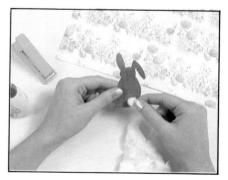

This cute rabbit tag tells the kids who their Easter present is from. Draw the shape of a rabbit on to white cardboard; if you're not good at drawing, you could cheat by tracing the outline of a rabbit from a magazine or book illustration. When you're happy with your design, cut it out.

Either paint the bunny shape, or cover it with brown paper (or whatever colour suits your gift wrap; a red or even green rabbit would be fun). Next take a piece of cotton wool and roll it into a ball for the tail; stick it in position with a dab of glue. Make a hole in the rabbit's head for some ribbon, write your message and tie the tag to the gift.

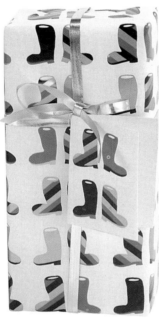

I f you have a long message for the recipient of your gift, this fold-out tag allows lots of room. Select a gift wrap design that has a fairly large repeat. One motif must have sufficient space around it so that it can be cut out without including any others. Draw a rectangle around the motif, ensuring that all the corners are right angles.

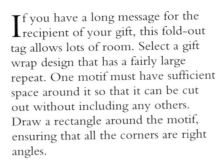

Cut the rectangle out with a craft knife. Next, cut out a piece of thin cardboard the same height as the chosen motif and exactly three times its width. Fold the cardboard in three widthways, creasing the folds well, then fold the top two sections back on themselves, as shown. Mark the folds in pencil first to be sure they are straight.

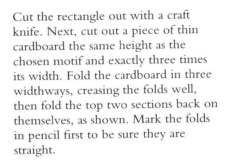

Cut the motif from the gift wrap precisely in half. Glue each half on to the top two sections of the folded card. They should fit exactly, but if necessary trim the top and bottom to form a straight edge. Try matching the colours of the lining cardboard with the gift wrap; in the example shown here, red or even black cardboard could have been used instead of white, for a different effect.

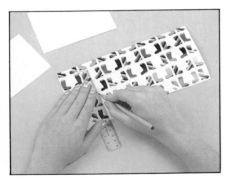

G ive your presents a co-ordinated appearance by creating matching tags. For simple fold-over tags you need to select wrapping paper which has a small design. Take a piece of gift wrap and rule a rectangle on it, twice the width of the required tag. (Outline a section of the design where the motif is visible when isolate.) Ensure the corners are perfect right angles, then cut the tag out.

Paste the tag on to thin cardboard; choose a colour which picks up a shade in the gift wrap. When the glue is dry, cut around the piece of gift wrap. Fold the card in half and punch a hole in the corner. Thread a ribbon through the hole and tie it on to the gift. Alternatively, you can cut out a single image, stick it on to cardboard and cut around the outline, as with the panda tag.

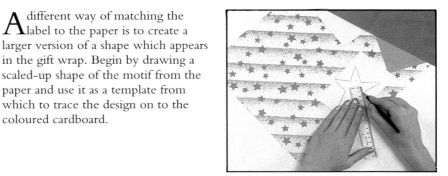

A different way of matching the label to the paper is to create a larger version of a shape which appears in the gift wrap. Begin by drawing a scaled-up shape of the motif from the paper and use it as a template from which to trace the design on to the coloured cardboard.

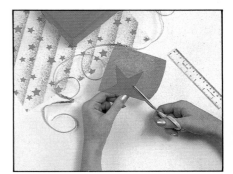

For this idea to be really effective, the colour of the tag should be as close as possible to that in the gift wrap. A layer of tissue laid over the cardboard of a near-match, as shown, might make all the difference to duplicating the final colour. Cut out the shape, and punch a hole to enable you to tie it to the gift.

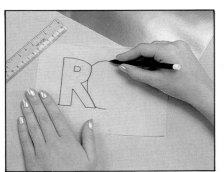

There can be no doubt who these presents are for! It's fun to make a tag out of the initial or - even better the whole name of the recipient. First draw the shape of the letters you want on to a piece of tracing paper. Make sure that the letters in a name interlock sufficiently.

When you're happy with the result, trace the letters (or single initial) on to coloured cardboard, pressing hard to make a clear outline. Use a ruler where there are straight sections to a letter.

Next, cut out the shape using a craft knife, carefully following the traced lines. Punch a hole in a position where the weight of the tag will make it hang well on the gift.

Incorporate a motif from the design of your gift wrap to make a fun three-page tag. It will work with any design involving a trailing string – balloons, kites, balls of yarn and so on. The motif is stuck on the sloping top edge of the middle 'page' of the card. Cut out the motif from gift wrap. Then experiment with a sheet of white paper to get the best shape for your card.

The slanting angle of the top edge is achieved by cutting a truncated triangular shape. Having worked out the shape you want, trace around your experimental tag on to thin coloured cardboard. Don't forget to leave a bit of card protruding from the top slanting edge in the shape of the motif, as shown. Cut out the tag.

Score the two fold lines of the tag using the back of a craft knife and crease them firmly. Glue the motif in position on the middle page and draw a long string trailing down. Close the card and draw another string on the front, making sure it is continuous with the string on page two. Write the recipient's name as if it were part of that string.

Create a stylish effect by matching the tag to the ribbon. Plain ribbon with a strongly patterned paper is attractive but a tartan ribbon with plain paper can look stunning. And if you don't have any ribbon, even a strip of fabric cut out with pinking shears will suffice! Glue a length of ribbon or fabric on to thin cardboard to make it rigid.

Trim away any excess cardboard. Fold the stiffened ribbon over and cut it to the length you want the finished tag to be. Punch a hole through your newly-created tag and thread a piece of contrasting narrow ribbon through the hole to tie it to the parcel. Trim the edges of the tag to match the ends of the bow.

Used greeting cards can often be turned into very acceptable gift tags. Sometimes, as here, the design lends itself to forming a tag. Cut very carefully around the lines of the motif you want to use. Make a hole with a punch, thread a ribbon through the hole and no one would guess the tag had a previous life.

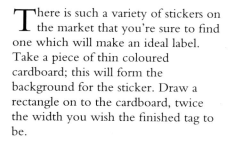

There is such a variety of stickers on the market that you're sure to find one which will make an ideal label. Take a piece of thin coloured cardboard; this will form the background for the sticker. Draw a rectangle on to the cardboard, twice the width you wish the finished tag to be.

Cut out the rectangle with a craft knife and score down the centre to form the fold; crease well. Remove the sticker from its backing and place it in position on the front of the tag. Punch a hole in the back 'page' of the tag, near the fold. Write your message inside and hang the tag on the gift.

Sometimes a little imagination is needed to give the tag a new and ready-made look. Here, the shape of the tag is outlined on the cardboard in red with a felt-tipped pen. Draw the outline lightly in pencil first to be absolutely sure it is the right size and shape to create the finished label.

What fun for a child to see Frosty and know that the snowman's hiding a gift! Wrap up a cylindrical gift in paper to form the body of the snowman. Crush newspaper into a shape for the head and stick it on top of the gift. Cover the body with cotton wool, sticking it on with dabs of glue. Create a face from bits of paper and stick in place.

For the hat, you need a strip of cardboard, plus a circle big enough to make the brim. Draw an inner circle in the brim, the diameter of Frosty's head; cut it out to form the 'lid' of the hat. Roll the strip of cardboard up to form the crown of the hat; stick it in place with tape.

Stick on the top of the hat, then attach the brim, putting strips of tape inside the crown. Paint the hat with black poster paint; it'll need two or three coats. Wrap around the red ribbon to form a cheery hat-band and put it on Frosty's head. Fray the ends of some patterned ribbon to form a scarf and tie it firmly in place.

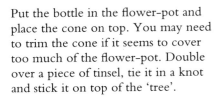

Bottles of seasonal spirits make an ideal present – but hide such an obvious-looking gift under the decorative guise of a Christmas tree. Find a flower-pot just big enough to take the base of the bottle. From thin cardboard cut out a third section of a large circle and make a deep cone about 8cm (3in) shorter than the bottle. Cover the cone with suitable wrapping paper.

Put the bottle in the flower-pot and place the cone on top. You may need to trim the cone if it seems to cover too much of the flower-pot. Double over a piece of tinsel, tie it in a knot and stick it on top of the 'tree'.

This heart of woven paper can hold a Valentine's Day gift. Lightweight paper in contrasting colours gives the best effect. Cut a strip of paper 25cm by 10cm (10in by 4in) and draw the template on page 253 on to it. Cut the shape out and fold it in half. Then cut the two slits as indicated on the template. Repeat with another strip of paper in a different colour.

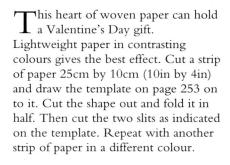

Hold a section of the heart in each hand, as shown, with the strips pointing upwards. Weave the two sections together, starting with the two inner strips. You need to open out each strip to slot the other strip through it, as illustrated.

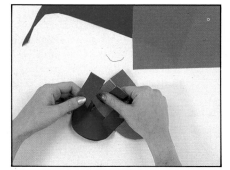

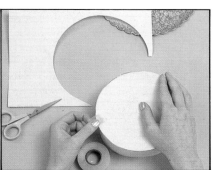

A cake, plus candle, is just the right disguise for a birthday present! First, make a drum-shaped frame for the cake; cut a strip of thin cardboard just wider than your present, curl it in a circle big enough to cover your gift and stick it in place with sticky tape. Cut a circle to fit as a lid; attach it with strips of tape.

Continue doing this until all the strips are interwoven. It is fairly fiddly but does work; it's clear at this stage why you need lightweight but strong paper! The finished item will open out like a basket, so that it can hold small gifts. The basket would also be very pretty made in felt.

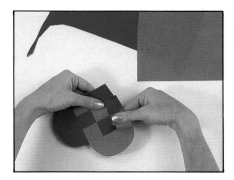

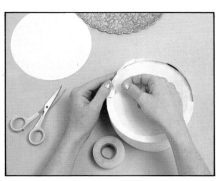

Cut a strip of white paper to cover the sides of the drum and glue it in position. Tuck one edge of the paper under the open end of the drum and trim the other edge close to the top of the drum to leave a small turning. Cut a series of small nicks in the turning and fold the flaps over, taping them to the lid. Cut a circle slightly smaller than the circumference of the drum and glue it in place.

Place the present inside the cake and put it on a cake stand. Cut two lengths of cord to fit round the circumference of the cake and glue the ends to prevent them from unravelling. Glue one piece to the top of the cake to form 'icing', and the second piece around the bottom, to fix the cake to the stand. Finally, put the candle in the holder and pierce through the centre of the cake.

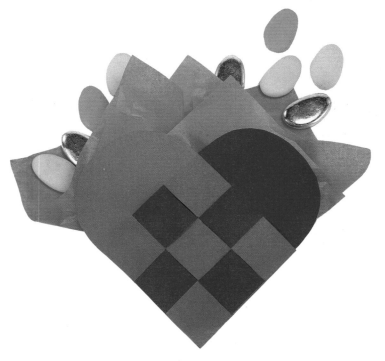

A romantic padded heart containing a little gift is perfect to give on Valentine's Day! Cut out two heart shapes from cardboard, one about 4cm (1½in) larger all round than the other. From red lining fabric, cut out a heart shape a little bigger than the larger heart. Take a gift box, wrap it in cotton wool and place it on top of the smaller heart.

When there's enough padding, cover the heart in the red lining, stretching it over the heart shape and sticking it firmly in position on the back with plenty of tape. You'll need to snip the fabric around the inverted point of the heart so that the fabric can open out to fit properly.

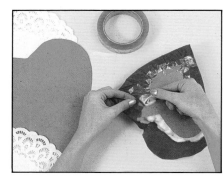

Cover the larger heart in white tissue paper, otherwise the brown surface may show through the lacey doily. Cut off a frill of about 5cm (2in) from the edge of four or five doilies, and pleat them up around the edge of the large heart, fixing them with tape as shown. When the whole heart has been edged like this, apply some strong glue to the middle and place the padded heart in position.

This simple but effective idea is just right for a wedding. Cover your gift with plain paper. Buy some rose petal-shaped confetti. Alternatively, you could make the petals yourself from softly-coloured tissue paper; fold a piece of tissue into about eight and cut out an oval shape; repeat for as many petals as you need.

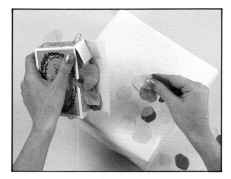

Arrange a cluster in a flower-shape on each corner of the gift. Stick each petal into position with a small dab of glue right at one end of the petal. When the glue is dry, bend up the petals to give a 3-dimensional effect. You could use this idea for a silver anniversary gift by wrapping the parcel in aluminium foil and using petals of just one colour.

A gift wrapped up as a prayer book makes an unusual and moving present for a wedding or confirmation. Wrap up the gift in gold paper so that it will look like the closed pages of the book. The last flap should not be folded in the usual way, but should be cut precisely to fit the side of the gift as shown; glue it in place.

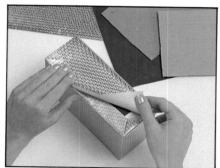

Take two pieces of thick cardboard slightly larger than the size of the gift. You will also need a long strip of thin cardboard measuring the width and length of the gift. Use tape to stick the thick cardboard on to either side of the thin cardboard to make a book cover for the gift. Cover the outside with plain paper as shown; glue all the edges down firmly.

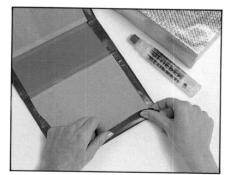

Spread glue over the inside of the book cover, and place the gift firmly on one side of it. Wrap the cover over the other side of the gift, making sure it's stuck properly. Cut out gold crosses (or other appropriate symbols relevant for your recipient's religion) and stick them in place. This idea is also good for christening or anniversary gift.

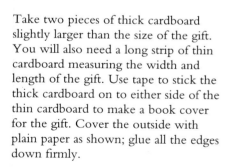

This pretty cradle makes a charming decoration for a baby girl's christening present. From thin cardboard, cut out a small box shape to make the framework for the crib. Fold up the sides and stick them in place with tape.

Cut a piece of ribbon one and a half time the length of the perimeter of the cot. Sew the ends together to make a loop, and run a gathering thread around the top. Apply some glue to the outside of the box and put the gathered frill over it, positioning it on the lower half. Repeat with more ribbon, sticking the frill over the first one, right at the top edge of the box.

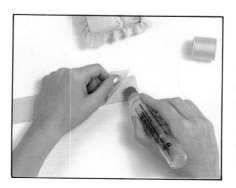

Put some cotton wool, a scrap of lace and a piece of wide ribbon in the cradle. Take another piece of ribbon, wider than that used for the frills, and cut a strip long enough to make a canopy. Cut a matching strip of cardboard; spread it with glue and cover with the ribbon. Fold it in half and stick in position over one end of the crib.

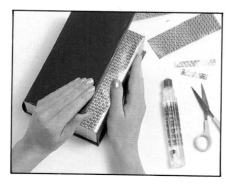

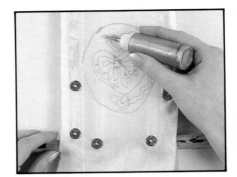

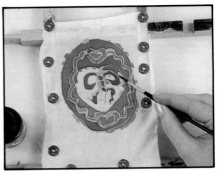

If you really love someone, you'll want to send him a beautiful Valentine's Day card, hand-crafted by you. To make it easier, you can buy the card blanks in most craft shops or haberdashery departments. The designs here are painted on silk. Stretch a piece of white silk over a frame (available from craft shops) and outline the design with gold gutta.

Make sure the gutta lines are continuous so that the paint can't bleed through once the design is painted on. When the gutta is dry, apply the silk colours with a fine brush. Do not be over generous with the paint as the silk can only take so much before it is saturated and the colours start to bleed.

When the silk is dry, fix it according to the paint manufacturer's instructions. Then glue the silk in position on to the blank card and stick the mount down around it.

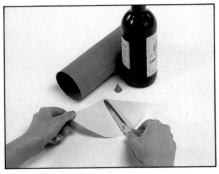

Disguise a bottle as a pencil and keep the recipient guessing! Make a cylinder, about 5cm (2in) shorter than the bottle, from light cardboard, join the sides with tape. Draw a third section of a circle – about 7.5cm (3in) radius – on pale cardboard and cut it out. Roll it in to a cone shape, running the flat edge of a pair of scissors along it to help it curl. Tape in place.

Make a small cone for the lead of the pencil and glue it on to the larger cone. Attach several lengths of sticky tape to the inside edge of the cone and, putting your arm inside the cylinder, stick the tape down to hold the cone in position. Fit the pencil over the bottle and secure with two strips of tape across the bottom.

HATS OFF!

Any little girl would be thrilled if her present looked like a hat. This idea obviously will only work on a gift that is circular and flat, so that the gift itself can form the crown. Cut a brim from a circle of thin cardboard and cover it with a circle of plain, pastel-coloured paper. Wrap the present by rolling it in matching paper, as shown.

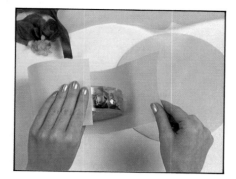

Make sure the paper fits tightly around the base by folding it in a series of small triangles. Trim the turning on the top of the gift to leave a small edge; fold that in neat triangles too. Stick the triangles down on to each other with tape, making sure that the surface is left as flat as possible.

Place the gift in the centre of the brim and stick it in position with glue or double-sided tape. Cut another circle of wrapping paper slightly smaller than the diameter of the crown; glue it in place. Tie a ribbon around the junction of the crown and brim, leaving the ends trailing. Cut a 'V' in the ribbon ends and glue on a couple of artificial flowers for a finishing touch.

BUTTONS AND BOWS

Make a small present look that extra bit bigger! Wrap the gift into a ball shape, then cut a strip of paper about three times the width of the gift and long enough to form loops on each side of it. Fold the edges over. Gather small pleats at each end, securing them with sticky tape. Pinch-pleat four gathers in the middle of the strip and secure.

For the trailing sections of the bow, cut a five-sided piece of paper as shown. Fold over the edges in to the centre at the back and secure with tape. Gather pinch pleats at one end and secure. At the other end cut out a V-shaped section to form a nicely-shaped tail. Repeat the procedure a second time.

Turn the pleated ends of the long strip to the middle to form the loops, and secure with double-sided tape. Stick the tails under the bow with more tape. Finally, put double-sided tape over the join on top of the bow and stick the gift in position. Puff out the loops so they look nice and full.

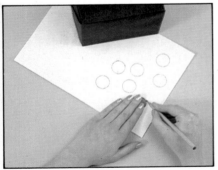 

Cube-shaped presents will look more interesting disguised as dice – and it's fun if a small, flat gift becomes a domino. For the dice, make sure the gift is a perfect cube by measuring it; the idea won't work well unless it is. Cover the gift with black paper. Then draw several circles on white paper; an easy way of doing this is by tracing the outline of a suitably sized coin.

Cut out the circles carefully and lay them on the box; glue them in place. Look at a real dice to get the juxtaposition of the sides correct. The domino can be treated in the same way.

Brighten up a dull-looking, flat gift by turning it into a playing card. Wrap the present in plain white paper. Make a template for the spade by folding a piece of paper in half and drawing half the outline against the fold; this way the design will be symmetrical. Trace around the template on to black paper and cut the shape out. Stick the spade in the centre of the 'card'.

Cut two small spades for the corner designs. Then, using a ruler, draw an 'A' in two of the corners, being careful to make them both the same. Glue the small spades underneath. Cut a piece of patterned paper – smaller than the card – and stick it on the back. You could vary the idea by making the King or Queen of Hearts for your husband or wife, or the ten of clubs for a ten-year-old.

H ere's an attractive way to add sparkle to the Christmas tree. You can buy these plain glass balls from craft suppliers, so look in craft magazines for stockists or try your nearest craft shop. As you are decorating a curved surface, it is advisable to keep the design simple. Draw the outlines of your design using a fine multi-purpose felt tip paint pen.

Try to place the motifs evenly, remembering you will see the far side of the design through the glass ball. Fill in the design with the same colour you used for the outlines. You can rub out any mistakes with a cloth soaked in turpentine.

Outline your motifs in a contrasting colour, combining colours such as red and green, yellow and black, pink and purple. Add tiny dots between the motifs using the same colour as that used for the outline. Hang the baubles from your tree with gold gift wrapping thread.

W hy not decorate your Christmas present as if it were a Christmas tree – with glittering baubles and tinsel? Wrap the gift in some elegant paper; something plain but shiny will set off the baubles better than a more complex Christmas design – you could use aluminium foil. Then thread Christmas baubles on to a length of tinsel.

Decide where you want to put the decoration and cover the area with a few strips of double-sided tape. If the parcel is rectangular, put the baubles in one corner; if the parcel is square, the middle would be better. An upright parcel like that shown here looks best with the decoration on the top. Group the baubles into a bunch on the gift, wrapping the tinsel around them to form a nest.

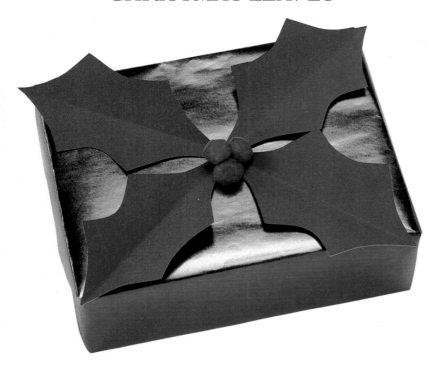

Holly leaves are an attractive shape and perfect for decorating a festive gift. Measure the length of the diagonal across the top of your parcel. On a sheet of plain paper draw a large holly leaf, the 'vein' of which measures slightly more than half the length of the diagonal.

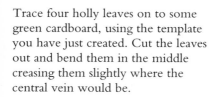

These Christmas bells ring out gaily from your present. Make two paper templates, both bell-shaped, with one showing the outline of the clapper from the bottom edge. From thin cardboard, cut out two of each shape.

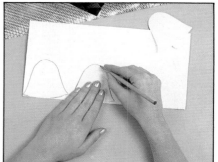

Trace four holly leaves on to some green cardboard, using the template you have just created. Cut the leaves out and bend them in the middle creasing them slightly where the central vein would be.

Cover all the cardboard shapes with gold paper (or any colour which would co-ordinate with your wrapping paper). Cover both sides, and trim away all the excess paper. On the bell shapes with the clapper, cut a slit from the curved top of the bell to the centre of the bell. On the others (the plain ones) cut a slit from the middle of the bottom edge, also to the centre.

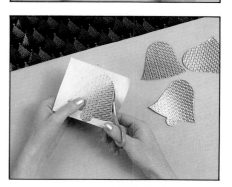

Make the berries from a ball of cotton wool wrapped in two squares of red tissue paper. Put a dab of glue inside and twist up the tissue tightly at the base. When the glue is dry, cut off as much excess of the twist as possible. Group the leaves and berries on the parcel; attach with glue or double-sided tape.

Pierce a hole in the top of the plain bell shapes and thread them with a length of ribbon. Then slot the pairs of bell shapes together (i.e. the plain one, and the one with the clapper) so that they form three-dimensional shapes, as shown here. Tie a group of as many bells as you like on to your gift. This idea can also be used for decorating a wedding gift.

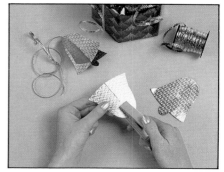

This cheery chick will brighten up any Easter gift. Cut two cardboard circles the same size, then cut a small circle from the centre of each to create two wide rings. Put both rings together and wind yellow wool around them, passing the wool through the centre. Continue doing this until the rings are well covered and the inner circle is almost full of wool.

Snip through all the wool along the outer edge of the cardboard rings. Pass a length of wool between the two rings, wind it tightly around all the strands of wool and tie it firmly, leaving long ends. Cut off the cardboard circles and fluff out the ball. Make a bigger ball for the body from two larger rings, and before cutting, pass a pipe cleaner through the rings to form the legs.

Tie the two balls together firmly. Bend the 'legs' up at the ends and wind a section of pipe cleaner around each foot leaving a V-shape on either side so that each foot now has three 'claws'; paint the feet and legs red. Make eyes and a beak out of felt and glue into position. This would work just as well with a Christmas robin decoration, using red and brown wool.

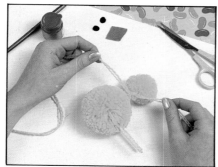

Paste the recipient's age in a great big number on the side of their present so that *everybody* knows how old they are! Draw around the present, so that you know exactly what size the numbers must be to fill the side of the gift and make a big impact.

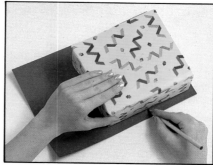

Draw the appropriate number using a ruler and measure carefully. Choose thin cardboard or plain paper in a contrasting colour to the wrapping paper.

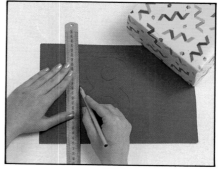

Cut the numbers out and stick them in position on your gift. You could make a numerical tag to match. This idea could be adapted for use with gifts celebrating wedding anniversaries – 25, 50 and so on.

203

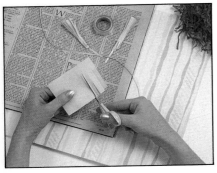

Disguise the unmistakable shape of a record by making it look like a cushion. First create paper tassels. Cut a piece of coloured paper into narrow strips leaving about 2.5cm (1in) at the bottom uncut so that you create a fringe. Roll up the fringe, catching in a short length of narrow ribbon. Secure the tassel with coloured tape.

Take some wrapping paper that is more than twice the size of the gift, fold it in half around the record and cut it so that it is just a little larger. Join two of the sides together with coloured tape along their full length, attaching the ends of the tassels at the corners as you do so. Put a strip of tape over the folded edge of the 'bag'.

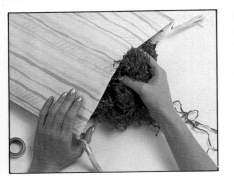

Stuff the inside of the 'bag' on both sides of the record with shredded tissue, being careful to put some in the corners. Don't use too much or the wrapping paper will wrinkle. Seal along the remaining open edge with tape.

Here's another clever idea for disguising a record. Take two large squares of cardboard; the side of a box will do. Position the record in one corner as shown and draw a line from the bottom right corner of the record to the top right corner of the cardboard. Draw a second rule from the top left corner of the record to complete the kite shape. Repeat for the other square.

Cut out the shapes and sandwich the record between them. Cover one side in coloured paper, folding over the edges and fixing them with sticky tape on the reverse. Cut another piece of paper slightly smaller than the cardboard shape; glue it in position on the back of the kite.

Draw two lines joining the four corners of the kite, and put contrasting tape along them; take care not to stretch the tape as it will pucker the paper. Cut out as many paper bow shapes as you want for the kite's tail. Attach the bows with double-sided tape or glue to a length of ribbon and stick the tail in position behind the longest point of the kite.

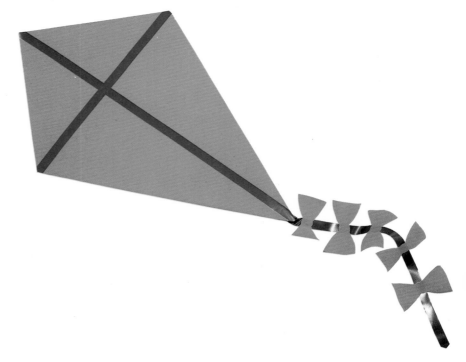

STENCILLED GIFT BOXES

Decorate some pretty boxes with stencils and stencil crayons. You can either buy the stencils from a craft shop or make your own. Position the stencil over the box lid and tape it firmly in place. Now rub a little stencil crayon on to one corner of the film. Pick up some colour with a stencil brush and apply it to the stencil cut-out with a circular motion, starting at the edge and working inwards.

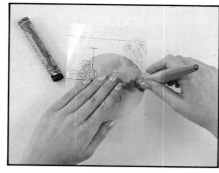

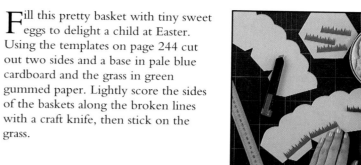

Once you have finished the first colour, change stencils and apply the second colour. Use a clean brush at this stage or your colours will appear muddy.

After you have completed the lid, stencil the sides of the box. Be sure to tape the film firmly in position to stop it from slipping.

EASTER BASKET

Fill this pretty basket with tiny sweet eggs to delight a child at Easter. Using the templates on page 244 cut out two sides and a base in pale blue cardboard and the grass in green gummed paper. Lightly score the sides of the baskets along the broken lines with a craft knife, then stick on the grass.

Fold the sides backwards along the scored lines and join end to end in a ring by gluing each end tab under the opposite end of the other side. Glue the base under the base tabs. Cut a strip of pale blue cardboard for the handle measuring 30cm × 1cm (12in × ⅜in). Stick the ends inside the basket.

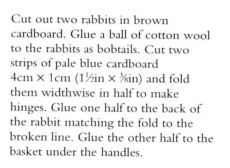

Cut out two rabbits in brown cardboard. Glue a ball of cotton wool to the rabbits as bobtails. Cut two strips of pale blue cardboard 4cm × 1cm (1½in × ⅜in) and fold them widthwise in half to make hinges. Glue one half to the back of the rabbit matching the fold to the broken line. Glue the other half to the basket under the handles.

POTPOURRI CONE

Fill this pretty cone with potpourri and allow the scent to waft through your home. Draw a 30cm (12in) diameter semi-circle with a compass on a piece of mottled peach-coloured paper. Cut it out and bend into the cone shape. Cut away a slice so the ends overlap smoothly and glue the overlapped ends together. Leave to dry.

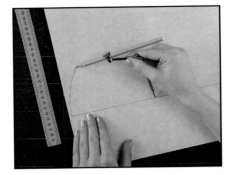

Cut out motifs from a white paper doily and stick to the cone with spray glue. Coat the cone all over with PVA medium. Set aside until the medium has hardened and become clear and then apply two more coats.

Cut a strip of paper 25cm × 1.5cm (10in × ⅝in) for the handle. Glue the ends inside the cone and coat with the PVA medium. Hang the handle over a door handle to dry. Tie ribbons in a bow and glue to the cone below the handle.

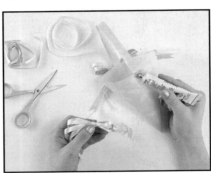

PAISLEY POUCH

Use a sophisticated print like a paisley design to set off this pouch which is ideal for holding a small gift. Apply giftwrap to one side of thin cardboard with spray glue. Use the template on page 244 to cut out two pouches and mark the position of the holes and broken lines. Cut the tabs off one pouch and punch holes on the other one.

Score both pouches along the broken lines on the right side and fold the tabs backwards. Stick the pouches together with double-sided tape on the tabs.

Thread cord through the holes and knot the ends inside. To close the pouch hold the sides between your thumb and finger and gently squeeze the pouch open. Now press down one of the ellipses. Close the other ellipse on top.

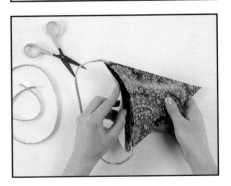

GREETING CARDS

Colourful puffins, cut from a sheet of wrapping paper, keep a lookout from their perch. Cut card 28 by 13cm (18 by 5¼in). The card is blue on the inside and white on the outside. On the outside, from the left, score 9cm (3½in) and 19cm (7½in) across and fold. Turn card over and on the inside, from the left, score and fold 20cm (8in) across.

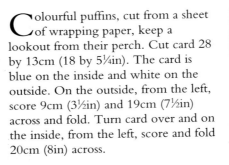

This card, in party mood, could be used for birthday, engagement or congratulations. Cut a piece of purple glossy card 20 by 30cm (8 by 12in). Score a fold down the centre of card (15cm/6in across). Cut two triangular shapes and bases from pink sequin waste and a piece of iridescent film to fit the width of the card. Mark with pencil dots where the glasses should be placed.

Cut out three puffins and spray glue the first on outside of far right-hand panel of card, facing right. Cut round him with a craft knife leaving him attached by his tail. The score line on the outside will allow him to stand forward.

Using a spray booth, spray glue on to the back of the iridescent 'table' and smooth down to remove creases. Trim away any excess. Spray glue on to the back of cocktail glasses and position on dot marks. Spray the bases at the same time.

Glue the other two puffins in place on the inside. Any wrapping paper with a distinct animal motif can be used in this way to make a striking card.

With a rubber-based glue, stick down strips of very narrow ribbon for the stems, then bases. Curl two narrow pieces of ribbon, and place sequin 'bubbles' over glasses. A pair of tweezers will make this an easier task. Glue curls of ribbon on the 'table' and leave for a few minutes for glue to set. Any residue may be gently rubbed away when dry.

A live teenage motif badge for sewing on to jeans and jackets makes a card and gift – it can be carefully peeled off the card at a later date and sewn on to a favourite garment. To put our pop singer in the spotlight we cut glossy red card 15 by 22cm (6 by 8½in). Score and fold 11cm (4¼in). Draw a spotlight shape on silver paper or plastic film using a ruler.

Cut out with a craft knife and trim the curve with a pair of small scissors.

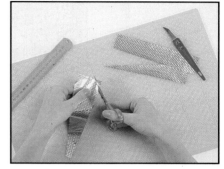

The bouquet on this bright and cheerful greeting card is made up of coloured gummed paper squares torn into simple shapes. Cut a rectangle of white cardboard measuring 38cm × 25cm (15in × 10in). Score across the centre widthwise using a craft knife. Fold the card in half along the scored line.

First glue down the spotlight and trim any overhang on the edge of the card. Stick down the pop singer with rubber-based glue and hold firmly in place for a minute or two until glue dries. The discs on the main picture are buttons purchased from a specialist button shop.

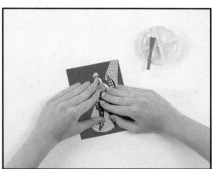

All the shapes have straight edges. Press a ruler down a gummed square, lift one edge of paper and pull it up against the ruler to tear it neatly. Now tear across the paper again either diagonally or straight across to form the various shapes.

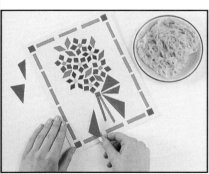

Arrange the pieces on the front of the card within a border of narrow strips and squares. Moisten the back of the gummed pieces to stick them in position.

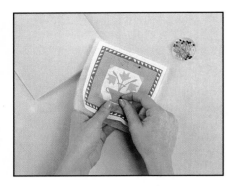

This small piece of quilting is from a ready-printed panel. It will shrink a little when it has been quilted, so measure and cut window from card *after* you have finished the piece. You will need very thin wadding (batting) to back the cotton panel. Cut a piece of card 45 by 15cm (18 by 6in) and score two folds 15cm (6in) apart. Pin panel to a slightly larger square of wadding.

On a larger piece of work, muslin would be used as a backing fabric, but in this instance it has been left out so that there is less bulk inside the card. Working from the centre, tack the two layers together, making sure the picture covers the wadding.

Cotton thread gives best results in hand quilting. Starting from the centre, with a knot on the back, sew with tiny running stitches. Finish thread with a double back stitch. Take out tacking stitches or you will lose quilted effect. Measure finished piece and cut window from centre of 3–fold card. With double-sided tape, stick down quilted panel and back flap of card.

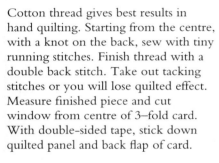

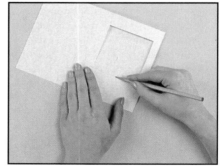

A window-box full of spring flowers is sure to bring cheer. We have used a ready-cut, 3–fold card with window. Fold under left-hand side of card (looking from the inside), marked with a cross in our second picture. With a sharp pencil, draw through window outline and cut out second window using a craft knife and steel ruler.

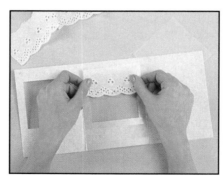

Place 1cm (½in) of double-sided sticky tape around the centre window and edges of the card. Cut a piece of broiderie anglaise and a piece of tracing paper cut slightly larger than aperture. Peel off tape backing and stick down the curtain, then the tracing paper. Peel off tape backing on the edges of card and close the left–hand side over. Light will filter through.

Apply 'stick-on' flowers (purchased on a strip) in a line half on the card and half on the tracing paper, then finish with a strip of satin ribbon or paper for the window box. Add a couple more flowers to the top of the window if you wish.

This top dog with a smart tartan bow makes a super greeting card. Cut out a cardboard pattern of the template on page 244 and mark the broken lines. Place the pattern on a 20cm (8in) square of blue cardboard with the lower edges level and the dog's nose against one edge. Draw around the pattern, score along the broken lines and cut along solid lines.

Here is a card that will appeal to cat lovers everywhere. Cut a rectangle of coloured cardboard 26cm × 6.5cm (10¼in × 7¾in). Use the template for page 244 to draw the design on the right-hand side of the card. Score along the broken lines with a craft knife and cut out the long window edge, window panes, cat's eye and the edge of the windowsill.

Fold the card in two along the scored line and trace around the dog on the lower section of the card. Now cut out this dog leaving the fold intact and cutting away the base of the tail on a neat curve.

Fold the card in half along the scored line and then open out the inside of the card. Cut a rectangle of pretty wrapping paper measuring 12cm × 6.5cm (43.4in × 2½in). Glue the paper inside the card over the top window panes.

With the card opened out flat, peel the backing off a square of black flocked sticky-backed plastic and press onto the card. Turn the card over and cut around the two Scotties. Fold the card in half and glue a ribbon bow to the front.

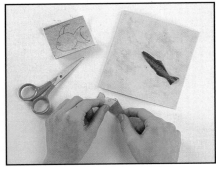

Cut out card 25 by 14cm (10 by 5½). Score and fold 12.5cm (5in) across. Trace out fish on the smooth side of bonding web. Cut out the fish just outside the pencil outline and place the rough side of web on to the back of your fabric. Press with a warm iron to melt the glue. Cut out on the outline. Peel off the backing and position on the card. Press with a dry iron.

Diagonal lines of spotted ribbon and self-adhesive labels give this card a 'dotty' air. Cut a piece of black card 25 by 16cm (10 by ¼in). Score and fold 12.5cm (5in). On the inside top left-hand corner measure 4cm (1½in) along the top of the card and down the side edge, mark with dots and score. Fold the corner back to the outside of the card.

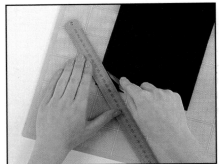

Draw in eyes and details of the fish with felt-tipped pens. Alternatively, you can use sequins for the eyes. Cut rocks and stick down in place with spray glue.

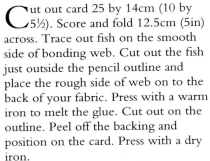

Rule a diagonal line across the front of the card from top left to bottom right. Measure and cut ribbons to fit either side of this line. Cut them slightly longer, to be trimmed later. Cut a triangle of ribbon to fit behind the turned-down corner. Spray backs of ribbon with glue in spray booth. Place in position, smooth down and trim edges.

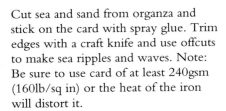

Cut sea and sand from organza and stick on the card with spray glue. Trim edges with a craft knife and use offcuts to make sea ripples and waves. Note: Be sure to use card of at least 240gsm (160lb/sq in) or the heat of the iron will distort it.

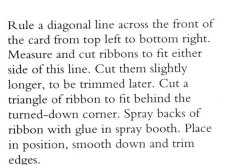

On the front bottom left-hand corner of the card, stick on self-adhesive dots and also on the folded-over, top right-hand corner.

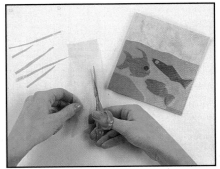

A favourite Victorian pastime was to make greeting cards from printed 'scraps'. Cut a piece of cardboard 42cm × 25cm (16½in × 10in) and score across the centre widthwise. Fold the card in half. Cut out a large heart from mottled pink paper and glue it to the middle of the card.

Offcuts of shot silk or other fabrics are woven into a landscape of green fields, hedges, yellow corn, blue sky and pink evening sunset. A ready-cut, 3–fold card was used. Mark the top left-hand corner inside the card with a cross. Cut canvas about 10cm (4in) square. Lay the card with oval aperture over the canvas and mark edges lightly. Rule a square just outside these marks.

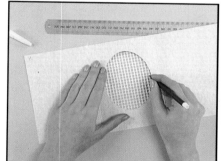

Cut out sprays of flowers from reproductions of sheets of Victorian scraps, available at craft shops and some museums. Alternatively, use pictures from seed catalogues. Arrange the flowers along the edge of the heart and when you are happy with the design glue them in place. Glue on single flowers to fill any gaps in between.

Cut strips of fabric approximately 1cm (½in) wide and 12.5cm (5in) long. Do not worry if they fray as this adds to the charm. Thread a large tapestry needle and starting from the bottom weave green strips. Continue with yellow fields, hedges and sky.

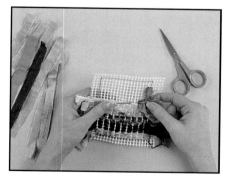

Highlight the flowers with a fine gold pen. Use a thick gold pen to draw a line 2cm (¾in) from the ends of the card. Cut two 1.5 (⅝in) wide strips of marbled paper and glue along the ends of the card with spray glue. To finish, stick a butterfly or other motif in one corner.

Attach double-sided tape around the oval window and along three sides of the panel, as shown. Trim canvas 6mm (¼in) outside the ruled square and peel off backing from double-sided tape. Stick canvas in place and close the card – the left side with the cross is the side to fold in. Smooth from the folded edge to the outside so that the card stays flat.

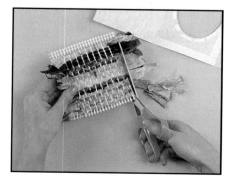

Windows open to reveal flowers cut from wrapping paper which could also wrap a gift. Cut glossy green card 22 by 15cm (8½ by 6in). Score and fold 11cm (4¼in). Cut a 4cm (1½in) equilateral triangle template. Open card flat and on the inside front draw four triangles. With a steel ruler and craft knife cut two sides of triangles and score the third.

Cut nine heaps of lurex, silk and satin. Cut two pieces of acetate film 10cm (4in) and 9.5cm (3¼in). Draw a 7.5cm (3in) grid of 2.5cm (1in) squares with a chinagraph pencil. Use polyester thread and machine two centre horizontal lines and left-hand vertical. Stuff the centre square. Machine right vertical to close the centre square. Stuff squares on left; top and bottom centre.

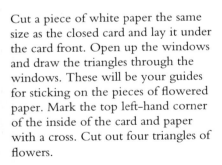

Cut a piece of white paper the same size as the closed card and lay it under the card front. Open up the windows and draw the triangles through the windows. These will be your guides for sticking on the pieces of flowered paper. Mark the top left-hand corner of the inside of the card and paper with a cross. Cut out four triangles of flowers.

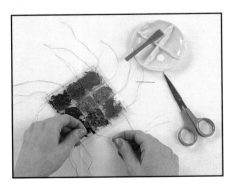

Machine the left-hand edge, and then top and bottom edges to close the squares. Stuff three right-hand squares and machine the right-hand edge to close. Pull threads to the back and knot. Trim and put a dot of glue on each knot to hold it.

Glue flower triangles on the paper where marked in pencil. Place a line of glue along all four edges on the front of paper and attach face down on inside front of card. Open up the windows and you will see peeping flowers.

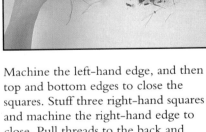
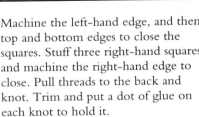

Make or buy a 3–fold card and cut a double window mount (see page 210). Mark the inside top left-hand corner with a cross. Put double-sided tape around centre window of card and edges. Pull off backing tape and place patchwork parcels in window. Close card and add cord and tassel.

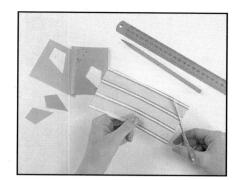

K ites flying in a high spring sky are always a cheerful sight and these three are made from wrapping paper and narrow satin ribbon. Cut pale blue cord 22 by 15cm (8½ by 6in). Score and fold 11cm (4¼in). Cut out kites in three different sizes and papers using a ruler. Arrange and stick on card using spray glue.

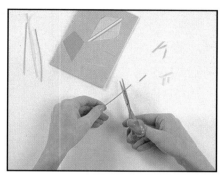

Cut narrow satin ribbons slightly longer than card so they will hang below bottom of card. Cut short lengths of ribbon for bows.

A theme card to give to a musical friend. The treble clefs are buttons. Cut red glossy card 22 by 15cm (8½ by 6in). Score and fold 11cm (4¼in). Draw a square 5.5 by 7.5cm (2¼ by 3in) on white paper. Rule two staves – groups of five lines 3mm (⅛in) apart – using a fine black felt-tipped pen. Cut out the square.

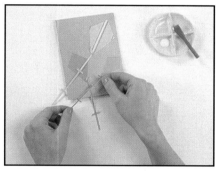

Glue and hold in place for a moment since satin ribbon tends to resist glue at first. Some of the bows can be a 'V' of twisted ribbon.

Centre the square of music paper on card so that you have an equal margin on three sides. Visually, it is better to have a larger margin at base of card. Mark corners of music lightly on card and stick down using spray glue. Place opened card on a piece of felt and pierce two holes for the buttons using dividers or a thick needle.

From the back sew on buttons through the holes you have pierced, then knot the thread and trim. Finish knots with a dab of glue.

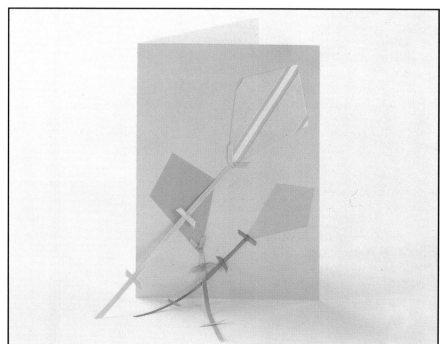

Use mono thread 'lockweave' needlepoint canvas 8 holes to 2cm or 10 holes to 1in, cut 18 by 14cm (7 by 5½in). Find the centre of the canvas and mark a centre hole on four sides. Draw two crosses in different colours either side of centre and side holes. Without counting centre hole, count 29 holes either side lengthways. Rule a border line.

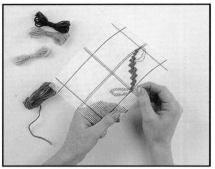

You will find a chart to follow on page 251. Thread a tapestry needle with either double-knitting wool or tapestry wool and counting holes, work long stitch in the pale lilac colour first.

Continue working towards the centre, finishing four corners last. Cut a 3–fold card 45 by 20cm (18 by 8in), score and fold at 15cm (6in) intervals. Measure the finished piece and cut a slightly smaller window in centre panel of card. Trim canvas to 6mm (¼in) all round and mount using double-sided tape. Close the card and stick down.

Cut card 22 by 22cm (8½ by 8½in) across. Centre your compass point horizontally 5.5cm (2in) from the top of the card. Draw an arc so that it touches the sides and top edge of card, then cut through both thicknesses. You could make a template of this shape if you wanted to make several cards.

Brightly coloured origami paper is perfect for this exuberant card. Either draw on the back of paper or cut freehand a collection of shapes and colours.

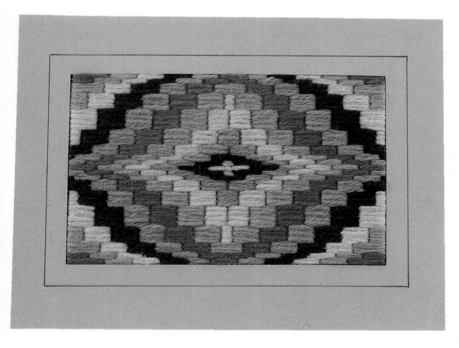

Arrange paper shapes in order of gluing and stick them on to card. Tweezers will help you to apply glue to the tiny star shapes, not your fingers!

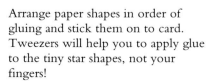

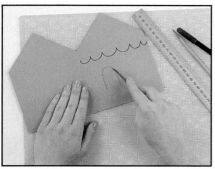

A detachable finger puppet of a jolly circus clown will delight a child. Cut card 18 by 25cm (7 by 10in). Score and fold 12.5cm (5in). Mark 5.5cm (2¼in) down sides of folded card. Measure across the top 6cm (2¼in) and mark. Cut through both thicknesses of card to form the apex of a 'marquee'. Draw the roof of the marquee. Cut a 'stand' for the puppet.

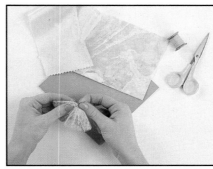

Just the card to please a young girl who dreams of becoming a ballet dancer. Cut card 30 by 15cm (12 by 6in), score and fold 15cm (6in). Cut the skirt from a piece of net 30 by 7.5cm (12 by 3in). Fold in half down its length and press with warm iron. Sew, with small running stitches, along this fold. Make a double stitch to start, gather tightly and finish with a double stitch.

Trace out templates 10, 11 and 12 on page 248 and transfer on to thin card to make your own templates. Cut out two balloons from card and satin ribbon strings. Using turquoise felt, cut two hats, two hands and a bow-tie. Cut two heads from white felt; two circles, one for his nose and one for his hat, from pink felt. Cut eyes from narrow black satin ribbon.

Use marbled paper for the background. Cut 13cm (5in) square. Cut the mirror from silver paper or foil. Details of how to draw a curve are given on page 216. Cut the bodice from satin and straps from satin ribbon.

Glue the balloons and ribbons in place. Sandwich the clown's hands between the two pieces of felt for the head, holding in place with a dab of glue. Sew, with a running stitch, round the clown's head. Glue on hat, bobble, eyes, nose and bow-tie. Place the clown on the stand and he will appear to be holding the balloons.

Centre background paper and attach with spray glue. Then glue the bodice and mirror. The straps will be easier to put on with rubber-based glue. Mark where the skirt is to be attached and pierce two holes each side with dividers. Sew from the back of the card, tie a knot and dab with glue. Make two more holes in the same way for the ballet shoes brooch. Finish with a silver star.

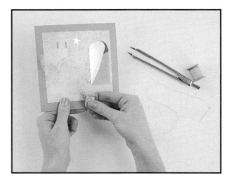

BOYS AND GIRLS COME OUT TO PLAY

Cut card 30 by 13cm (12 by 5in), score and fold 15cm (6in). With the fold on top find the centre and mark with a pencil dot. Measure down 6cm (2½in) on each side. Rule a line from each side point to middle mark to form roof. Stick down ribbon forming a mitre at the apex of the roof. Cut two pieces of medium weight wrapping paper 20 by 7.5cm (8 by 3in).

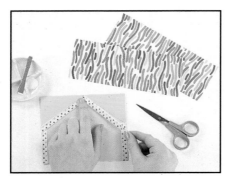

Trace out templates 14 and 15 on page 248. Fold a length of wrapping paper in half then in half twice more. Draw on half boy or girl making sure hands are on folds. Cut out. When you draw the second child, check folds are in the opposite direction, so that when they are opened they are left and right of card. Open out boys and girls and refold alternate ways.

On green and pink paper cut a boy and girl. Glue them to the blank side of the folded figures. Glue the last girl and boy to the card so that their feet are on the bottom edge. Fold figures flat to fit in an envelope.

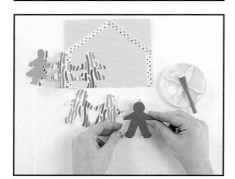

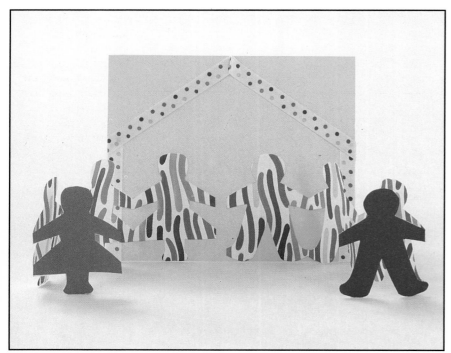

BIRTHDAY BALLOONS

Cut yellow card 22 by 33cm (8½ by 12¾in). Score and fold 11cm (4¼in) and 22cm (8½in). Trace out template 13 on page 248, transfer to card to make a template. Place over folded card, mark around the balloon outline at the top and cut through all three thicknesses. Open out the card and trace out balloon shapes on to centre panel and cut.

Place double-sided tape around the balloon holes on the inside centre of the card. Cut small pieces of narrow ribbon and stick across the neck of the balloons. Using the balloon template, cut three satin balloons slightly larger. Remove double-sided backing and stick them in place. Stick down the left side of the 3–fold card using double-sided tape.

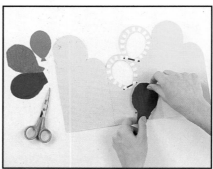

Cut three 'reflection' squares out of white or silver fabric and glue on to the three balloons. Cut four lengths of narrow ribbon, one shorter, so that it will appear to pass behind the red balloon. Using a sharp pencil, rule guide lines for where the ribbons will be placed. Glue them down, leave for a minute or two for glue to dry and then trim ends.

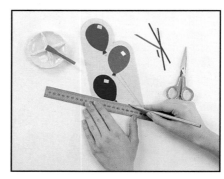

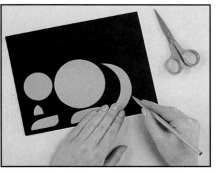

Our mischievous black cat seems not to have noticed the little mouse! Cut card 23 by 18cm (9 by 7in), score 11.5cm (4½in) across and fold along top of card. Trace out cat templates 16–21 on page 248 and transfer on to thin card to make your own templates. Draw around pieces on to black paper or card. Keep paws and tail the right way round.

Cut card 30 by 20cm (12 by 8in), score and fold 15cm (6in) across. Trace out templates 22–25 on page 248. Transfer the designs on to thin card to make your own templates. Cut out from thin card two arms, two legs, head and body. From brown felt cut out the same pieces but slightly larger. Glue felt to card – make a left and right leg. When glue is dry trim edges.

Cut out a black cat, a tree shape from tissue paper or card and two green eyes. Mark with a sharp pencil where the pieces will fit on card and stick on in order using spray glue: the tree, body, paws, tail, ears and eyes.

Tear green tissue-paper to resemble hills and hedges and cut gingham tablecloth. Glue them to card and position 'stick-on' flowers. Glue on Teddy's head and punch holes in the body, arms and legs. Mark shoulder holes on card, since Teddy will be attached through them. Punch or cut out with a cross, so that brass paper-clips will pass through.

Use stationers' self-adhesive dots for cat's nose and pupils. Finish by drawing whiskers using white chinagraph pencil. Draw around limbs and ears with a soft pencil to make the cat stand out.

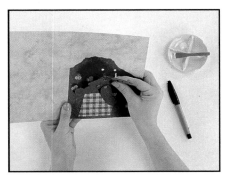

Join Teddy's legs to his body with brass paper-clips. Pass paper-clips through holes at top of the arms, body and card and open out on the back to secure him. Glue on small black beads for eyes and nose. With a fine felt-tipped pen, draw in his snout and mouth.

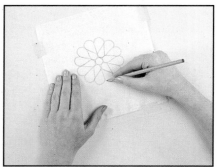

The card is a ready-made 3–fold with window. Cut out a circle in the left-hand section to match the window (see page 210). Trace out template 35 on page 249. Put masking tape in each corner to hold tracing still, then place silk over tracing, holding it firm with masking tape. Trace through on to silk using a soft pencil.

Cut glossy red card 18 by 23cm (7 by 9in), score and fold 11.5cm (4½in) across. Cut on bias four strips of Christmas fabrics 2.5 by 30cm (1 by 12in) long. Fold strips lengthways, machine 3mm (⅛in) seam allowance. Leave a length of thread at end, thread with bodkin and knot. Thread bodkin back through the tube with damp fingers.

Place silk in an embroidery frame and draw over lines of design with gutta. This will stop the silk paints from running into each other. Leave to dry thoroughly – it may take an hour. A hairdryer will speed up the process.

Thread a length of double wool through each tube. Pin ends of tubes to a firm surface. Plait by laying four strands over the left hand, take left strand over two middle strands and right strand over one. Continue to end. Ease into a circle, cross over ends and sew through to secure. Trim and finish with a bow.

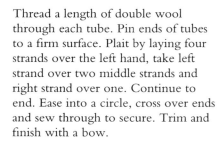

Shake or stir fabric paints and using a clean damp brush flood each petal area with paint in one swift stroke. When paint is dry place a piece of fabric under silk and iron on the wrong side for two minutes to set paint. Wash out gutta from silk and dry if you wish. Trim to just larger than the window, stick down fabric and left-hand card section with double-sided tape.

Bind trimmed ends with embroidery cotton, tie and knot and trim. Draw an arched border (see page 216) using a gold pen. Centre finished wreath and pierce through card with a thick needle or point of dividers. Sew through from back of card, knot thread, trim and finish with dot of glue to hold firm.

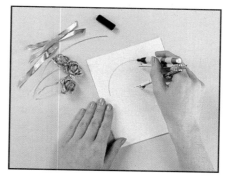

A bunch of golden roses to celebrate 50 golden years together. Cut card 16.5 by 25cm (6½ by 10in), score and fold 12.5cm (5in). Find horizontal centre of card and draw a circle with gold pen taped to compass. Cut three 10cm (4in) pieces of gold gift-wrap ribbon and cut ends diagonally to use as leaves.

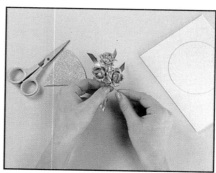

Arrange gold roses with leaves and hold in place by binding together with fine wire. Cut a piece of gold paper in a triangle shape, curving the top.

On red fabric draw in pencil four 9cm (3½in) squares and cut out. Fold in a 6mm (¼in) seam allowance and press. Find centre of square by folding diagonally each way and mark with tip of iron. Fold down one corner to this mark and pin. Continue with other corners to make a square. Catch centre points with a small stitch. Fold in again and sew. Complete all four squares.

Wrap paper around flowers and glue at the back to secure. You may like to put a dab of glue to hold roses in place. Apply glue to back of bunch of flowers and stick in place on card. Add golden birds and hearts and a large '50' cake decoration.

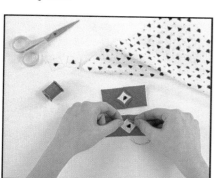

Cut four 2cm (¾in) squares from fir-tree fabric. Place two red squares right sides together and sew down one side to make a double square. Pin a fir-tree patch diagonally over the seam on the right side and curl back folded edges surrounding the patch. Slip stitch to hold in place. Repeat to make another double square.

Sew double squares together and place third and fourth fir-tree patches over seams. Sew tiny beads in corners of 'windows'. Cut card 25 by 18cm (10 by 7in), score and fold 12.5cm (5in). Mark top centre and sides 6cm (2½in) down with pencil. Cut through card to form a point. Glue finished square centred horizontally on to card. Add gold border.

CANDLELIT CHRISTMAS TREE

Cut card 15 by 20cm (6 by 8in) and score down centre. Trace template 32 on page 249, transfer on to thin card and draw round on green paper. Cut out using the craft knife. Set your sewing machine to a fairly wide satin stitch. Sew moving card from side to side to form garlands. Pull threads through to the back, tie off with knot and finish with dab of glue.

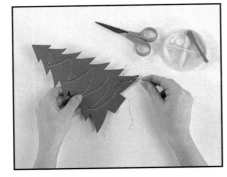

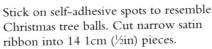

Stick on self-adhesive spots to resemble Christmas tree balls. Cut narrow satin ribbon into 14 1cm (½in) pieces.

Glue them in place at end of the branches on the back of the card. Tweezers will help you to hold them steady. Leave until glue dries. Cut tops diagonally to look like candles. Add the finishing touch – a red star on top of the tree.

THE FRIENDLY SNOWMAN

The snowman at the window invites us to come outside to play in the snow. Cut off the left-hand side of this 3–fold card so that light will shine through the window. Cut a piece of film slightly smaller than the folded card. Draw snowman and trees on to paper to fit between window bars. Place paper under film and on the right side draw the outline of the snowman and trees.

Turn over film and colour in trees and snowman using a white chinagraph pencil.

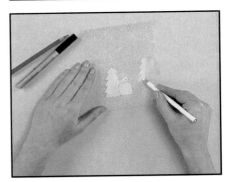

Turn back film on to the right side and draw in scarf and nose with a red chinagraph pencil. Add face details in silver. Attach film to the inside of the card with double-sided tape and place a silver star where it can be seen shining through window.

Asimple, easily-made card in unusual colours for Christmas. Cut card 11 on page 248 by 20cm (4¼ by 8in), score and fold 10cm (4in). The fold is at the top of card. Cut a strip of green plastic from an old shopping bag. Tear four strips of tissue in shades of orange and yellow. The fir-tree is from a strip of self-adhesive 'stickers'.

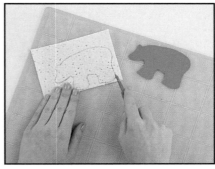

Cut card 23 by 18cm (9 by 7in), score 11.5cm (4½in) and fold along top. Trace out template 33 on page 249 and transfer on to thin card to make a template. Place on polystyrene wallpaper and draw round with a soft pencil. Cut out with craft knife. Cut out ice caps and ground from iridescent plastic or silver paper.

Arrange strips so that colours overlap and produce new colours and tones. Stick down the tree. Spray glue on to back of strips and stick down.

Glue down mountains, ground and polar bear, placing the latter in front of the peaks. Glue on silver sequin stars.

Trim excess paper from edges of card with a steel ruler and sharp craft knife.

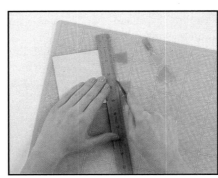

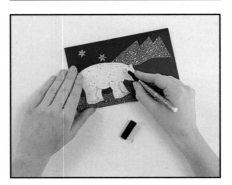

With a silver pen, draw in the polar bear's features: legs, paws and ears. The polar bear could also be made from white felt.

Cut card 15 by 22cm (6 by 8½in), score and fold 11cm (4¼in) along top. Mark the centre top of the card with a pencil dot. Cut a triangle from sequin waste, place on card and mark two sides at the bottom of the tree. Glue along edges of tree and hold in place on card until glue dries. Any residue glue can be rubbed away when dry.

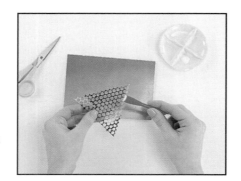

Cut a base for the tree from a piece of card or paper. Curl over scissors a number of narrow pieces of ribbon cut about 9.5cm (3¼in) long.

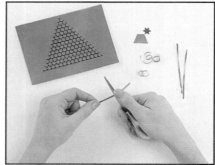

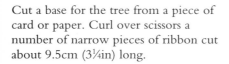

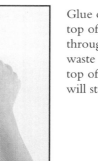

Glue on base and add sequin star to top of tree. Slip curled ribbons through every other hole in sequin waste and every other row, starting at top of tree. No need to tie them; they will stay in place.

The attraction of this card lies in combining circles cut from a variety of materials of a single colour. The feather adds a final touch of frivolity. Cut card 23 by 18cm (9 by 7in), score and fold 11.5cm (4½in). Find sequins of different sizes but similar colours, then paper, sequin waste, satin paper and foil. Sequin waste can be marked with dividers.

Draw circles of different sizes on your chosen materials. Any round objects can be used for this, or use a pair of compasses. Cut out.

Position circles and sequins to make an interesting arrangement and glue in place. Finally glue on a feather of matching colour.

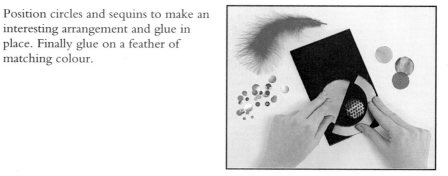

A dove of peace for New Year. It is made from a paper doiley with calendar dates falling from its beak. Cut deep blue card 30 by 20cm (12 by 8in), score 15cm (6in) and fold. Draw freehand two curves at top of card to represent clouds and cut with craft knife.

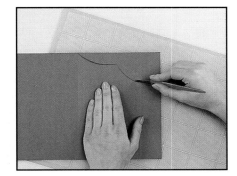

Trace dove template 34 on page 249 and transfer to thin card to make your own template. Trace out dove on to white paper doiley and cut out, together with dates 1 and 31 from an old calendar and strip of translucent film waved along upper edge to resemble hills.

Spray glue all pieces and place on the card together with four star sequins. Using a silver pen, draw line along edge of cloud curves.

This card could be used for the New Year or Christmas. You will see from template 31 on page 249 that only two sides of the 3–sided card are shown. The left-hand portion is a repeat of the right but with 7cm (2¾in) added to the bottom, so it stands taller. Trace out template adding extra section to make left-hand part of card. Rub soft pencil over back of tracing.

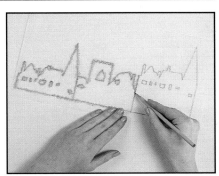

Cut a piece of white card 33 by 15cm (13 by 6in), lay tracing over right side up, lining up lower edges, hold in place with masking tape and draw over outline to transfer drawing.

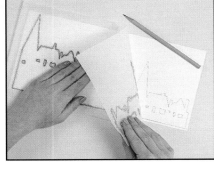

Use a ruler to help keep lines straight and cut out. Score and fold into sections. Trim lower edge and 1mm (1⁄16in) from one side of card so that it will hold flat. You will need an extra piece of card in the envelope to protect the points.

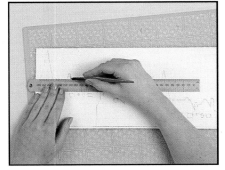

Cut card 22 by 15cm (8½ by 6in), score and fold 11cm (4¼in). Trace out heart 37 on page 250 and transfer to a thin piece of card to make your own template. Cut out a heart in thin white card. Place the template on the front of the card at a slight angle and draw round in pencil. Cut round pencil line leaving enough uncut at bottom to enable card to stand.

Glue dried flower petals on to a white heart working in rows from outside to centre. Use a rubber-based glue; tweezers will help to hold petals steady. Finish with a whole flower in centre.

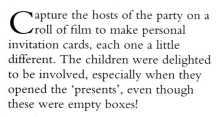

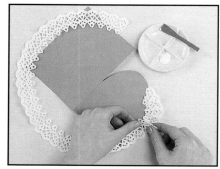

Cut a border from a paper doiley. Spread a thin line of glue on outside of main card heart. Pleat doiley border on to glue all round heart. Stick petal heart over pleated doiley, cover with a piece of clean paper and smooth down. Hold for a minute until glue dries. Lastly stick on Victorian angel motif on top right-hand corner of card.

Capture the hosts of the party on a roll of film to make personal invitation cards, each one a little different. The children were delighted to be involved, especially when they opened the 'presents', even though these were empty boxes!

Make a mask to fit the 'sunken plate' area of the card mount and mark the corners of photographs with a compass or sharp pencil point. Cut the photograph with a sharp craft knife and ruler and use spray glue to affix.

Invitations can be hand-made by children too — a great way to keep them happy and involved in party planning. This rabbit is for an Easter football party given by a nine-year old boy. He drew the picture, then photocopied it a number of times. Each invitation can be hand-coloured before being glued to cards.

SWEET-HEART

Use a mould from a cake decorating shop and fill it with tiny cake sweets. Cut a 3–fold card 42 by 19cm (16½ by 7½in), score and fold 14cm (5½in). Tape heart to the back of the tracing paper. Turn over and rub along the edge of the heart to make a template. Line up heart tracing in the centre of the middle section of card and transfer outline. Cut out.

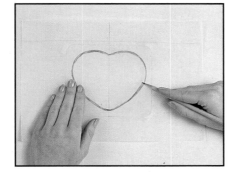

Place double-sided tape round heart aperture and around edges of the left-hand portion of card, marked with a cross. Remove backing from tape around the heart and place mould in position. Press to stick firmly. Put narrow line of double-sided tape around edge of heart.

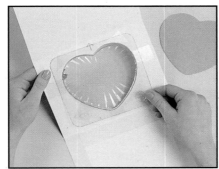

Pour sweets into the heart until full and pack out with a piece of wadding cut to heart shape. Take off backing from tape around heart and from left-hand portion of card, fold over card and press down. A pretty pink bow is the finishing touch.

EASTER BONNET

A doll's straw bonnet forms the basis of this card and is decorated with spring-coloured ribbons, flowers and a butterfly. Cut card 15 by 22cm (6 by 8½in), score and fold 11cm (4¼in). Cut length of yellow ribbon and cut inverted 'V' shape at ends. Hold in place around hat and sew leaving tails at centre back. Repeat with a length of slightly narrower ribbon.

Trim stems of small fabric flowers and pin in place on the ribbon at regular intervals around the hat.

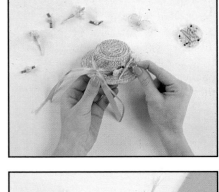

Sew flowers in place using double thread. Finish with a butterfly at the front. Centre bonnet on card and attach by sewing through brim of hat and knotting threads on inside of card. A dab of glue will make knots secure. Arrange ribbons prettily.

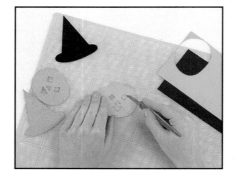

A fun for Halloween card, quickly and easily made from paper and sequins. Cut red card 22 by 16cm (8½ by 6¼in). Score and fold 11cm (4¼in). Trace out templates 39 and 40 on page 250 and make your own templates. Cut out a witch's hat from black paper. Cut pumpkin head from orange paper or card, then cut out eyes and mouth.

Position head and hat on card and mark with a sharp pencil. Glue pieces in place.

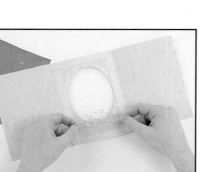

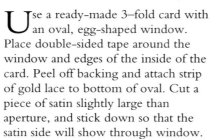

Use a ready-made 3–fold card with an oval, egg-shaped window. Place double-sided tape around the window and edges of the inside of the card. Peel off backing and attach strip of gold lace to bottom of oval. Cut a piece of satin slightly large than aperture, and stick down so that the satin side will show through window.

Add sequin stars and moons using rubber-based glue, holding them in place for a moment while glue dries. Tweezers make handling the sequins easier.

Glue a large, jewel-like bead in centre of 'egg'. Arrange beads, sequin leaves and petals, then glue in position. Tweezers will make it easier to place them accurately.

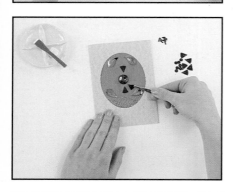

Finish with a smear of rubber-based glue around the edge of the egg on the outside of the card. Leave for a moment to become tacky, then press down to gold braid. Neatly trim the end of the braid.

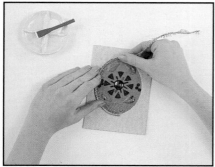

The flowers we used are Victorian scrap or motifs. You could also cut flowers from magazines or old birthday cards. Cut card 25 by 19cm (10 by 7½in), score and fold 12.5cm (5in) for top of card. Trace out template 42 from page 250. Place tracing over gold card and draw again using a sharp pencil which will indent soft gold card.

Measure a border around edges of card and mark in pencil. Go over the border again in gold pen.

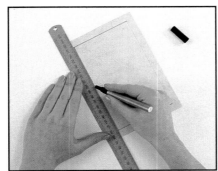

Glue the cornucopia on to the card, then the flowers and fruit tumbling out. Add a white dove.

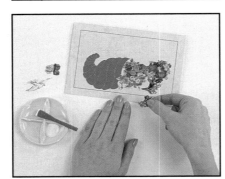

A lace sachet of pot pourri could be detached and used later to perfume a drawer. Pot pourri can be bought in a variety of colours and perfumes. Cut card 23 by 18cm (9 by 7in), score and fold 11.5cm (4½in). Cut out two lace flowers, pin together and oversew leaving a gap to fill with pot pourri.

Make a funnel from a piece of paper and fill a lace sachet with pot pourri. Oversew to close. Make a bow from narrow satin ribbon and curl ends over scissors.

Cut three tissue paper leaves and glue on to the card. Sew bow on to sachet. Using a point of dividers or a thick sharp needle, make two holes at either side of the card, for positioning the sachet. Sew through and knot on back, securing with a dab of glue.

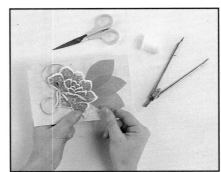

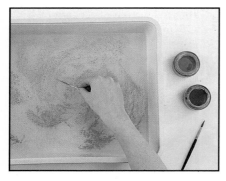

Cut card 22 by 19cm (8½ by 7½in), score and fold 11cm (4¼in) for top. Into a plastic tray put two pints of cold water, mixed with 14g (½oz) of wallpaper paste. Leave for 15 minutes. In a small jar mix 2.5cm (1in) of oil paint from a tube and a little turpentine substitute. Apply drops of the mixed paint on to the surface of the water. Disperse with an orange stick.

Place piece of paper larger than card gently on top of water and remove again fairly quickly, as soon as the paint has taken to surface of paper. Leave to dry on a sheet of newspaper. Press flat, if necessary, when dry. Cut to fit card and glue down.

Trace out a car from a magazine or postcard and transfer to glossy white paper. Cut out and glue down. Trace 'chrome' details on to silver paper or card, cut out and glue in place. Add details with silver pen.

Cut card 23 by 18cm (9 by 7in), score and fold 11.5cm (4½in). This is a spontaneous arrangement, so no two cards will look the same. Lay out a selection of blue materials: ribbon, sequin waste, buttons, feathers, tissue and silver paper. Tear tissue-paper and cut chosen papers into random shapes. When you overlay strips of tissue, more shades of blue will occur.

Spray glue your materials and place in your favourite arrangement and trim any excess. Tie a bow from narrow satin ribbon on to the base of the feather and trim ends diagonally. Attach to the card by sewing through.

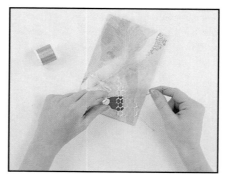

To attach the duck button, make two holes with sharp needle or point of dividers, checking which way the button shank lies. Sew on the duck button from the back using double thread. Finish with a knot and secure with a dab of glue.

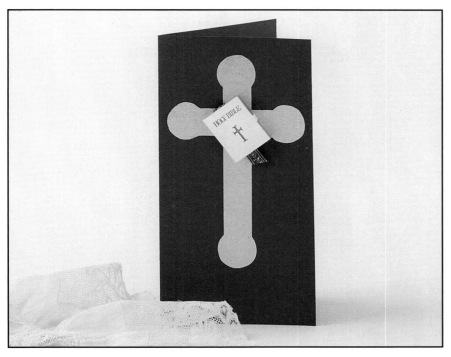

Cut grey marble-effect card 28 by 19cm (11 by 7½in), score and fold 14cm (5½in). Trace out template 43 on page 250. Cut piece of silver card to fit, turn over and hold down with masking tape. Place tracing over card and attach with masking tape. Trace through on to card with a sharp pencil. Trace base on to a piece of black card.

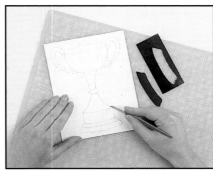

With a sharp craft knife, cut out cup and base. Burnish edges of silver card by rubbing gently with the back of your thumbnail.

The tiny Bible is from a doll accessories' supplier. Cut card 23 by 22cm (9 by 8½in), score and fold 11cm (4¼in). Trace cross template 41 on page 250 and transfer on to thin card to make your own template. Trace out on to gold paper and cut straight edges with a craft knife and ruler. The curved ends can be cut with scissors.

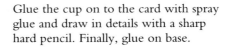

Glue the cup on to the card with spray glue and draw in details with a sharp hard pencil. Finally, glue on base.

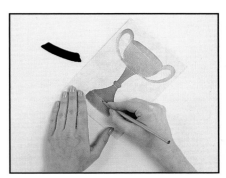

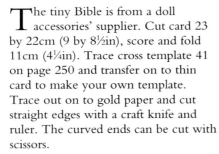

Lay the template on the card to position cross and mark with pencil. Spray glue on wrong side of the cross and attach to the card.

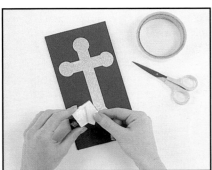

Stick a piece of double-sided tape on the back of the Bible, peel off backing and attach to the cross at an angle.

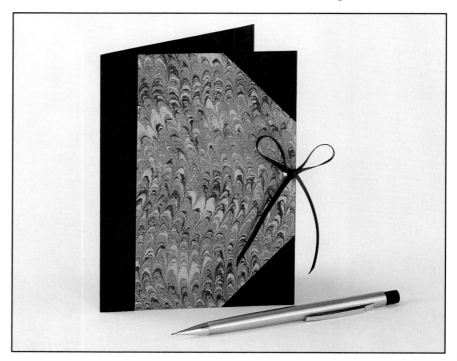

Cut a circle of card 3cm (1¼in) in radius. Take approximately 1 metre (3ft 2in) of single-sided 2.5cm (1in) wide pink satin ribbon, pleat and machine sew round edge of card circle. Machine an inner circle of pleated blue ribbon. A wide zig-zag stitch will hold pleats in place. Fold ends under to finish. Keep excess lengths of ribbon.

Cut green card 22 by 15cm (8½ by 6in), score and fold 11cm (4½in). Cut piece of traditional ledger-look marbled paper 15 by 9cm (6 by 3½in). Cut away top and bottom right-hand corners by measuring 4cm (1½in) along top and right-hand edges and bottom and right-hand edges.

Cut a circle of pink metallic paper or card 2.2cm (⅞in) in radius. Using left-over ribbon, cut two tails, one from each colour and one longer than the other. Cut an inverted 'V' shape at ends.

Spray glue on the back of the paper and attach to card so that there is a 2cm (¾in) margin of green card on left-hand side. Punch a hole in the centre along right-hand edge of front of card.

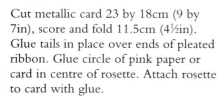

Cut metallic card 23 by 18cm (9 by 7in), score and fold 11.5cm (4½in). Glue tails in place over ends of pleated ribbon. Glue circle of pink paper or card in centre of rosette. Attach rosette to card with glue.

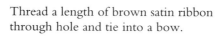

Thread a length of brown satin ribbon through hole and tie into a bow.

Purchase a 3–fold window card in a pale colour whichever size you prefer. Mark inner left-hand portion of card with a cross. Select an attractive picture, or focus on a detail from a magazine and lay a window over the picture. Mark four edges and corners with pencil dots.

Cut out picture slightly larger than the window. Place double-sided tape around the edges of the window inside the card and stick down the picture using pencil guide marks to position. Fold over and stick down left-hand portion of card using double-sided tape.

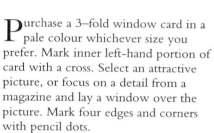

The cats are purchased from a bead shop and attached to card with rubber-based glue. Hold in place for a minute or two until glue dries.

Make your own template from the dove 46 on page 250 and cut an extra template for the wing alone (see finished card). Draw round the dove twice on dark blue felt so that the birds face opposite directions and cut out. Cut two pieces of muslin 18 by 11.5cm (7 by 4½in), position doves between two layers and pin. Tack layers together to hold doves in place.

Using two strands of embroidery thread, sew tiny running stitches around doves and stitch feet (see finished card). Place wing template over doves and lightly draw round with a sharp pencil. Quilt along these lines. When finished, take out tacking thread and lightly press.

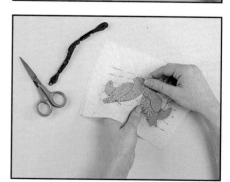

Purchase a 3–fold window card to fit quilted doves. Cut out a matching window from the left-hand section of card (see page 210). Trim muslin to about 6mm (¼in) larger than the window. Stick down using double-sided tape. Add tiny round bead for the doves' eyes and pearl beads to the corner of window.

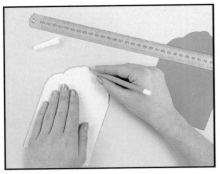

Cut card 22 by 16cm (8½ by 6¼in), score and fold 11cm (4¼in). Trace out template 48 on page 250 and transfer to thin card adding 10cm (4in) to depth, to match the card. Cut out and place on folded card. Draw round the church window shape at the top of the card and cut through both thicknesses. Draw a border with felt-tipped pen.

Place several layers of different shades of pink tissue-paper together in a pile on a cutting board. Cut round template 38 (page 250) to make approximately 10 hearts.

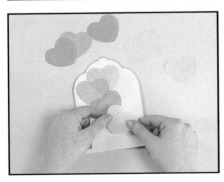

Spray glue hearts and position on the card so that they overlap. You could stick more hearts inside the card and also leave some loose so that they scatter when card is opened.

Colours can be matched to those of the bridesmaid's dresses. Cut card 15 by 30cm (6 by 12in), score and fold 15cm (6in). Bind a turquoise felt-tipped pen to a compass and draw a double circle on the centre of card. Sew a line of running stitches along the edge of strip of lace half a metre (1ft 6in) in length. Gather into a circle and sew seam.

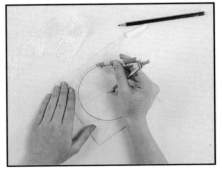

Sew ribbon flowers on to the centre of a lace circle. Cut a strip of flower braid into single flowers and sew around ribbon flowers.

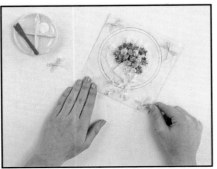

Sew on a couple of strings of ribbon flowers or braid to hang from the bouquet. Using a sharp needle or compass point, make several holes in card and sew on the lace bouquet from the back of the card using double thread. Tie a knot and add a dab of glue to secure. Glue on satin bows in four corners.

POP-UP WEDDING CAKE

Cut card 30 by 15cm (12 by 6in), score and fold 15cm (6in). Trace template 47 (page 250) and transfer to piece of white card. Cut a piece of white card 2.5 by 9cm (1 by 3½in) and score across 1.25cm (½in), 2.5cm (1in), 4cm (1½in) and 1.25cm (½in) for the stand. Decorate cake using felt-tipped and silver pens before cutting out.

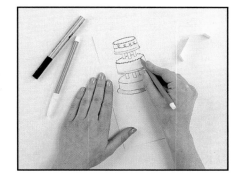

Glue down doiley tablecloth on the base of the card. In pencil, draw two lines 2.5cm (1in) either side of the fold in the centre. This is your guide for placing cake stand. Glue a 4cm (1½in) section to the back of the cake, then place bottom 1.25cm (½in) section on guide line and glue. Glue silver bows, bells and horseshoes in place.

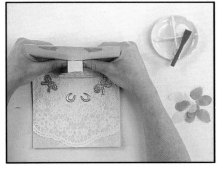

Glue the final 1.25cm (½in) section of the stand to the back of the card and hold until glue dries. Cut some tissue-paper confetti in colours to match the cake, glue some to the tablecloth and leave some loose. Punch holes in four corners of the card. Thread curled silver ribbon through to tie and close card.

GET WELL DAFFODILS

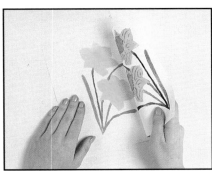

Cut card 22cm (8½in) square, score and fold 11cm (4½in). Cut out a window 9 by 16.5cm (3½ by 6½in). Trace daffodils from a catalogue or book and transfer on to cartridge paper. Paint with transfer paints. When dry, place over a square of polyester or poly-cotton fabric and press with a hot dry iron for two minutes. Carefully lift off paper.

Place print in an embroidery frame the opposite way from hand embroidery and pull until taut. To machine embroider, use same thread on top and bobbin. Take off présser foot and drop 'feed dog' so that teeth will not hold work and you will be able to move it freely. Place embroidery ring under needle and drop pressure lever.

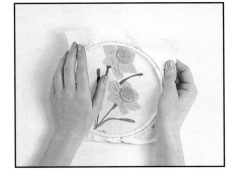

Moving machine wheel by hand, draw up bobbin thread to top and hold to start. Move ring, keeping your fingers on the edge of the frame and slowly paint with your needle. Experiment with stitches – length 0 and zig-zag are good. Sew outline first then colour in. Press on reverse, mount with double-sided tape and back with white paper.

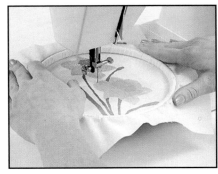

Cut card 45 by 20cm (18 by 8in). Score and fold at 15cm (6in) and 30cm (12in) to form 3–fold. Follow chart on page 251. You may vary the wools and use up odds and ends. Most wool is used double on 12 holes to 2.5cm (1in) canvas. Find the centre point of the canvas and draw on the fireplace design with felt-tipped pens.

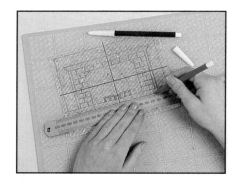

Start in the centre, working the fire in random long stitch and tent stitch, varying the colours of the flames. Next, work the fire basket in tent stitch.

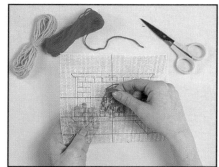

Cut card 22 by 15cm (8½ by 6in), score and fold 11cm (4¼in). Trace templates 44 and 45 (page 250) and transfer on to green card for bedhead, and brown for bunny's head. Cut them out and an oblong of white paper for a pillow. Trim edges of pillow with pinking shears.

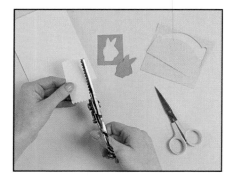

Continue with the copper fireguard in slanting satin stitch, fire surround in tent stitch, brickwork in long stitch, carpet in tent stitch and walls in long stitch. For the rug, lay a cocktail stick across the canvas and work stitches over the stick. Cut loops to make pile. When finished, trim and cut a window in 3–fold card to fit piece. Mount with double-sided tape.

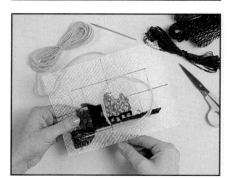

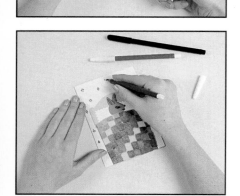

On good quality cartridge paper, draw a patchwork quilt and fill in squares with transfer paint following manufacturer's instructions. Iron the painting on to a piece of bonded interfacing or man-made fabric and trim to fit bed.

Spray glue backs of all pieces and attach to card in order: bedhead, pillow, bunny and quilt. Draw in bunny's features with a fine felt-tipped pen. Add wallpaper pattern using groups of four dots to look like flowers.

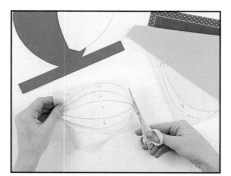

Trace out template 52 (page 251) and transfer outer balloon on to blue card, inner balloon on to white card and also on to the tracing paper side of bonding web. Number each segment and cut out. Mark on the blue balloon where the inner balloon will fit. Iron balloon segments on to the wrong side of three fabrics. Cut out carefully and peel off backing.

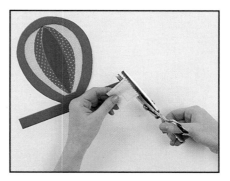

Place balloon segments on to white card balloon and press with a dry iron. Trim edges and using the guide on the main blue balloon, glue down. Cut a small piece of fabric for the basket with pinking shears and glue in place.

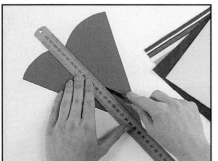

Idyllic lazy days, beachcombing in yellow sand under blue sky. Trace template 51 (page 251) and transfer to blue card. Score down the centre.

Draw in ropes then the basket design on fabric using a brown felt-tipped pen. Score the base of balloon where indicated on the right side and fold back so that the balloon will stand. If being mailed, this card should have an extra piece of card in the envelope for protection.

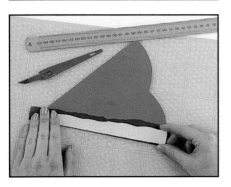

Tear blue tissue-paper to resemble the sea. Cut a piece of yellow paper with a curved top edge to make it appear that waves are breaking. Place the pieces wrong side up in a spray booth and spray glue. Fix to the card and trim to fit.

Cut a piece of striped fabric or paper to make a beachtowel. Draw fringe on the towel with a felt-tipped pen. Glue in place. Punch two holes and insert a beach umbrella.

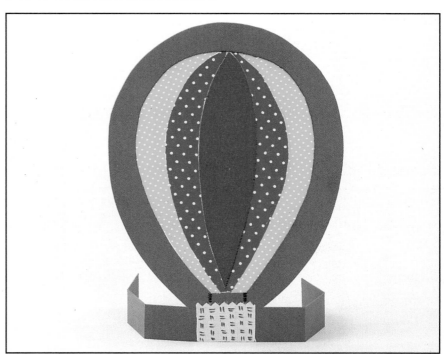

On good quality cartridge paper, draw a 12cm (4¾in) square. Using a postcard or photograph as a guide, roughly draw in mountains, lakes and grass. Colour in with transfer paint, applied sparingly. The colours will not be true to the end product since they will change according to fibre content of material on which you print.

When paint is dry, place the paper over poly-cotton and press for two minutes with a hot dry iron. Try not to move the paper. You can make several prints from one painting. Mount the picture in an embroidery ring as shown. Follow your sewing machine's instructions for free machine embroidery. Using a selection of threads, fill in areas using satin stitch and straight stitch.

Tie ends of satin stitch on the back when finished and press. Cut card 14 by 28cm (5½ by 11in). Cut a window 11.5cm (4½) square. Attach finished picture behind window using double-sided tape, then cut a piece of white backing paper and attach to back of your work. Trim excess paper.

Cut card 22 by 15cm (8½ by 6in), score and fold 11cm (4¼in). Draw a border around the card, first in pencil then pink felt-tipped pen. Roll out a piece of white Fimo modelling material until thin and cut a kite shape. Cut edges again with pinking shears.

Roll out lots of tiny pink balls for flowers and some long green sausages to be cut for stems. Roll out some flat lengths of pink clay to make a bow.

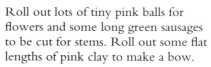

Fashion a wrapping paper shape from 'kite' and place on a piece of baking foil. Slip green stems inside and press on flower balls with a cocktail stick. Make a bow by folding pink lengths and shaping. Lay on foil and bake for 15–20 minutes on 130 C (275 F/Gas mark 1) to harden. Leave to cool, glue to card and attach bow.

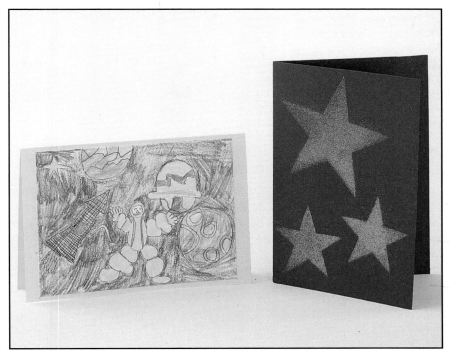

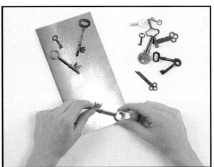

An unusual way to mark a 21st birthday and the traditional receipt of the key of the door. Cut a piece of bright silver card 22 by 22cm (8½ by 8½in) and score a fold down the centre. Collect together some interesting shaped keys. Using a spray booth, place folded silver card inside and lay keys on the card in a pleasing arrangement.

Stencilling is a good way of making several cards quickly. We used gold spray paint. Stencil card is firm and flat so the paint does not spread under the edges. Cut a piece of stencil card large enough to cover cards. Using templates 49 and 50 (page 251) cut out stars with a sharp knife and ruler.

Our cosmonaut was drawn by a six year-old boy. Draw several squares 9 by 14cm (3½ by 5½in) and ask a child to draw some pictures. Photocopy it several times. The child will have great fun colouring in these drawings, perhaps each one in different colours. Cut card mounts to fit and stick down drawings.

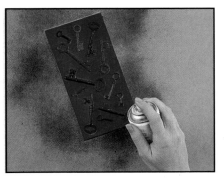

Use spray car paint, holding the can 20–25cm (8–10in) away from the card, and spray in a few short bursts to cover the whole card. Allow the first coat to dry for a few minutes and then spray a second coat. To ensure even distribution you should carefully turn the card between coats. You may wish to spray a third coat. Use in a well-ventilated room.

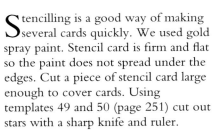

Shake a can of paint for a minute or two, then spray from a distance of 30cm (12in). A couple of coats gives a deeper colour and paint dries quickly. The stars you have cut from the stencil can also be used to make reverse image cards.

When completely dry, remove keys. You will not be able to get the cellulose paint off the keys easily, so be sure to use keys you no longer need. Other objects such as old clock and watch parts, can also be used to make theme cards.

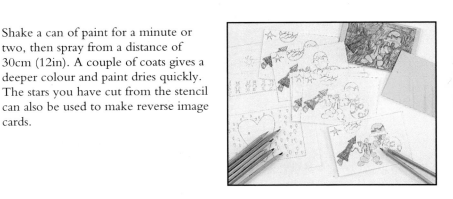

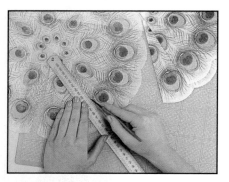

Gossamer-fine Japanese paper napkins make quick cards. Simply cut out designs and glue them to cards. With a sharp craft knife, cut a fan shape from a circular peacock napkin, so that the two large 'eyes' are at top. Spray glue the back of fan, position and smooth on to a card.

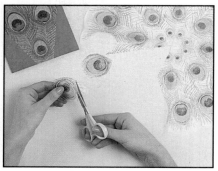

Cut two further eyes from the napkin. Arrange, spray glue on the wrong side and smooth down on to the card.

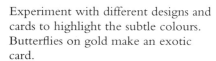

Experiment with different designs and cards to highlight the subtle colours. Butterflies on gold make an exotic card.

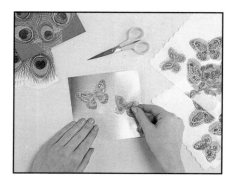

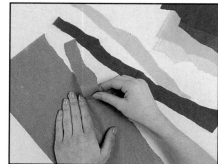

This magical, ever-rolling landscape is all in the imagination. It is made from layers of torn tissue-paper and plastic iridescent. Cut pieces of card 16 by 25cm (6¼ by 10in). Score and fold 12.5cm (5in). Roughly tear several strips of tissue-paper and cut iridescent film.

Arrange them on a sheet of A4 (21 by 30cm/8 by 12 in) typing paper so that colours overlap and shade. When you are happy with your arrangement, turn strips over and spray glue. You will find one side of tissue-paper has more shine than the other. If there are gaps, you could fill them in with silver pen.

Divide a sheet of paper into six or more pieces and cut with a sharp craft knife. Each landscape can now be positioned on a card and glued.

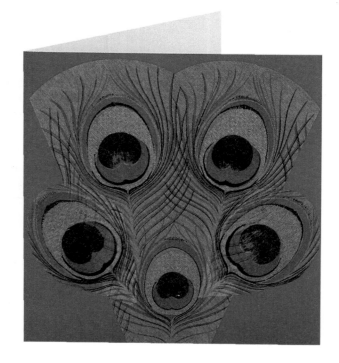

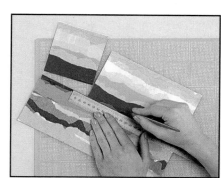

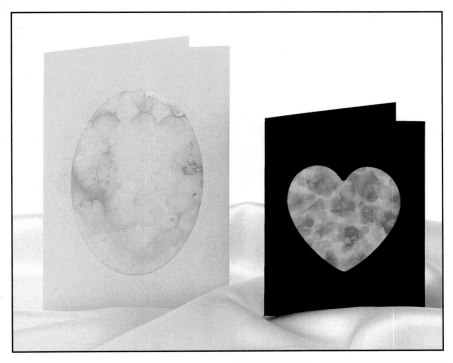

Wonderful abstract patterns can be produced by sprinkling salt on freshly painted silk. Cut a piece of fine white silk lining and place in an embroidery frame, pulling taut. Select colours of silk paints you wish to use, shake and carefully open jars. Wet brush, apply paint fairly swiftly and immediately sprinkle on salt. Fill frame with designs.

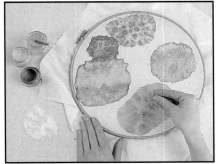

Potato cuts make quick but 'impressionistic' prints. Choose a medium-sized potato to fit comfortably into your hand. Cut in half and lay on it a motif cut from a piece of paper. Cut along the edge of the image, then slice potato away all the round shape so that the image is raised. Dry on a paper towel.

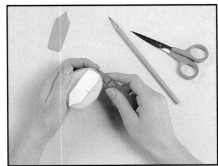

Leave to dry, then brush off the salt. The silk will yield a variety of effects, so place different ready-cut window cards over the most attractive patterns. Mark area to be framed in a window, then cut out slightly larger. The smaller the window, the more designs you can make. You could also add embroidery, beads and sequins to your designs.

A water-based, poster or even fabric paint can be used. Apply paint to the potato image, turn over and press gently but firmly on to card. Clean off paint with tissue when you want to change colour and continue, making sure overlapping colours are dry.

Mount silk in centre window of 3–fold card, using double-sided tape. Stick down left-hand portion of card over the back of the silk.

Some cards will be better than others, but this is part of their charm. Finish off a candle card with gold pen flame and 'surround'.

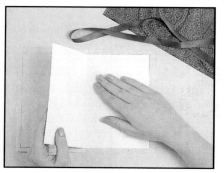

Cut pink glossy card 15 by 22cm (6 by 8½in), score and fold 11cm (4¼in). Draw out cake shape on to thin card and cut out to make template. Warm a ball of Fimo modelling material in your hands and roll out until thin. Place template on clay and cut round with a knife. Make a little dent in top centre where candle will fix.

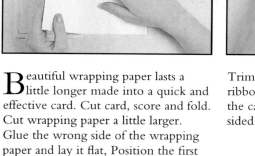

Beautiful wrapping paper lasts a little longer made into a quick and effective card. Cut card, score and fold. Cut wrapping paper a little larger. Glue the wrong side of the wrapping paper and lay it flat, Position the first half of the card on paper and smooth. Bring up wrapping paper to adhere to the other half of card but leave room for fold. Smooth down.

Trim edges with a sharp knife. Affix ribbon on four sides on the inside of the card with a little piece of double-sided tape. Tie ribbon in a bow.

Carefully transfer to baking foil with a spatula or knife. Bake cake according to manufacturer's instructions. Cake may stretch, but you can trim with scissors after baking. Glue doiley tablecloth on card. Cut spotted ribbon and fold around the base of the cake. Attach with double-sided tape or glue and add second ribbon trim.

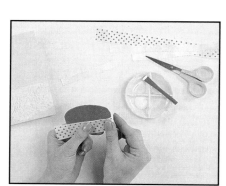

Photographs of flowers can be mounted on cards and sent to friends during winter months. Make a collection over the summer. Make a mask of the right size so that you may frame the most effective image. Mark four corners with a compass or sharp pencil point. Cut off excess with ruler and craft knife. Spray glue to mount.

Wipe back of cake with lighter fuel to remove any grease. Dab rubber-based glue on the back of the cake and wait until tacky before fixing to card. Spread a fine line of glue along candle and apply to card. Hold in place for a minute or two until glue dries.

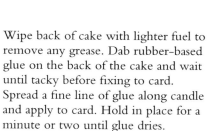

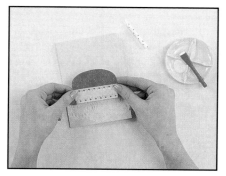

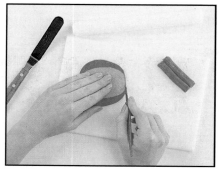

TEMPLATES

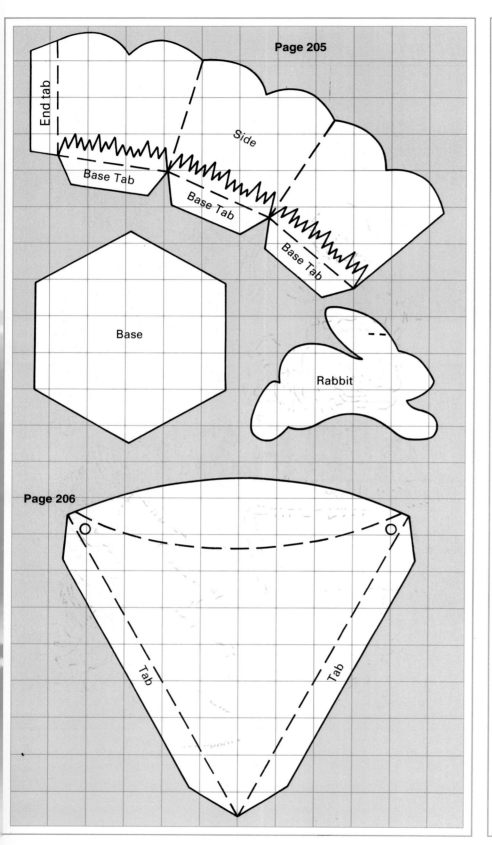

Page 205

End tab

Side

Base Tab

Base Tab

Base Tab

Base

Rabbit

Page 206

Tab

Tab

Page 211

Page 74

Page 211

Harvest storage jars (page 62)

Brilliant boxers (page 68)

Rosy Scarf (page 69)

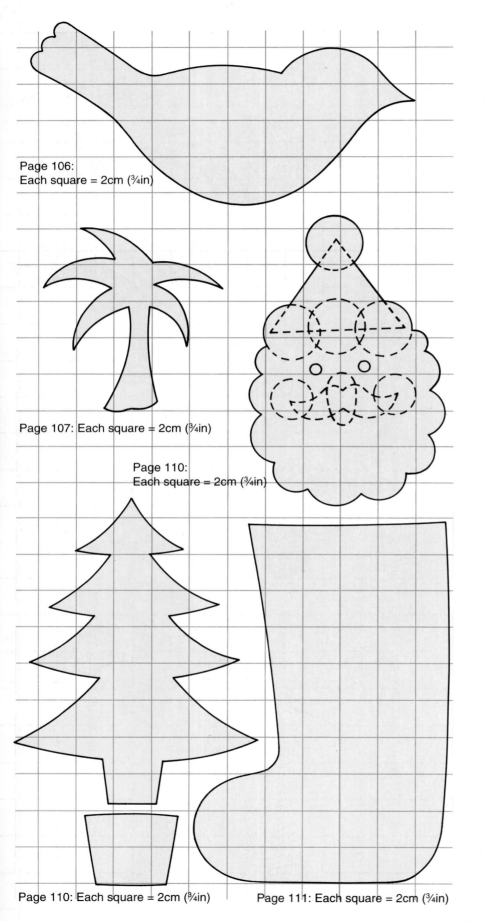

Page 106:
Each square = 2cm (¾in)

Page 107: Each square = 2cm (¾in)

Page 110:
Each square = 2cm (¾in)

Page 110: Each square = 2cm (¾in)

Page 111: Each square = 2cm (¾in)

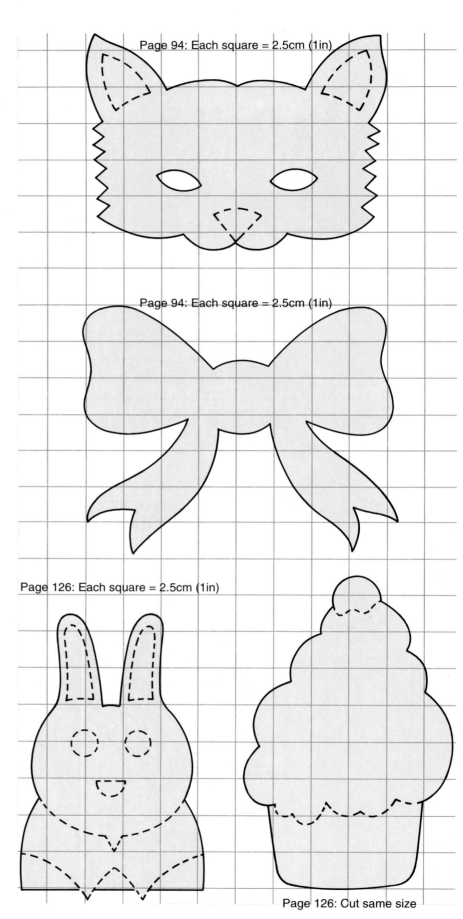

Page 94: Each square = 2.5cm (1in)

Page 94: Each square = 2.5cm (1in)

Page 126: Each square = 2.5cm (1in)

Page 126: Cut same size

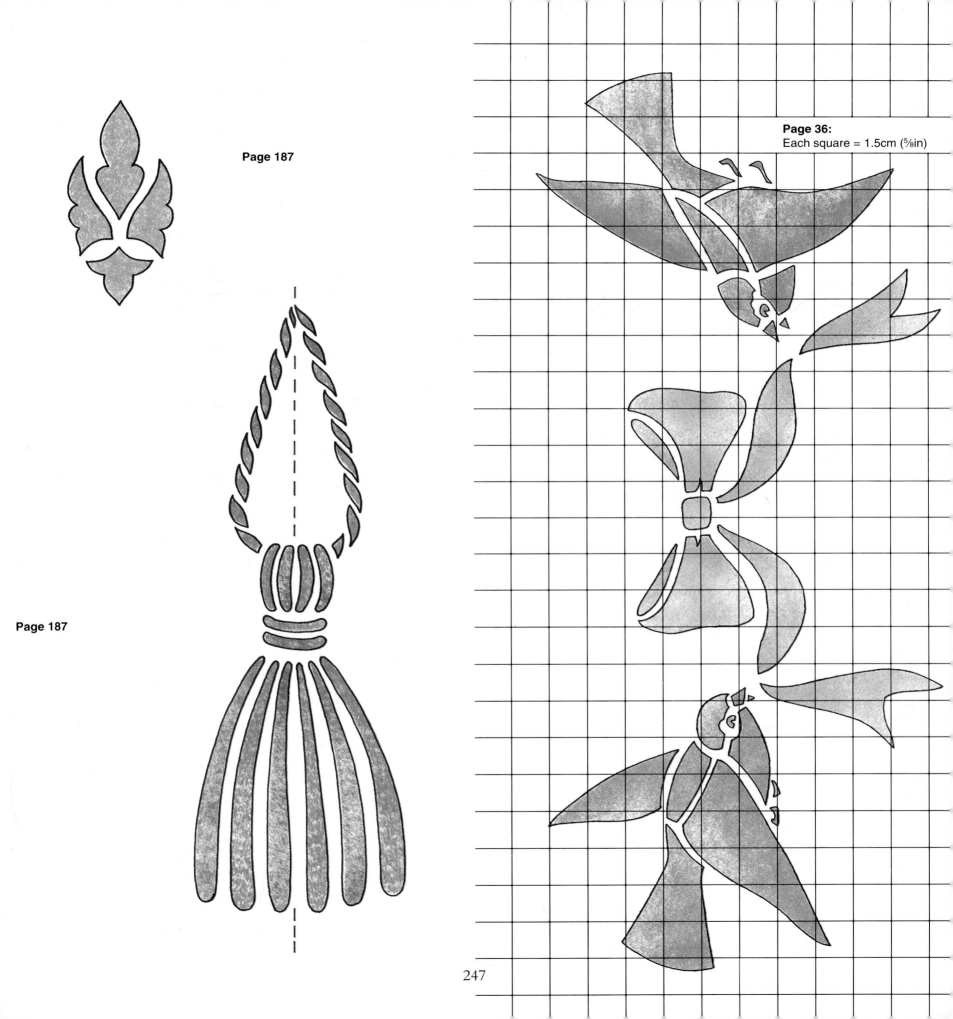

Page 187

Page 187

Page 36:
Each square = 1.5cm (⅝in)

247

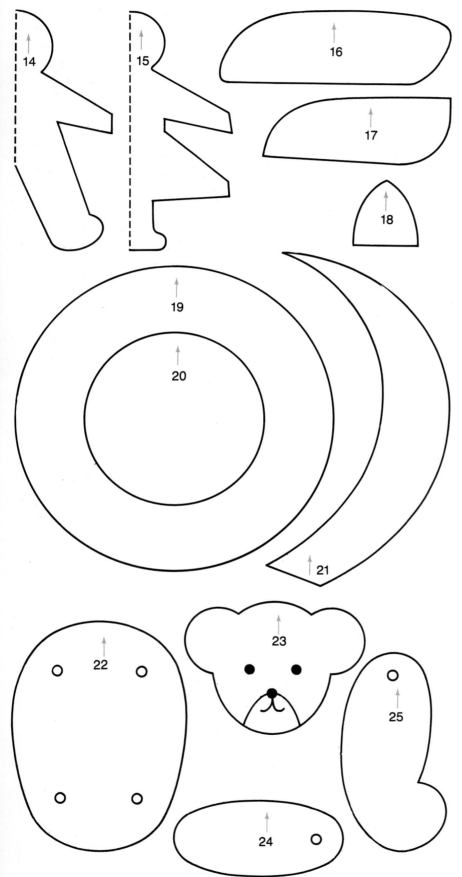

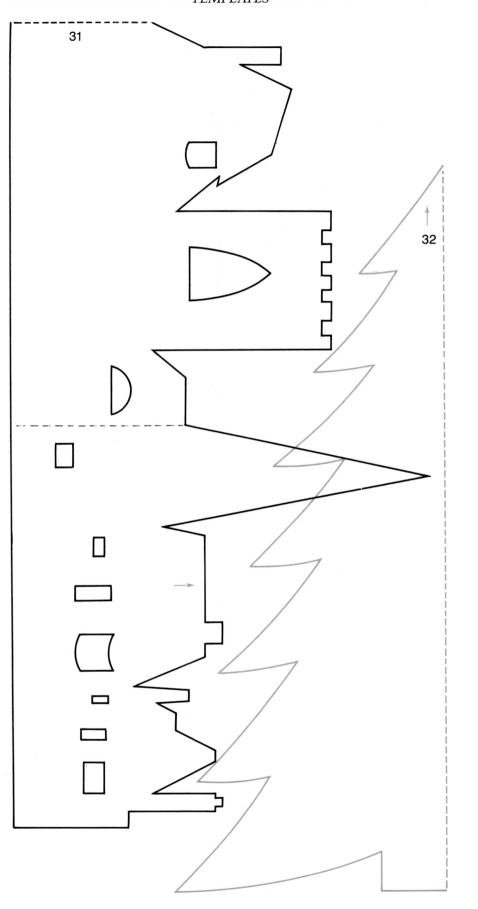

31

32

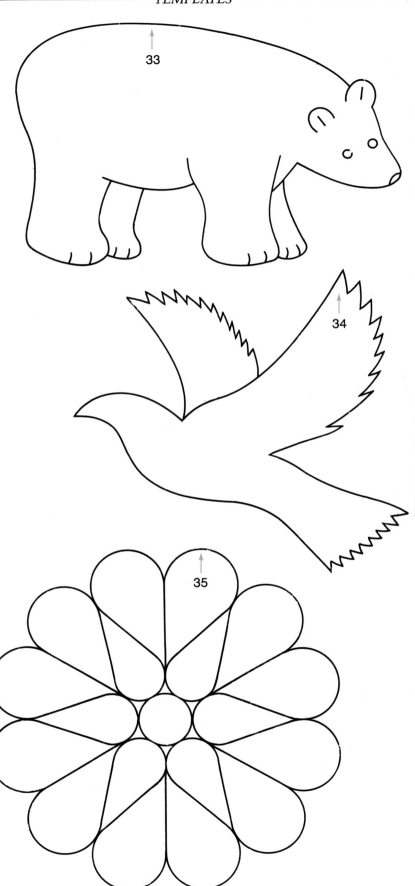

33

34

35

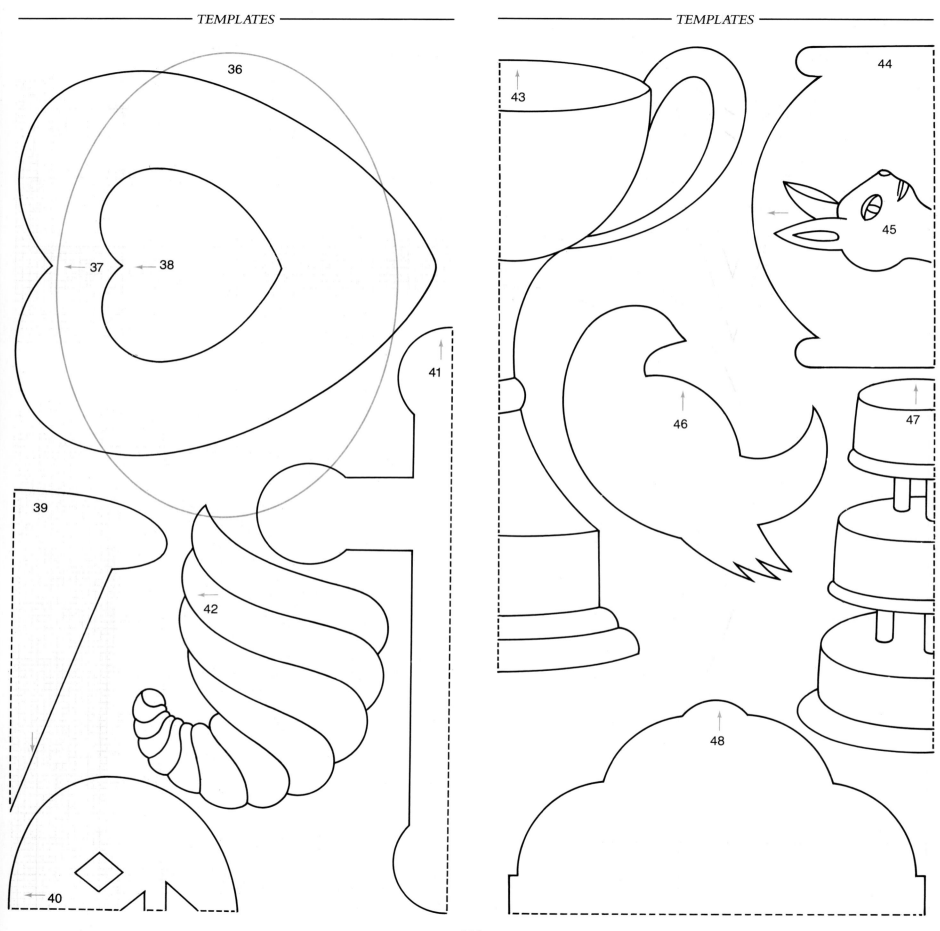

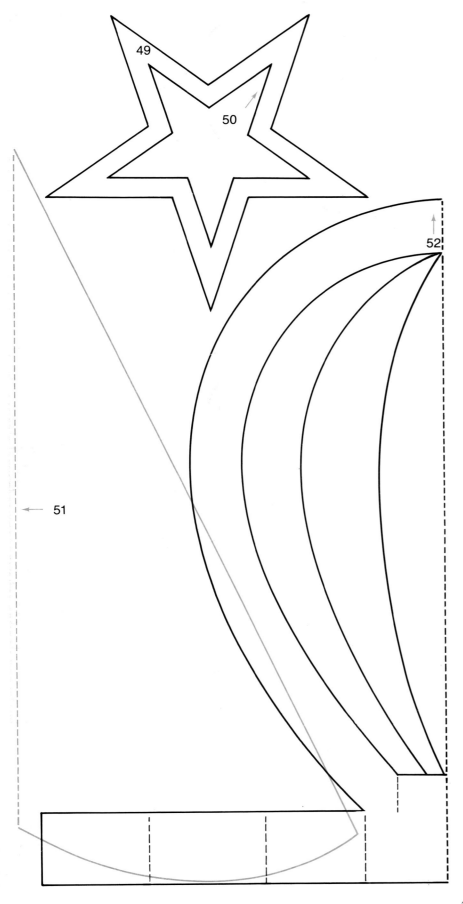

49

50

52

51

Needlepoint in Lilac (page 216)

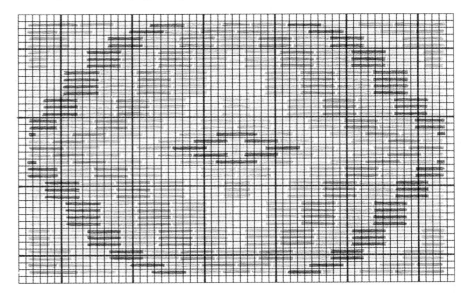

A Warm New Home Welcome (page 236)

251

The following are designs for the various boxes described in this book. Draw the templates out carefully, following either the metric or the imperial measurements – do not use a combination of both. To score the fold lines run along the dotted lines – on the inside of the box – with the back of a craft knife or the blunt edge of a pair of scissors; this will help you to fold the box more easily. If you wish to increase or decrease the size of your box just scale the measurements up or down as required.

Squared Up (page 162)

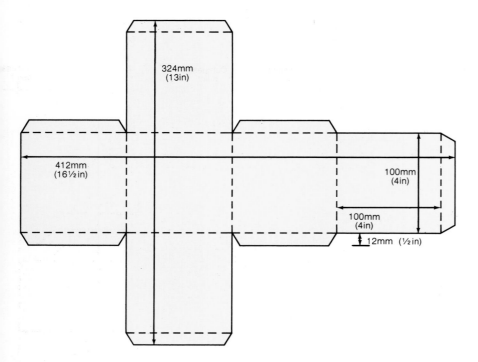

Diamonds Are Forever (page 163)

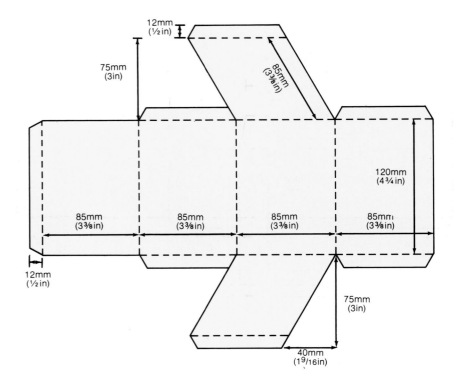

Floral Tribute (page 164)

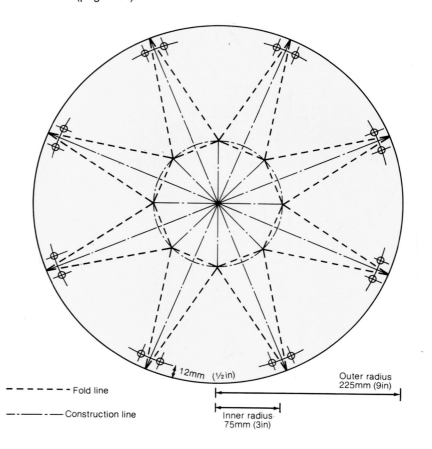

Box Clever (page 162)

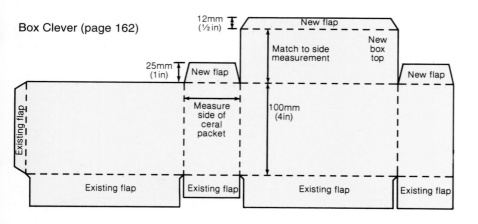

Handle With Care (page 164)

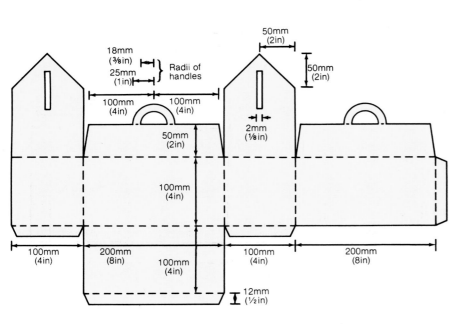

The Pyramids (page 165)

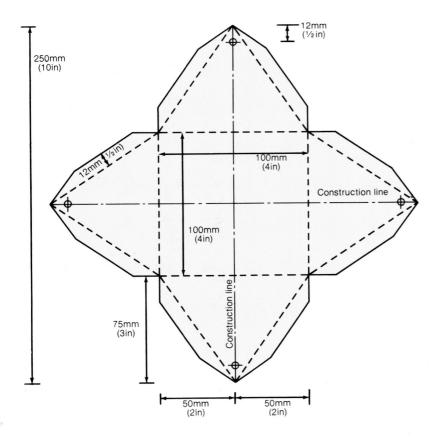

Smart Sachets (page 166)

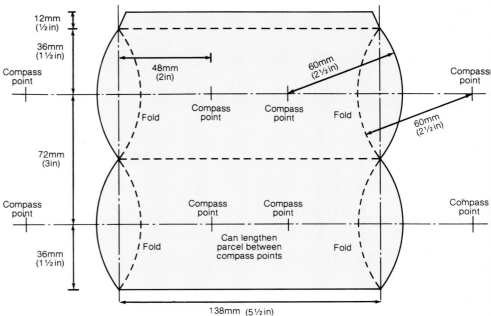

Boxed In (page 167)

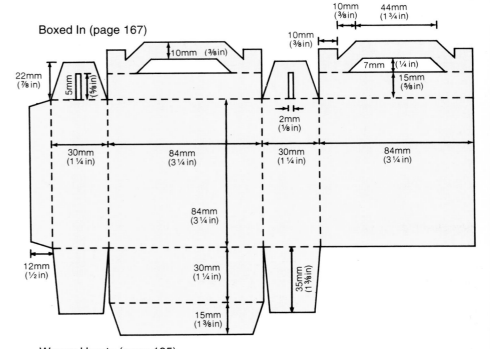

Woven Hearts (page 195)

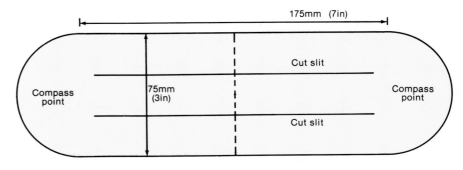